W9-AGV-083

CultureShock!
A Survival Guide to Customs and Etiquette

USA

Esther Wanning

Marshall Cavendish
Editions

This edition published in 2008 by:
Marshall Cavendish Corporation
99 White Plains Road
Tarrytown, NY 10591-9001
www.marshallcavendish.us

© 1991 Times Editions Pte Ltd
© 2002 Times Media Private Limited
© 2005, 2008 Marshall Cavendish International (Asia) Private Limited
All rights reserved

No part of this publication may be reproduced, stored in a retrieval system
or transmitted, in any form or by any means, electronic, mechanical,
photocopying, recording or otherwise, without the prior permission of
the copyright owner. Request for permission should be addressed to the
Publisher, Marshall Cavendish International (Asia) Private Limited, 1 New
Industrial Road, Singapore 536196. Tel: (65) 6213 9300, fax: (65) 6285 4871.
E-mail: genref@sg.marshallcavendish.com

The publisher makes no representation or warranties with respect to the
contents of this book, and specifically disclaims any implied warranties or
merchantability or fitness for any particular purpose, and shall in no event be
liable for any loss of profit or any other commercial damage, including but not
limited to special, incidental, consequential, or other damages.

Other Marshall Cavendish Offices:
Marshall Cavendish International (Asia) Private Limited. 1 New Industrial Road,
Singapore 536196 ■ Marshall Cavendish Ltd. 5th Floor, 32-38 Saffron Hill,
London EC1N 8FH, UK ■ Marshall Cavendish International (Thailand) Co Ltd.
253 Asoke, 12th Flr, Sukhumvit 21 Road, Klongtoey Nua, Wattana, Bangkok
10110, Thailand ■ Marshall Cavendish (Malaysia) Sdn Bhd, Times Subang,
Lot 46, Subang Hi-Tech Industrial Park, Batu Tiga, 40000 Shah Alam, Selangor
Darul Ehsan, Malaysia

Marshall Cavendish is a trademark of Times Publishing Limited

ISBN 10: 0-7614-5503-5
ISBN 13: 978-0-7614-5503-5

Please contact the publisher for the Library of Congress catalog number

Printed in China by Everbest Printing Co Ltd

Photo Credits:
All black and white photos from the author except page 264 (Corel Stock
Photo Library); pages 39, 118 (Marcia Lieberman); pages 76, 89, 139, 149;
(Kristy MacDonald) and pages 21, 24, 206, 210 (The Weekly Packet) pages
x-xi, 4-5, 132-133, 170-171, 204-205. 212-213, 249 (Photolibrary).
Colour photos from Getty Images pages d-e, h, j-k, l-m, p; Photolibrary
pages a, b-c, f-g, i, n-o ■ Cover photo: Photolibrary.

All illustrations by TRIGG

ABOUT THE SERIES

Culture shock is a state of disorientation that can come over anyone who has been thrust into unknown surroundings, away from one's comfort zone. *CultureShock!* is a series of trusted and reputed guides which has, for decades, been helping expatriates and long-term visitors to cushion the impact of culture shock whenever they move to a new country.

Written by people who have lived in the country and experienced culture shock themselves, the authors share all the information necessary for anyone to cope with these feelings of disorientation more effectively. The guides are written in a style that is easy to read and covers a range of topics that will arm readers with enough advice, hints and tips to make their lives as normal as possible again.

Each book is structured in the same manner. It begins with the first impressions that visitors will have of that city or country. To understand a culture, one must first understand the people—where they came from, who they are, the values and traditions they live by, as well as their customs and etiquette. This is covered in the first half of the book.

Then on with the practical aspects—how to settle in with the greatest of ease. Authors walk readers through how to find accommodation, get the utilities and telecommunications up and running, enrol the children in school and keep in the pink of health. But that's not all. Once the essentials are out of the way, venture out and try the food, enjoy more of the culture and travel to other areas. Then be immersed in the language of the country before discovering more about the business side of things.

To round off, snippets of basic information are offered before readers are 'tested' on customs and etiquette of the country. Useful words and phrases, a comprehensive resource guide and list of books for further research are also included for easy reference.

CONTENTS

FOREWORD

Foreign vacationers to the United States are likely to return home delighted by our country. The vastness and landscapes surpass expectation, the richness of ordinary homes seems astonishing, and above all, the friendliness of the people to strangers is unforgettable.

Culture shock is what happens when you stick around a little longer. It is the most natural—and elusive—of ailments. "If one were to offer men the choice of all the customs in the world, they would examine the whole number and end up by preferring their own," wrote the Greek historian Herodotus almost 25 centuries ago, describing culture shock. But we rarely are insightful enough to realize that it's cultural differences that separate us. We don't see our own ways of doing things as conditioned in the cradle. We see them as correct, and we conclude that the people from the other country have grave failings.

So our longer-term visitors start to complain: "These Americans are always in a hurry; they are so materialistic; they aren't sincere; the children are spoilt; they don't care about their families." The points vary according to country of origin. Brazilians find us work-crazed, Japanese think we are self-indulgent, Chinese think we're selfish, British consider us unsophisticated, and Mexicans see us as greedy.

This book attempts to explain why we act the way we do, and in what ways our behavior is in accordance with our cultural values. Some of these values may seem questionable to you, but if you grasp what makes Americans tick, your stay here—whether long or short—will be far more interesting, and your culture shock minimized. And perhaps you will be more forgiving of the aspects of American behavior that trouble you.

If you have come to stay for good, it is all the more important that you try to be sympathetic to American culture. In fact, you will do best to acquire some American qualities yourself if you want to succeed. Furthermore, you don't want to end up in one of those enclaves of foreigners which nourish themselves on disdain for America—while their children are becoming more and more American. (This is not the

ACKNOWLEDGEMENTS

Any book that attempts to generalize about culture must begin with a disclaimer. No amount of research frees a writer from her own particular background. This is mine, which undoubtedly affects my outlook: I'm a native of the state of Massachusetts, which makes me a 'Yankee'. My forebears were mainly Scottish, English, Irish and Dutch. I spent part of my childhood in a small farming town in New York State's Hudson River Valley and treasured this experience of small-town life in a place that clung to old-fashioned American values. As an adult, I lived for a dozen years in New York City and have spent the last 29 years in California, where I married into a Jewish family of Hungarian and Eastern European origins.

I have my grandmother, Mary Hannah Augusta Fife Emerson, to thank for early instruction in correct behavior. Her emphasis on points of etiquette left me more observant of the lapses of others than I would sometimes wish to be.

However, the fish do not have the necessary perspective for reporting on their own sea, and this book could not have been written without the help of the many immigrants I interviewed, some of whom were old friends. Their reflections make up the backbone of this book. My greatest thanks go to Ali Awartani, Ridvan Bircicek, An-Ching Chang, Rani Devadasan, Uwe Dobers, Mufeed Droubi, Ocean Epstein, Angelo Garro, Brian Gitta, Bernadette Glenn, Greg Gorel, Agneta Heijl, Sid Irwin, Lakshmi Karna, Lata Karna, Fauz Kassamali, Dorothy Kino, Fusao Kiuchi, Ashis Mukhopadhyay, Joanna Oliveira, Lourdes Quesada, Mike Pham, Edda Piccini, Elizabeth and Marian Price, Carolina Rosales-Wyman, Dagmara Svetcov, Alice Leong Smith, Citania Tam and Regina Waldman.

Kathleen Wolf directed me to some rare texts (such as Judy Winn-Bell Olsen's unpublished Little Glimpses) and also arranged for me to meet her language classes and those of Josephine Lewis at Alemany Community College in San Francisco. For a fresh and updated outlook for this latest edition, she assigned my questions to her students at City College of San Francisco and once again arranged for me to meet with them. In all cases these roomfuls of students from around the world produced wonderful insights.

For editorial help, my utmost gratitude is due to Katherine Wanning Major. Earnest thanks also go to Andrews Wanning, Beth Gutcheon and Robin Clements, Suzanne Mantell, Jim Churchill, and Nikki Meredith. For other kinds of help, I am grateful to Kristy MacDonald, Sally Taylor, Patricia Emerson Watson, Rufus Wanning, Molly Wanning, Bill Wilson, Kathy Stein, Lynn Ferrin, and Elsa and Alfred Lipsey. For generosity with photographs, Marcia Lieberman and The Weekly Packet of Blue Hill, Maine. For hospitality above and beyond the call of duty, the Press family of California. For her good work and being supportive, thanks are overdue to my agent, Heide Lange.

Finally, I must thank those many cultural analysts who went before me, whose books are listed in the bibliography at the end.

Esther Wanning, 2005

Many people's first impression of the USA are that it is filled with huge cities with high-rise buildings as seen through television and the movies. But the country has vast rural areas devoted to the cultivation of wheat, corn, and other grains.

MAP OF USA

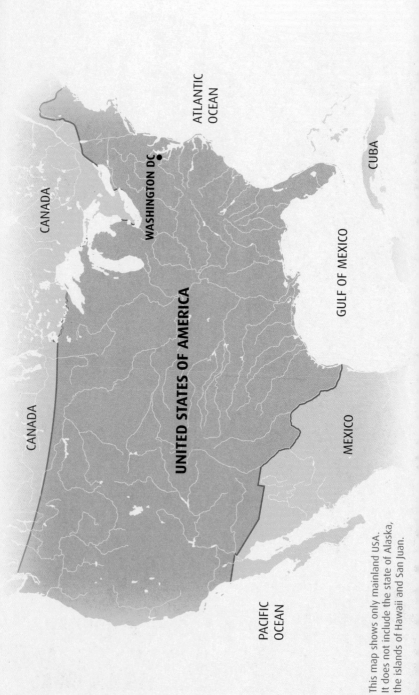

ATLANTIC OCEAN

CUBA

CANADA

WASHINGTON DC

GULF OF MEXICO

UNITED STATES OF AMERICA

CANADA

MEXICO

PACIFIC OCEAN

This map shows only mainland USA.
It does not include the state of Alaska,
the islands of Hawaii and San Juan.

FIRST IMPRESSIONS

CHAPTER 1

'America is so vast that almost everything said about it is
likely to be true, and the opposite is probably equally true.'
—James T Farrell

LANDING

No matter how long you stay, you will always remember your first impressions of the USA. But different people react differently—because they come from different countries or maybe just because they saw different American movies. One Asian who landed in San Francisco was surprised that the airport wasn't bigger! TV had made our airports look huge and confusing. Other visitors are instead overwhelmed by the airport's enormity.

A well-travelled Russian was bowled over by how quick and efficient it was to go through customs. "Everything is easy in America," he notes.

Says a New Zealander, "As soon as I landed at the NYC airport, I went to the McDonalds and was super-excited about eating their burgers in America (even though my cheeseburger was terrible). Then I took the bus to Manhattan, and it blew my mind to be really in New York seeing the things I'd seen on TV and soaking up the magnitude of everything—New York is the coolest city in the world."

Many are thrilled by the clean, fresh air, especially those coming in to the West Coast. Says one Brazilian, "It was like coming from a catacomb into the bright sun."

Some are not so happy about the fresh air. They want to smoke, and in many airports there are only a few smoking lounges, and in some you can't smoke at all. Serious smokers may have to exit the airport building to smoke.

Arriving in the City

"Everything looked big—the houses, the people, the size of a soda. The freeway had five lanes," says a Chinese man. But other people are surprised that most buildings aren't tall and that so many houses are made of wood.

Many people note, "There's hardly anyone walking on the streets. Just cars."

A woman from Mongolia was amazed to see Starbucks everywhere. "Everyone must be addicted to caffeine," she said. At restaurants, people immediately are struck by how big portions are in restaurants. Often, too, they're disappointed by the food: "Too oily." "Snacks are either too sweet or too salty." "The cold sandwiches aren't good." But one Chinese man happily adds, "In Chinatown, the food is as good as in China!"

Astonishing to many is the number of homeless in most of our cities, sleeping on the streets and asking for spare change. At the same time, there are so many new, expensive cars on the road. So the big gap between rich and poor is immediately obvious.

Most people are amazed at how clean the streets are. "They have a special machine for cleaning streets," notes a Guatemalan. "And there are garbage cans on every corner."

There's some surprise at how casually Americans dress. "They never dress up. They have no style," says a Brazilian. "They just wear jeans and sweat suits, and women don't wear heels." "They're very casual, but clean," says a Mexican. "You can wear anything," said one visitor. "It's very easy to dress."

Many people, whether landing at New York, San Francisco, or Chicago, are surprised at how cold it is and wish they'd brought warmer clothes. Perhaps they've seen movies made in Los Angeles—where it actually can be chilly too.

"I liked the sense of space," says a Malaysian. "There are no fences between the houses, and people's doors are open." Everyone finds the suburbs remarkably clean. But a Chinese man says, "Bring a lot of tapes from home. It's so boring." "So many different birds," another person pointed out. "In China, they'd be on the table."

Aerial view of Manhattan reinforces the stereotype that 'things are big' in the USA.

This American's warm smile makes up for his lack of formality in greeting his guests.

THE PEOPLE

The number of fat people is striking to many. The number of tattoos is also a shock. Visitors, especially those in San Francisco, are astonished to see gay people kissing. "Lots of churches," a Chinese woman was surprised to observe when she arrived.

Very often the friendliness is the first thing people notice. "The customs officer was very friendly." "They smile to strangers and open the door." "They are very polite." "American people talk well to strangers."

To an Indonesian, American manners were disconcerting. "People looked at me straight in the eye. This is how they portray sincerity and honesty, but it's rudeness in my country, so when I arrived it was intimidating."

A woman from El Salvador says, "I always tell newcomers that they don't have to be afraid of the police—or of men. There are laws against men harassing women, and if anyone bothers you, you should report him."

One Chinese arrived in New York City just in time to see an anti-war demonstration. He was astonished. "You couldn't do this in my country," he says.

OTHER SURPRISES

You don't take off your shoes indoors... Students may be disrespectful to teachers and chew gum in class... Disabled people can get jobs and use the buses... Lots of people swear... At some streets there's a beeper at the stoplight so that blind people can cross... People treat their dogs like babies... You have to tip everybody... Rent is very high... There are lots of places where you can play basketball and tennis for free... Nothing happens at night... After 9:00 pm, almost everything is closed... People don't really carry guns.

'I only regret that I have
but one life to lose for my country.'
—Nathan Hale, last words,
September 22, 1776

THE COLONIAL PERIOD

When Christopher Columbus, celebrated as the discoverer of America, landed in the West Indies in 1492, he found a generous and friendly people whom he called Indians (because he thought he had discovered the westward route to India). He was not kind to them. He killed some, captured others and enslaved more to mine for gold.

When the English settlers arrived in the 17th century, many Indians mistakenly thought there could be room for both themselves and the Europeans; the Indians did not understand the concept of private property that drove the newcomers. They also lacked European firepower, and when driven to defend their land, their bows and arrows proved no match for guns.

Directly and indirectly, the Whites massacred the Indians throughout the first two hundred years of their occupation, until the Indian population was reduced to a small proportion of its original size and pushed onto reservations in the infertile West. The last major battle wasn't fought until 1890, but it was clear much earlier that the Land of the Brave had passed to European hands.

American culture acquired a few agricultural tips and some place names from the Indians, but little else. Our language, institutions and religion came directly from Europe. For many years so did the livestock, fine clothes and furniture, literature, and music.

The Declaration of Independence

As the victors in a series of wars between European nations, the English became the rulers of north-eastern America, but the colonists chafed against English rule and taxation. In 1776, they rebelled. In the famous Declaration of Independence ('We hold these truths to be self-evident, that all men are created equal; that they are endowed by their Creator with certain inalienable rights; that among these, are life, liberty, and the pursuit of happiness'), the colonists declared themselves an independent nation. Five years of fighting ensued—the War of Independence—at the end of which the British surrendered and went home, and the original thirteen colonies became a free nation, the United States of America.

The United States Constitution

In 1789, the American government was formally established according to the United States Constitution, which includes the Bill of Rights. The Bill upholds individual rights against those of the government. The Constitution is vastly quoted in American life; the most frequently quoted parts are those that deal with freedom of religion, free speech, freedom of assembly, and freedom of the press.

It is because of these constitutional rights that prayer is not allowed in schools; that newspapers may criticise the government; that the police may not search your home without a warrant; and that any group may form a political party. The determination of constitutional rights lies with the Supreme Court, which decides how the Constitution relates to specific cases.

States' Rights

Many rights and responsibilities were reserved for individual states, which causes confusion for visiting foreigners. Many laws (such as the laws regarding divorce, drinking, wages, guns, education, and driving) vary from state to state. When corporations establish their headquarters in a particular state, they must follow the laws of that state. Each state has its own school and taxation system.

The system of government outlined in the Constitution derived from English traditions—limitation of executive power, bicameral legislature, trial by jury, and protection of individual rights. Although some assert that the system has best served the interests of the landowners who created it, the system has, nevertheless, provided a government of unusual stability.

One Creed/One Nation

The ideals of democracy, equality, and freedom served an important purpose as the country grew older. As a nation, America was singularly bereft of unifying concepts. Whereas most peoples are unified by race, language, culture, traditions, and history, America's immigrant population had little in common other than the initiative to get ahead. In the days when communication was slow, the country was too big for a strong centralised government. Instead, democracy became the faith, the unifying theme, of the new nation.

> America may be the only country in the world founded on a creed.

During the first half of the 19th century, the doctrine of equal rights was developed to mythical proportions. A. A. Bennet wrote in 1827, "We may look forward to the period when the spark kindled in America shall spread and spread, till the whole earth be illuminated by its light." Individual liberty, in the American mind, became synonymous with America, and Americans consider themselves the world's freest people.

Until the last quarter-century, Americans were generally very proud of their democratic political system. We thought of our government as uniquely democratic, run by representatives of the people, chosen in honest elections. This was not necessarily so, but it was not much called into question.

Today, the amount of campaign money required to win high office is so great that candidates are forced to seek money from those who have it. Without money, a candidate for national office can't buy television advertisements, and those who don't advertise on TV make little impression on voters. Consequently, there is widespread opinion that corporations and the very rich acquire disproportionate power through making campaign contributions. It is apparent that businesses with special interests in the laws that are passed get the ears of their legislators through these donations.

Some states limit contribution amounts, and a new law was passed in Congress in 2002 limiting corporate contributions. However, there are loopholes in the new law, and nobody expects that money will not continue to affect politics. One particular factor has been the Supreme Court's ruling that the right of free speech gives people the right to spend as much of their own money as they want to win office.

But Some weren't So Equal

Despite America's creed of equality, in reality constitutional rights have been unevenly distributed throughout our history. Each immigrant group has been subjected to discrimination; the Chinese in particular suffered from laws that once prohibited Chinese land ownership, marriage with whites, and other such rights. African-Americans have had a long and unique history of discrimination, even after slavery ended. Women were not allowed to vote until 1920, and it is only in the last twenty-five years that discriminatory laws against women have been struck down. Today, all discrimination according to race, color, sex, or creed is illegal, but it nonetheless continues in various forms.

Intractable as America's race problem seems, at least philosophically we are against prejudice. Most Americans do not accept the idea that some people are born inferior to others, and it is not socially acceptable to make slighting statements about people on the basis of their race. (However, people are less delicate about references to nationality, and jokes about the Polish, the Irish, the Chinese, the Scottish, etc., may be heard.) To dislike people because of their color is considered ignorant and stupid, and no responsible citizen makes outright racist statements.

Continued on the next page

Continued from previous page

Since the attacks of 9/11, the status of Muslim-Americans is more problematical. Americans generally understand that most Muslims deplored the attacks. And yet the visa process has become much stricter, and Muslims may find themselves often searched at airports and meeting with suspicion elsewhere. The fear that members of Al-Qaeda could be lurking in our communities, planning further attacks, makes people forget that moderate Muslims consider violence antithetical to their religion.

With this possible exception, most foreigners interviewed for this book (from all parts of the world) held that racism has not been a big problem for them. Today there are many more women, African-Americans, Hispanics, Asians, and other ethnic groups in government than in years past; it's the economic pie that has not been so readily shared.

DEMOCRATS, REPUBLICANS

There are only two major parties in the United States: Democrat and Republican. In most states, people must register themselves with their chosen one party to vote in the primary election, in which the candidate for the party is chosen. Except in non-partisan local races, 99 per cent of elected offices are held by Democrats or Republicans.

Democrats traditionally found support among blue-collar workers, labor unions, environmentalists, and ethnic minorities. The Republicans got many of their votes from white Southerners, farming communities, and corporate boardrooms. Yet, despite a Democratic predilection for increased social services and a Republican emphasis on lower taxes, the parties were in many ways similar. Both regularly promised a strong military, free trade, individual liberties, and (in recent years) smaller government.

However, so much has changed politically since the election of George W. Bush in the year 2000 and the bombing of the World Trade Center and the Pentagon on September 11, 2001, that even astute political analysts are bewildered. The parties are far more polarized than they were in the 20th century. Washington observers say they have never seen so little compromise and such maltreatment of foes.

Ideologically, the splits are profound. Furthermore, the 2000 election was contested and after an unheard-of 32-day delay finally decided by the Supreme Court. Some Democrats continue to doubt Bush's legitimacy. There were also problems in voting in the 2004 election, in which Bush won by 51 per cent, and Democrats are leading a movement, resisted by Republicans, to improve and regularize the election process.

Red States, Blue States

The divisions in Washington are exemplified by the extremes in the 'blue states' and the 'red states'—catchwords that took root during the 2004 election. The 'red states' are in the South and in the heartland of America. These are the Republican states where President Bush's support is strongest. In these states, evangelical Christians are a dominant force and have a significant influence on elections.

Anti-abortion sentiment is profound in the red states, along with the beliefs that homosexual practices are sinful (and gay marriage offensive), and that the government should reflect Christian beliefs. Family values and patriotism are very strong. And yet the abortion rate, the divorce rate, and the number of teen births are highest in the red states. Perhaps it is not surprising that the fervor against these practices is highest where they present the greatest problem.

The 'blue states' contain the more heavily populated, urban and coastal areas—such as New York, California, and the New England states. These are the more 'liberal' areas—which generally mean that they favor increased social services, spending money for such matters as education, libraries, and rehabilitating prisoners and are concerned with fairness for minorities, with civil rights, conservation, and gun control. Socially, they are permissive, less moralizing, less absolute about Biblical meaning. They vote Democratic, and many people in these states deplore the policies of President Bush.

However, visitors should not think that the divisions between red and blue are black and white. There are plenty of gays and lesbians in the red states and born-again Christians in the blue states. Even in Republican strongholds, substantial minorities voted against George Bush, and in some of the 'red states', the election was close.

Besides Democrats and Republicans, there are scattered very minor parties, which hold no important offices. Because we have a winner-take-all system, offices only go to those who have won a majority of the votes, unlike in a parliamentary system. It should also be borne in mind that while any citizen over aged 18 is entitled to vote, for most elections fewer than half the voters turn out.

Foreigners often find Americans naive about politics and ignorant of foreign affairs. Do not expect that Americans will know anything about your country's government, wherever it is.

RECENT HISTORY
The Rise of the USA
The United States, despite its burgeoning wealth, was not a major power until the 20th century. Foreigners often considered Americans ignorant, uncultured and unsophisticated. Before modern communication systems, Americans were too far from the European capitals to follow their fashions and too busy working the land to care about them.

After the two world wars in the 20th century, however, the USA could no longer be regarded as a backwater. Whatever its cultural deficits, its farms provided food for the world and its factories exported much of the world's manufactured goods. American jazz and American movies stamped the USA onto world consciousness.

The Vietnam War
The Vietnam War, which engaged American troops from 1964 to 1973, caused much conflict between Americans. It gave rise to the largest anti-war movement the country had ever known; there was acute division in the country between those who did and did not support the war. At the end, despite the deaths of 50,000 Americans and the

dropping of seven million tons of bombs, America withdrew in defeat. There is still bitterness in the country over the war, which was stirred up by the 2004 presidential election because the Democratic candidate, Senator John Kerry, though a Vietnam War hero, first achieved name recognition as an anti-war activist.

The Sixties

The Vietnam War gave rise to a rebellious generation. Students led the anti-war movement, which led from questioning the government's Vietnam policy to questioning the entire history of the United States as it was represented in their history books. The civil rights movement had been a precursor of the anti-war movement, and the anti-war movement, in turn, led to support of women's rights, Indian rights, and farm workers' rights, among others.

A broad spectrum of young people—who became known as 'hippies'—experimented with communal living, sexual freedom, and drugs, while proclaiming the power of love. Long hair and imaginative clothes distinguished hippies from 'straights'. Rock music provided the theme songs.

However, the establishment hardly stumbled, and by the late 1970s the ageing young rebels found it politic to join society as it was. Society had certainly changed—for economic as well as political reasons. The affluence of the 1960s was over. Many more women held jobs than ever before. In some respects the appearance of egalitarianism was more pronounced. Many social rituals were out, dress was more casual, and discrimination less blatant. But the inequities of wealth and privilege remained; some of the Sixties' generation went on to fight for environmental causes, while others turned inward to focus on personal self-fulfilment.

End of an Era?

For over a hundred years, the USA enjoyed extraordinary economic growth, and we came to expect this growth would continue forever. We got used to having an ever-increasing Gross National Product to solve our problems. We could talk about equality without having to make sacrifices.

Taxes remained low, individuals profited, and there was enough left over to pay for social programs. But after 1972, there was a serious recession, combined with double-digit inflation. It wasn't until the 1990s that the country really recovered, and the recovery didn't last long. Fast on the heels of extraordinary stock market highs, the USA followed Asia into a recession at the start of the 21st century.

Social services in the USA have never been on the same level as Europe's, and the safety net for the system's losers is inadequate. Since the 1990s, social services have been cut back even further, in the name of making big government smaller. Union membership has now dropped to 13 per cent of the work force, and few people have job security. With welfare benefits low and home prices high, unemployment quickly leads to an upsurge in homelessness.

Adding to insecurity has been a wave of home foreclosures for people who have been unable to make mortgage payments, often people with poor credit histories holding "sub-prime loans". These are people who were not able to qualify for a regular loan, but instead bought a house by paying higher and sometimes adjustable interest rates. When house prices fall, as they have done in much of the country, they are out of luck as they are unable to refinance.

The US economy remains basically strong, although the government maintains a very large deficit. This debt will have to be faced someday, but few politicians dare mention raising taxes.

September 11, 2001

On September 11, 2001, Muslim extremists hijacked four U.S. airliners. Two planes were deliberately crashed into New York's World Trade Center, which both collapsed, and another plane plunged into the Pentagon in Washington, America's military headquarters. Passengers of the fourth plane overpowered their hijackers, and the plane crashed in a Pennsylvania field. The combined death toll from the terrorist attacks exceeded 3,000.

The effect on the USA was devastating. Americans had never before been attacked on their own soil in such a manner. It became clear that Osama Bin Laden, the exiled Saudi Arabian leader of the terrorist organization Al-Qaeda, was behind the attacks. The U.S. turned the full force of its military against Osama Bin Laden and his Afghanistan hosts, the Taliban, a month after the September 11 attacks.

The Taliban was easily defeated, but at this writing Al-Qaeda remains operative, along with other terrorist organizations. In early 2003, President Bush went on to attack Iraq, for reasons that may always be hotly debated. President Bush said at first it was because Saddam Hussein was developing nuclear weapons; he later said it was to establish democracy in the Middle East. Support and opposition to the Iraq War divides the country, with much more support in the 'red states'.

Since the invasion, the U.S. has been embroiled in a controversy reminiscent of the time of the Vietnam War. It is generally acknowledged by all sides that the US made disastrous mistakes from the beginning in its occupation of Iraq, which led to sects fighting the Americans and each other. At this writing, there is little support in the U.S. for continuing the war, but withdrawal is very difficult. Al-Qaeda has now become a force in Iraq, although it wasn't before the war, and the overall breakdown of order is for some a reason to leave and for others a reason to remain.

What is indisputable is that around the world anti-Americanism has exploded since the U.S. attack on Iraq. It has been a complicated and growing force since the end of the cold war, and Americans are puzzled by it. We have always regarded ourselves as the good guys. President Bush has claimed that the reason for it is that evil hates liberty; few others would regard that as a satisfying explanation.

Simply the fact that the U.S. military budget is greater than that of all other countries combined probably is a sufficient reason for people to focus on and fear the U.S. Ivan Krastev, a leading Bulgarian political scientist, considers that anti-Americanism gives many groups in other countries a handy vehicle for expressing anger by many groups in many countries. It gives them a focus for disappointment with democracy and the market: "Governments are trying to convince frustrated publics that America is the problem."

But there are a number of people in the U.S. who think our foreign policy really is the problem, that America disregards the damage it does in pursuing its own interests. The growing disparities between rich and poor worldwide may contribute both to religious extremism and to hostility toward America—and to the growth of terrorist groups.

A fear often discussed in the U.S. is that important American freedoms may be compromised in the effort to track down terrorists. While we do not want our enemies freely plotting deadly attacks by e-mail, neither do we want the government reading our e-mail. According to one survey, nearly half of Americans thought that there should be some curtailment of liberties for Muslim Americans. Slightly more thought there should not. The more frightened people are by terrorism, the more they are willing to sacrifice civil rights. The reverberations from 9/11 seem likely to continue for many years.

IN GOD WE TRUST

The American viewpoint on religion is paradoxical. We extol the separation of Church and State (and the freedom to worship in the religion of one's choice), but in public life few people dare admit to having no religious belief at all.

The Supreme Court keeps watch over freedom of religion—prayer is not allowed in schools or during public sports events.

Religion is supposed to be a private matter, between the individual, his conscience, and his Church.

Nonetheless, the idea is widespread that decent people believe in God and that ethical standards spring from religion; this notion extends beyond the religious right. Politicians frequently assure the electorate of their faith in God. The President Bush has spoken often of being "born again," and he says in his State of the Union address, "God is near," and the White House holds regular prayer breakfasts. Religious belief jibes with American optimism and the faith that justice will prevail, if not in this world, then in the next.

Our coins all have 'In God We Trust' cast on them; the Pledge of Allegiance to the Flag calls us 'one nation, under God'. The legality of this phrasing is regularly reviewed by the courts.

The religious right has devoted its energy to becoming a huge political force and to electing Christians who support a Christian fundamentalist platform. Their success in registering new voters in 2004 led to the election of George W. Bush for a second term.

However, despite this religious upsurge, the U.S. remains a very secular society—in the minds of some visitors, too secular. They see a country in moral decline, where people have so much personal freedom that society is in chaos.

Nobody could deny that a great deal of what meets the eye—billboards, television, magazines—is vulgar. However, people should not imagine that American's lives are truly reflected on the advertising space or on television shows. Even the many, new reality programs generally expose bizarre characters in strange situations, not reality.

The Christian Majority

It's the Christian God that most people have in mind when they invoke Him. In the United States, 77 percent of the population describe themselves as Christians; 3 percent are Jewish; Muslims and Buddhists are 0.5 percent each. About 14 percent claim no religion, and the rest are divided between thousands of other religions, old and new. The only national religious holidays are Christian holidays, but employers must

This man, bowing his head in prayer in a coastal town in Maine, is prompting his dog to bow its head in prayer too.

respect the demands of anyone's religion and grant leave of absence when religion requires it.

Nine out of ten Americans claim to believe in God, and one-half are affiliated with a religious group. However, even churchgoers aren't necessarily deeply involved with their religions (although some are). For many, the church serves mainly to provide a setting and a ritual for weddings and funerals.

Sectarianism

A majority (52 percent) of Americans are Protestants—Christians who do not follow the Church of Rome (Catholicism). As Protestants have no central

God and Country

Motherhood, God, and the Flag. Any United States politician who hopes to be re-elected must take these three sacred icons seriously. While most foreigners will easily comprehend the tributes paid to motherhood, the attitude to religion remains confusing to many and that towards the flag mystifying.

authority, there are hundreds of denominations. All adhere to one God and the Bible, differently interpreted. Some have very dignified services, whereas others involve a lot of emotional display. As a general rule, it's the dignified ones (Episcopalian, Congregational, Presbyterian) that are the more upper class, and many a rising salesman has switched from the Baptist to the Episcopalian Church when he moved to a better neighborhood.

Most of the remaining Christians are Catholics (24 percent), a group by and large reflecting Irish, Italian, French, and South American immigrants. The Catholics have known discrimination and even (unjustifiably) have been suspected of dividing their allegiances between the Roman Pope and their country. Until the election of John F. Kennedy, people thought that no Catholic could become president.

Abortion

No issue brings out religious divisions more strongly than abortion. Since 1973 and the Supreme Court decision of Roe vs. Wade, any woman who so desires may have an abortion. However, there is a strong movement (called 'Right to Life') to make abortion illegal once again. The campaign against abortion is rooted in the religious belief that all human life is sacred and begins at conception, but many feminists think that the real root is the desire to keep women subservient and pregnant.

The Catholic Church considers contraception as well as abortion immoral. However, Catholic women actually practice birth control as much as other American women do.

The only other Christian group of any size are the Mormons, which comprise 2 percent of the population. Besides these established religions, there are numerous religious cults. Religious cults have been prominent through our history, but most cults depend on a charismatic leader and usually don't outlast him or her. Cults demand a wholehearted commitment from the followers, and scandals erupt among them frequently.

Various Hindu and Buddhist leaders have attracted a significant following in recent years. Some of these leaders are learned messengers from the East, and others acquire power and wealth, while making a little learning go a long way

Born Agains

The 'Born Again Christians' are the most surprising among today's religious sects. Not long ago, intellectuals assumed that in the modern scientific age, belief in God would not last much longer. They were wrong. Instead, millions of people have joined a variety of evangelical groups. These people, who include President George W. Bush, are sometimes also called 'Born Agains' because they believe that their lives started anew when they accepted Jesus Christ into their lives. They believe in the importance of 'evangelizing'—introducing others to Jesus—because to them it is the only way to gain eternal life.

Evangelicals used to be largely uneducated and strongest in the South. Recently, however, they've been showing up in growing numbers on college campuses and in prosperous communities. This puzzles those who wonder how educated people can believe in miracles, but evangelicals wonder how others can fail to believe.

Charities

Judeo-Christian values emphasise the importance of aiding the poor and unfortunate. Many of the hungry are fed from church basements, and some of the country's largest charities are run by church groups. Hospitals, homeless shelters, workshops for the disabled, schools, teen centers, and countless other projects are church or synagogue-supported—although often run without any overt religious overtones.

Churches also often support missionaries who go to distant lands to spread the Gospel. Many of them also work as teachers, doctors, or nurses.

Evangelicals consider the Bible the word of God but may be willing to consider various interpretations.

Fundamentalists, a subset of evangelicals, consider every word in it literally true, despite contradictions—which leads to the problem of evolution.

Darwin or Adam?

The Bible says that God made the world and the first man and woman (Adam and Eve) in six days. (On the seventh, he rested, which is why Sunday is supposed to be a day of rest among Christians.) If this is true, the theory of evolution, as described by Charles Darwin, must be wrong. So say the fundamentalists. The evolutionists say that man evolved over millions of years.

The evidence is strongly on the side of Darwin, but there have been many court battles brought by those who cling to

These cub scouts in a Memorial Day parade are demonstrating their patriotism by waving flags.

the Bible's teachings and want to see 'creationism' taught in public schools. They have been losing their cases lately, and over this issue, many fundamentalists have withdrawn their children from public schools altogether and enrolled them in Christian schools.

Fundamentalist preachers can be seen on many cable television stations, and visitors should try to watch them at least once. However, they should not mistake these preachers as representing mainstream thinking.

THE FLAG

Patriotism comes close to being a religion in America. Patriots demonstrate their love of America and freedom through respect for the flag. Politicians constantly pay homage to flag and country and would not dare to suggest that the United States is not the greatest country in the world.

Citizens of other countries pay homage to their flags too, but the belligerence with which Americans proclaim their patriotism is surprising to outsiders. In many countries, to insist that your country is the best country of all is unpleasantly chauvinistic. But Americanism means believing America is a special nation chosen by God.

Professional sports events begin with the singing of the national anthem (whereupon men take their hats off and some people put their hands on their hearts). The flag waves above all government offices. Although the Supreme Court has ruled that the right to burn the flag is protected, there are still laws (mostly unenforced) about bringing the flag in after dark, not wearing it, and not trampling upon it.

Many schools begin each day with the students standing up and facing the flag with their hands on their hearts, saying "I pledge allegiance to the flag of the United States of America and to the Republic for which it stands—one nation, under God, indivisible, with liberty and justice for all".

PEOPLE

CHAPTER 3

'Perhaps this is our strange and haunting
paradox here in America—that we are fixed and
certain only when we are in movement.'
—Thomas Wolfe

THE ONLY REAL NATIVES IN THE USA are the American Indians (now often called 'Native Americans'). The rest of us spring from families who immigrated to this country within recent history.

Among Caucasians (or Whites), the Spanish and English were the first colonists, arriving in the beginning of the 17th century. They were soon followed by Dutch, French, Scottish, Irish and German settlers. In the 19th century, great numbers of Irish and Chinese immigrated, escaping famines at home. Thereafter, there were waves of Scandinavians, Italians, Russians, Jews and Greeks. Most of these people arrived poor and stayed poor; the high levels of immigration kept wages minimal. In 1922, Congress set immigration quotas, repealed in 1943, that favoured Anglo-Saxons and virtually barred Asians and Africans.

Many African-American families have been here longer than most as their ancestors were brought here forcibly from Africa as slaves. The African slave trade was outlawed after 1807 but continued illegally until all the slaves were freed by the Civil War, which ended in 1865.

Statistics show that, legally at least, immigrants from Mexico, the Philippines, India and China now predominate, once again changing the ethnic make-up of the country. Illegal immigrants arrive in large numbers from Mexico and Central America, slipping in through the southern border and adding to a large, low-paid labour pool.

Choice Grain

It is an axiom among Americans that we are an exceptional people because our forebears were those with the pluck to abandon their native lands and start anew here. As early as 1669, a William Stoughton wrote that God 'sifted a whole nation [England] that he might send choice grain over into this wilderness'.

The American humorist HL Mencken argued instead, 'the majority of non-Anglo-Saxon immigrants since the revolution, like the majority of Anglo-Saxon immigrants before the revolution, have been, not the superior men of their native lands, but the botched and unfit.' It was Mencken's view that it was easy to get ahead in America because the competition was third-rate. Unlikely as this is, it is a nice counter-balance to the sense of superiority Americans sometimes display.

VARIETIES OF AMERICAN LIFE

People have asked me, "How can you generalize about America when there are so many regional differences?" Americans—like most people—think most of their behavior is merely human, not cultural, and the few elements that vary, such as the Amish farmers or Southern cuisine, as the cultural part. In fact, the similarities in customs across the land, big as it is, are vastly greater than the differences.

It is the culture of the white middle class that is reflected in this book because it is their values and practices that shape America. Although many of our people are neither white nor middle class, most nonetheless subscribe to the majority outlook. Even people born elsewhere begin to change their ways after a few years' exposure. "I knew I was becoming an American," says an Iranian, "when I started wanting to have time to myself."

Regional Differences

Regional differences, such as they are, are most notable in the South. Family counts for more there, and money less. Time is a little slower, hospitality a bit fuller, the work ethic slightly less full-blown. The South lost a war that the North won (the Civil War or War Between the States), which has given the white Southerner a heritage of failure and defeat that Northerners are exempt from.

Yet the South does not feel like a foreign place. Airports are identical, the phones work the same way, and most of the merchandise is the same as everywhere else. The same hotel and fast food chains thrive all over the country. In the commercial centres, where international business people gather, only the hot weather may indicate it's the South. Anyone looking for regional variety should abandon the cities and explore small towns. Throughout the USA, and especially in the South, there are rural communities where the values described in this book appear subordinate to family ties and tradition.

Southerners were once considered to be more racist than Northerners, but this is no longer necessarily the case. Atlanta is the new Mecca for educated blacks, many the descendants of great-grandparents who went North to escape racism. Not only have attitudes changed in the South, the diversity is fast increasing. It was once hard to find a decent egg roll below the Mason-Dixon line, but the number of Asians has grown geometrically in recent decades, particularly in pockets in and around large cities, creating a much more varied culinary scene.

Southerners tend to be effusive and friendly, and visitors are likely to enjoy the famous Southern warmth and politeness. However, warns a disaffected Southerner, "Don't believe everything they say."

Southerners are traditionally less direct and frank than Northerners, less apt to tell you about their neuroses and their family problems. They may have deep roots in the places where they live and have an extended family living nearby. Consequently, social circles may be closed to newcomers—foreigners and American-born as well. Life in the South can prove lonely for those without secure contacts.

New England (the area made up of the states of Maine, Massachusetts, New Hampshire, Vermont, Rhode Island and Connecticut) was a Puritan stronghold in the 17th century, and some people think they can detect the origins in today's inhabitants. New Englanders, known also as Yankees, are theoretically reserved and quiet, more apt to speak in monosyllables than to babble. They are traditionalists, preferring the old to the new. They make no promises they cannot keep. They are slow to accept newcomers but will in time, should the newcomers prove reliable. The foreigner living in New England needs only patience. Friendships once developed are lasting.

Yankees would also like to think that they are less materialistic and less trendy than the average American. Many of the oldest and most respected schools and colleges are in New England, giving the region an intellectual reputation.

New Yorkers (residents of New York City) are in a category of their own, with a reputation for being impatient, fast-talking and rude. Nowhere else in the country is it necessary to put one's head down and elbows out to jam onto a subway or bus. And yet many people find New Yorkers remarkably friendly and helpful. Do appreciate their wit, which New

Yorkers have in abundance, and note their fast pace. One of the special pleasures is watching the speed at which the deli workers can slap together a sandwich.

Visitors to New York are most likely to see Manhattan, which is only one of the five boroughs of New York City (NYC). Manhattan is a lively and exhilarating place, jammed with every nationality, young single people, aspiring artists and actors and successful entrepreneurs. People go out a lot and stay up late. Should you find yourself in New York's outer boroughs, you'll see a very different kind of life, largely dominated by families and often by one or another ethnic group.

Midwesterners are credited with being plain-speaking, down-to-earth, and conservative. One thinks of Midwesterners as unglamorous but genuine. Midwesterners don't like 'phonies' so in the Midwest we can all relax and be ourselves. But you might not want to be your most outrageous self. They don't like 'show-offs' in the Midwest. You are likely to find office dress a bit more formal than elsewhere, in keeping with the old-fashioned, conservative spirit.

Your new neighbors in the Midwest may bring you a cake when you move in and be a little more excited about having a foreigner in their midst than in the more cosmopolitan parts of the country. This is the heartland—friendly, family-oriented people. The Midwest is known for its plains and farms—miles of corn and wheat—but you can also find anything else you might want to find, from sophisticated cities to excellent universities.

Californians are expected to be healthy, trendy, superficial and empty-headed. The beautiful blondes and the Hollywood money are concentrated in the southern part of the state. Northern California has the more intellectual and left-wing reputation, represented by the University of California at Berkeley (known as 'Cal'). Californians pride themselves on open-mindedness, and as the state is home to a vast mix of peoples, you ought to find ready acceptance wherever you're from.

Californians are heavily satirized for starting or buying into every kind of new-age, spiritual or healing art to come along. And it is true that crystals, astrology, visualization, past lives, homeopathy, you name it, all have centres in California. And you may find many people more interested in self-healing than in you. Or in hiking, bicycling, surfing, politics, environmental reform, or organic farming. Some people have left their families as far behind as possible in coming to California; they don't want to get tied down here either. Closeness of any kind could seem binding.

Yet, you may meet the best friends you ever had in California. All these stereotypes about America's regions may hold some grains of truth, but in fact you may have to work pretty hard to observe them. New England is full of chatty, emotional people and the South has its share of cold and quiet ones. The Midwest has plenty of artists; I've lived in California for decades and still can't categorise the people.

Food

Local distinctions in food are few but held dear. You must go to the South to find hominy grits (a form of corn). New York City, heavily under the influence of the Jewish deli, serves up a vast number of hot pastrami (smoked and seasoned beef) sandwiches. You won't get many crawfish outside of Louisiana. But 90 per cent of the dishes on any menu in the country are the same everywhere. Freezing, storage and growing techniques have seen to it that if Americans like something, they can have it wherever they go.

ETHNIC GROUPS

Cultural differences between ethnic groups are probably greater than regional differences. Many African-Americans have retained a somewhat separate culture with distinctive language and strong ties to the extended family. The outlook is likely to be more group-oriented than in the individualistic white culture.

Black culture tends to be matriarchal. Employment has always been easier for black women to find than for black men; the black woman's average income is higher than the black man's and more of the women go to college. The result can be male disappearance, and fathers are frequently absent. But uncles, aunts and grandparents may be very present. Families tend to be strict with children, although love and caring are strong. The church is important in African-American communities and provides leadership and hope.

Native American (Indian) tribes pride themselves on retaining their cultures, despite all the whites' efforts to obliterate them. Some, living on reservations, continue to speak their own language, practice their own religion and ceremonies, and follow customs extremely foreign to those of white Americans. That they have continued to do so, despite several centuries' efforts of missionaries and government first to annihilate and then to assimilate them, is a testament to the strength of their cultures.

Nonetheless, Indians have tremendous problems of poverty and alcoholism. Life on many reservations is bleak and hopeless. Casino gambling (see page 174.) has provided a source of revenue, but not all tribes benefit equally from it.

Scattered about in obscure pockets of land throughout the country are traditional white communities where the values are very different from those itemized in this book. Some have ideologies very far from the mainstream. The Amish, for instance, don't use electricity, plough with horses, and wear 19th century clothes. Here and there, religious groups live communally in defiance of the American passion for private property. Unless you are a sociologist, you are unlikely to meet any of these groups.

Less obscure are large urban communities of Chinese, Japanese, Irish, Poles, Russians, Vietnamese, Italians, Mexicans, etc. In some towns and cities you can also find enclaves of Scandinavians, Hungarians, Germans, Laotians and scores of other nationalities. Each group, to a certain extent, manages to retain aspects of their native cuisines, holidays and habits.

Despite its size, the USA is not as diverse a country as we sometimes like to think. We have institutions and businesses that impose unity on us all. People who have grown up in this country, on the whole, have gone to the same schools, watched the same television shows and movies, read the same magazines, shared the same historical events, taken in the same nightly news, worked for the same companies, and been subjected to the same advertisements in addition to speaking the same language.

However, some pundits believe this common ground is becoming fragile as the media presents more options for each point of view; a cluster of cable channels, radio stations, web sites, and blogs cater to each particular viewpoint. So both left-wing and right-wing people are increasingly getting all their news from their own corners, thus each group becomes more extreme and further from a middle ground. Or so they say.

Black Americans

The lot of African-Americans has been the most difficult of any American group. Until the Civil War, they lived under one of the most brutalizing versions of slavery in history. Afterwards, they began their lives as free people without property, skills, education, or civil rights, in a land in which they were widely regarded as inferior.

In the Old South (the Southeast) especially, blacks were segregated. They were not allowed to eat in white restaurants, stay in white hotels, or use white bathrooms. Schools, parks and swimming pools were all segregated. The worst jobs were reserved for blacks. It was not until 1955 when a tired black woman, Rosa Parks, refused to give up a seat on the bus to a white man that the civil rights movement started to gain any ground in integrating public facilities. In 1964, an omnibus Civil Rights Bill was passed by Congress, banning public segregation.

African-Americans also fought a long struggle in the North against unofficial segregation, which was not so blatant as in the South, but has proven perhaps even more entrenched. Blacks lived in separate neighborhoods and were the last hired and first fired. Attempts to guarantee African-Americans places in public universities and workplaces, called 'affirmative action', have been stalled recently and outlawed in some places, on the grounds that in no way should race be a factor in assessing potential candidates.

The unemployment rate for African-American men is now very high, and the problems in the poor communities are vast. Nonetheless, at least for some, the opportunities have greatly improved. The first black senator was elected in 2004, the son of a Kenyan black man and a white woman from Kansas. "In no other country on earth is my story even possible," says this man, Sen. Barack Obama.

Americanization

In many ways, American habits are a product of affluence and are spreading to other parts of the world. Extended families are less likely to live together when they can afford separate homes. It doesn't seem so bad to be alone when you're home with cable television, an Internet connection, an iPod in one ear, a phone in the other, and plenty to read. Small families indulge their children more than large ones ever could, and children who own cars become less dependent on their parents.

In other countries, when jobs become available for young people in distant cities, when television and computers begin to dominate home life, when ready-made foods appear in the markets, the culture appears more 'American'—although the resemblance could be entirely superficial.

AMERICAN VALUES

Like peoples everywhere, Americans don't think of themselves as having American values. We simply imagine that the qualities we hold dear are those that matter to all mankind.

In this we are mistaken. American values are uncommon. This becomes clear when an American advisor launches a project in an underdeveloped country. The American, who plans to bring prosperity to the natives, ends up in despair because nothing gets done. He cannot imagine that there are societies where getting things done isn't top priority. He is baffled to discover people who do not seem to want to improve themselves. He cannot understand individuals who are not eager to change their status in society. He goes home in defeat, thanking God that he is an American.

What he does not understand is that American values could only have been forged in a new country full of opportunity. We are a nation almost entirely of immigrants, steeped in the belief that anyone with talent can get ahead. We cannot comprehend people who think it is more important to go visit a sick mother-in-law than to put in a new sewage system.

American culture is commonly dated from the first permanent English settlement of 1607; from that point we see our history as a record of progress: from wilderness to space stations in a few centuries. We conquered the original inhabitants, overthrew the English rulers, cleared the forests, opened the West, built skyscrapers, won the World Wars and extended the comfortable life to the masses. We achieved all this—as we see it—because of dynamic individuals who never stopped seeking a better way.

This viewpoint may change in the 21st century. Certain realities are beginning to affect our sunny outlook towards the future: We no longer have the highest living standard in the world, and today's young people cannot assume that they'll be better off than their parents. The road to success looks more difficult than it did a generation ago. Terrorist attacks have made the world a scarier place. But our response at present remains to work harder, not to look for satisfaction elsewhere. Realities change much faster than values.

Equality

It is a sacred belief in America that all people should have an equal chance at success. Such an idea could only be taken so seriously in a nation of great opportunity, and it has been opportunity, as much as democracy, that has made America the 'Land of the Free'. Were resources scarce and possibilities limited, people would only be free to go nowhere, and equality would have had a very different meaning.

'The US, too, has its national customs and traditions, but underlying them is the ideal that each person is free to choose his own destiny, unfettered by the social chains of whatever old world one had escaped from. '
—Ian Buruma

When the USA was founded, the population was small and the resources were vast; those both aggressive and lucky could go far. In 1782, a Frenchman, St. John de Crevecoeur, noted that it was in going from a servant to a master that a man became an American. Actually, many people through the years remained downtrodden, but there have been enough examples of upward mobility to keep the myth of equality alive. Democracy could promise visible fruits. Everybody might not win, but everybody (so goes the myth) was eligible to get out on the racecourse. Family and connections were not required. Effort and brains and imagination were.

Because the country's natural resources seemed endless, Americans developed an economics of abundance. We do not see our personal wealth as having been gained at the expense of others. Instead, we think of the rich as creating opportunities and jobs for others. We are very frank about admiring rich people, and, despite ample evidence to the contrary, we consider wealth a sign of merit.

The American system traditionally contributes the sense that everybody plays by the same rules. The government's job is to keep the course equal, to protect the rights of every aspirant. When people at least believe that they have a chance, it seems worthwhile to try to advance themselves—and when they fail, to try again. If, on the contrary, they feel that only those in favoured positions can succeed, they are not inspired to make an effort. We like to think that anyone could become President of the United States—regardless of family, wealth, or background.

'Any man's son may become the equal of any other man's son,' wrote Fanny Trollope on visiting the United States in 1831, 'and the consciousness of this is certainly a spur to exertion.'

Much as conditions have changed since 1607—the frontier wasn't endless, industrial competition comes from around the world, and the greatest predictor of success is having successful parents—the conviction remains that each person is responsible for his or her own advancement. People who don't succeed tend to blame themselves, no matter how unlucky they may have been.

Future Outlook

Americans are profoundly future-oriented. While other societies look to the past for guidance, we cast our nets forward. We have a nearly exclusive respect for the future and what it will bring, and it's this belief in a brighter future that has given Americans their optimism. Whereas most peoples aren't surprised by cycles of good times and bad, we are accustomed to looking at our history as a record of forward progress. We trust that we have the power to affect the course of events. We do not believe that bad things are God's will, things to be endured.

Even these days, when statistics show the rich getting richer and the poor poorer—and when not all progress seems positive (environmental problems, job losses, community breakdown, etc.)—the belief remains that for every problem there is a rational solution. If it's ourselves we must change, we do so. Or perhaps it is all the government's fault.

The idea that life can always be improved accounts for Americans being in such a hurry. The contemplative man accepts the world as it is; the active man changes it. It is change that Americans believe in. Consequently, to say that somebody is 'very energetic' (no matter in what cause) is one of our highest compliments.

Future Shock

Because change comes so thick and fast, the American has been called 'the constantly jumping man'. Recent decades have been particularly fast-paced, in gadgetry as well as in mores. In the last few years, iPods, iPhones, digital cameras, MySpace, wireless internet, webcams, flat panel and high-definition TVs, and a medication for dogs that paralyses fleas have become commonplace. Alvin Toffler in his popular 1970 book, *Future Shock*, made the claim that all Americans are living in a state of shock due to the increasing tempo of change in our lives. Future shock, he says, is worse than culture shock because there is no resolution. The only resource is to become more adaptable than ever before, leading to a loss of identity.

Independence

Cowboys never were a large part of the population, and they're very scarce now, but in many ways they characterise the American ideal—self-reliant, tough, risk-taking and

Children are encouraged to do things for themselves at a young age.

masculine. The cowboy stands alone, pitting himself against the elements. His strongest tie is to his horse.

In many countries, people cannot conceive of themselves apart from the family or group they belong to; their loyalty is to the group and their achievements are for the group. In America, instead, self-reliance is the fundamental virtue. Each person is a solo operation, and independence is considered the birthright of every child. Our highest aspiration is self-fulfilment, and it's only the unencumbered person who can become his true self. Many decisions that would be made by the family or group in other cultures are made by the individual here.

Newcomers, especially those from tightly knit families, are frequently surprised to discover that American children quite regularly leave home—with their parents' blessings—at the age of 18. From then on, they will make most of their own decisions without their parents' help, having already been quite independent during their teenage years. A grown child who doesn't leave home is a source of concern. The child's job is to go out into the world and succeed. The job of the parents is to give the children every opportunity while they are growing up and then get out of their way.

While today's young people are unlikely to enjoy the job security or upward mobility of the past, our confidence in the American way remains. We still believe the deserving can and will succeed, without family interference. Even well-off parents fear to inhibit young people's efforts by 'handing it to them on a silver platter'. And when they do help them out, they will try to make light of their assistance. Children are not to be burdened with a sense of obligation.

Asian families, who by working together often quickly become home owners in the United States, are surprised to discover that American parents are not expected to contribute to the down payment on a house for their married children. Going it alone allows the children to be proud of their own success and not beholden to their parents. Often, parents do contribute though, especially when home ownership would be out of reach otherwise.

Many of the aspects of American life that seem most baffling to foreigners make sense in light of the freedom principle. Aged parents as well as children remain independent. If you want to go to Belize and open a boarding house, you do. If you want to walk alone to the North Pole, go ahead. You will be admired for achieving your goals. You don't have to stay home to take care of your elders.

In fact, sticking around your hometown could suggest a lack of backbone, a failure of imagination and courage. Psychologists like to see families in which each member is 'differentiated' rather than 'enmeshed'. People who are enmeshed with their families can't break away to follow their dreams. The majority of foreigners look 'enmeshed' to American psychologists.

To us, the individual comes first. We do not consider this selfish. A person serves society by living up to his potential. The classic American hero is someone who succeeds on his own, pulling himself up by his own bootstraps. The finest American literature, such as Huckleberry Finn and Walden, extols the rebel. "I did it my way," sang Frank Sinatra in a classic popular song.

Authority

It will not come as a surprise that a society that admires independence and progress does not have an automatic respect for authority. What deference people in authority do command is based on their actual powers rather than on their age, wisdom, or dignity. Old people are often seen as behind the times. It's instead the young who are expected to have special insight into the modern world. Not many American adults would consider consulting their parents before making a decision. They are more likely to consult their children!

After all, it was by overthrowing the King of England that the United States was born, and suspicion of authority has remained a pillar of American life. This attitude has helped establish the USA as the birthplace of innovations that have changed the world. If a better way of doing something comes along, we unsentimentally jettison the old way. But we also jettison people. In a society that changes as fast as ours, experience simply does not have the value that it does in traditional societies.

> 'One characteristic of Americans is that they have no tolerance at all of anybody putting up with anything. We believe that whatever is going wrong ought to be fixed.'
> —Margaret Mead

However, independent as Americans like to consider themselves, in the area of work they are not. Most corporations operate in a dictatorial manner and are not expected to accommodate complexities in employees' personal lives. If an executive's responsibilities require sudden travel, family obligations become secondary. Very long work hours are common. Most people think employers have a right to make these demands; the employee after all retains the freedom to find another job.

Land of the Too-Free

"I think one person should end where the other begins," said one US immigrant. Many foreigners agree that American freedom is excessive. Americans tend to leap to the conclusion that any limitation on their rights is an attack on the American way of life. Out on the frontier you could do anything you wanted because nobody was around to notice.

(The true frontiersman picked up stakes and moved as soon as he could smell his neighbor's smoke.)

But the right to self-expression, defended by the First Amendment of the US Constitution, is one we take very seriously. An art show that depicts Jesus Christ in an offensive manner may attract few viewers, but there is support for the artist's right to paint and show what she wants. Graffiti is even defended by some people on the grounds that it is a form of self-expression.

We are a rights-based society (rather than rule-based or group-based). We don't object to following rules, but we want to know that they're fair and the same for everyone. The idea that some people could have privileges that others don't infuriates your average American. Children are taught from a young age to 'stick up for your rights'.

> 'If you want to understand democracy, spend less time in the library with Plato, and more time in the buses with people.'
> —Simeon Strunsky

These equal rights are essential to the idea of America as a nation in which 'all men are created equal'. You may argue that equal rights are irrelevant in the face of great income disparity (as the French say, "So what if the rich have the same right to sleep under bridges as the poor?"), but we like to think that making money is a right open to all.

The Puritan Tradition

Although we have gone from a rural society to an urban one, some core American values are the traditional ones established by the European settlers in the 17th century.

The Puritans, a stern Christian sect, were among the first and most lasting settlers. Their values were well suited to survival in a strange new world: self-reliance, hard work, frugal living and the guidance of the individual conscience.

In addition, the Puritans considered earthly success a sign of God's favour and saw no conflict between making money and entering the kingdom of heaven. Americans continue to have few ideas about the holiness of poverty. It's a puritanical idea that people get what they deserve (adding to the difficulties of being poor or handicapped in the USA).

The Puritans would not have smiled on the conspicuous consumption of today, but they would have admired the unrelenting effort that goes into the acquisition of goods. Americans respect businesspeople. An Englishman who has made enough money may well be happy to retire to his country home. The American only wants to go on making more money, driven as much by the Puritan work ethic (often called 'the Protestant work ethic') as by the desire for more money.

The Puritan values still referred to today usually refer to a prudishness towards sex and enjoyment. Although the Puritans were not actually against good times, they did feel that people were basically sinful, and spontaneity revealed their inner wickedness. Today, to call someone 'puritanical' is generally not meant as a compliment, as it suggests that he or she is strait-laced and no fun.

However, Americans are positively schizophrenic about sex. Mass culture makes it look as if sex is completely open and free. Yet nothing will bring Child Protective Services to your door faster than the suggestion of inappropriate sexual behavior around children, and charges of sexual harassment in business are taken very seriously. Infidelity in marriage is the rationale for many divorces.

Good Works

Not all Americans are concentrating on staying young, losing weight and improving themselves. America is also a country in which individuals give a total of more than $199 billion a year to charity, and many give of their time as well. Small, local governments depend largely on unpaid citizens to run them. Public schools, water systems, hospitals, and many other public services are watched over by unpaid boards. Any number of charities—from soup kitchens to drop-in medical clinics—rely on volunteers. And many churches involve their parishioners in a range of good works, which can be anything from tutoring children to delivering a water system to a poor, small town in Guatemala.

This kind of active civic life is very important in a democracy and has been traditional in the US since the colonial days. The people involved generally find it highly rewarding and a source of strong community ties. In fact, there is an argument that America's economic success is built on these social networks.

Unfortunately, civic involvement in the US has fallen by practically every measure—from voting to bowling— since the 1960s. There are some obvious reasons: longer working hours, women in the workforce, long commutes, TV, videos, the Internet, and emphasis on self-improvement. When interviewed, people often report feeling socially disconnected and nostalgic for the old days when people knew each other. Perhaps this awareness will be a first step toward a reverse in the trend.

Efficiency: Time Is Money

If there is anything that warms the American heart, it's efficiency. Henry Ford was long regarded as a hero for implementing the assembly line. The assembly line reduced workers to cogs of machinery and ignored their boredom, but it produced goods fast.

'Time is money,' we say. Nothing is more American than the supermarket. Food is prepackaged, and shopping is impersonal, but the efficiency of the operation produces lower prices and less shopping time. The food's lack of taste has not created much customer resistance.

Fast-food operations calculate ways of saving a few seconds in each customer's waiting time. It's not just that we're impatient; lunch hours are short, day care centers charge extra if parents are late, and if the meter runs out, there's no getting out of paying the ticket.

Even when we're relaxing, we're watching the clock. If I go out to dinner in Spain, I won't expect any food to arrive at my table for an hour, and nobody will be surprised if dinner takes four hours. Here, even at a fancy restaurant, I want to be served promptly and be able to leave within two hours. I want to get more things done at home before the night is over.

Time Waits for No Man

According to anthropologist Edward T. Hall, we are a monochronic culture, meaning we operate according to schedules, doing one thing at a time. Sticking to the schedule is more important than the human interruptions to it. When the bell rings, the class is over, no matter how interesting the discussion at that moment.

> 'Early to Bed and early to rise, makes a Man healthy, wealthy and wise.'
> —Benjamin Franklin, *Poor Richard's Almanac*, 1738

There are some other Asian countries at least as efficient as the USA, but vast parts of the world cannot conceive of our concept of time. Time is all-important to us. We think of ourselves as people who are going places. Tomorrow is not going to be like today. Tomorrow, we'd like to be way down the road, and speed is going to get us there, not standing around chatting.

Consequently, we have come to see only practical and profitable activity as truly valuable. "How has so Spartan a philosophy descended on an age that hoped to make machines do all the useful work while man enjoyed his leisure?" asked Walter Kerr in his book, *The Decline of Pleasure.*

It does seem that Americans often lack the capacity to enjoy their achievements. We find more satisfaction in acquiring the trappings of the leisure life than in leisure itself. Activity—rather than family or community—gives us our identities, and very few people are able to rest on their laurels. The Puritan values still dominate.

THE NO-STATUS SOCIETY

In a status society, people learn their places and gain some dignity and security from having a place in the social order. Americans, however, are taught not to recognise their places and to constantly assert themselves. This can manifest itself in positive ways—hard work and innovation—but also in ongoing dissatisfaction. 'Democratic institutions most successfully develop sentiments of envy in the human heart,' wrote de Tocqueville.

As an American is always striving to change his lot, he never fully identifies with any group. We have no expressions such as in China where 'the fat pig gets slaughtered', or in Japan, where 'the nail that sticks out gets hammered down'. Here, nearly everybody is trying to stick out, which limits closeness between people. We say, 'It's the squeaky wheel that gets the grease.' According to Alan Roland, author of *In Search of Self in India and Japan*, in the United States 'a militant individualism has been combined with enormous social mobility', leaving very little group identity.

'Identity is the number one national problem here,' writes Eva Hoffman, the Polish-born author of *Lost in Translation*. 'Many of my American friends feel they don't have enough of it. They often feel worthless or they don't know how they feel.'

Loneliness is very common. Many people live by themselves and a great many spend nearly every evening alone. Telephones, televisions and computers ease the isolation, and most people have a few friends, but a sense of belonging to a group is largely absent.

Many people also suffer from a sense of failure. No success is good enough. Not everybody can reach the top, and those who don't blame themselves.

However, to someone who feels oppressed in another culture, American life can look wonderful. "Americans have a blank check, on which they can write anything they want," concluded one foreigner after ten years here.

The Status Seekers

"I just wanted to find a place where I would be accepted," said an East German who is happily settled in San Francisco. He is delighted that you don't have to be a doctor to be treated with respect and that people don't care who your father is. But the myth of equality should not fool anyone into thinking that America doesn't have a class system. We do, and speech, dress and level of education are strong markers. But it's a very fluid system, and penetration at most levels is possible for nearly anyone with enough money. Equipped with the money, one can acquire the taste, style and ideas that mark each class and launch a quick ascent of the social ladder.

There do exist a few clubs, societies and debutante balls that require old money for entry. People whose families were among the early arrivals in America may let it be known, but in point of fact, such lineage doesn't mean much (politicians prefer to advertise their humble beginnings) and one's level in society can be—like so many other things in American life—determined by one's own efforts. (Of course, only a few people actually do go from the bottom to the top. Most of the jockeying around is for levels in the middle class.)

Conformity

Despite the emphasis on independence, Americans do care a good deal what the world thinks of them. Only through the eyes of others can success have significance. The theory of culture analyst David Riesman (author of *The Lonely Crowd*) is that Americans are no longer primarily governed by inner values handed down through generations. Instead, he thinks Americans have become outer-directed people—guided not by their own consciences but by the opinions of others. To be liked, or at least envied, is crucial.

Money is the key to social position, and it is nearly impossible to be upper class without it (with the possible exception of Southern aristocrats). Thus the seriousness of money. If I make a lot of money, I can drive a Mercedes, buy a big house and join a country club. I will be accepted, not just because I have the money, but because the money proves that I have performed in society at a high level. If I am truly socially ambitious and have enough money to give large amounts to prestigious charities, I can hire a promoter who will guide me in an assault on high society. If I am hard-working, successful, generous and amusing on top of it all, nobody will mind how low-class my origins may have been. I would certainly do better not to pretend to advantages I did not have.

However, every generalization has exceptions, and not quite everyone admires money-makers. There are those who subscribe to a different code, called Class X by Paul Fussell in his book *Class*. Usually artists, intellectuals, or eccentrics, members of 'Class X' do their best to disdain the values of the rich. And yet, few are entirely unaffected by money envy.

THE CASUAL LIFE

Informality pervades our culture. The forms of our language do not change when we address a superior, as they do in many languages. People dress casually as much as possible. We use slang in nearly all circumstances. We slouch in chairs, lean against walls, and put our feet on desks.

There are, however, boundaries. In church, you sit up straight. You do not use slang before a judge. If your boss comes into your office and puts his feet up on your desk, you are flattered; he regards you as an equal. But you don't put your feet up on his desk. A lot of these distinctions are subtle, and foreigners can step on toes by trying to become American-casual before understanding the culture well.

Our degrees of casualness do leave a lot of room for confusion. Teachers who are informal ('Call me Janet') and friendly and open with their students want to be liked; they do not wish to be treated as any other friend. Should students respond by becoming too personal or forward with their teacher, they might discover a frosty barrier. A Brazilian remembers how hurt she was when she threw her arms around a friendly professor on seeing him in the street and he pulled away in alarm. 'I didn't understand the boundaries,' she says. 'After that, he became standoffish.'

Boye de Mente in his insightful book, *Etiquette and Ethics in Japan*, depicts the Japanese as difficult to penetrate on the outside and very open on the inside. Americans, he says, are the opposite. The top layer is very open and anyone can penetrate it. It is the inner layers that are hard to crack. Some Americans remain forever impenetrable.

Relaxed? No

Most of my countrymen will be eager to assure you that they live in a very casual, relaxed manner. This may be far from true. They may keep their houses spotlessly clean, never open their doors to strangers, and live a rigidly planned life, but it remains an article of faith that the good life is the relaxed one. Relaxing is a synonym for having a good time, as seen in the many advertisements which picture people lying around in the sun. However, much as people look forward to relaxing, they rarely actually do it.

It's hard to take it easy when time represents opportunity. The conviction that you succeed or fail by your own efforts—rather than by the whims of fate—is one that adds a high degree of tension to life. And without family and community to fall back on, success of some sort becomes critical.

The whole concept of achievement, whether in career or hobby (e.g. gourmet cooking), makes passing the hours in idle conversation seem like a waste of time. As that sage Ben Franklin said, 'Time lost is never found again'. Too much sitting around, and the American gets nervous and wants to be up doing something. Even on vacation, Americans want to 'improve each shining hour'.

It's not just that we work hard. Our leisure activities are demanding too. Besides the pursuit of health and fitness, any number of adult Americans are taking night classes, involving themselves in children's schools, coaching soccer, running church groups, bird watching, and redecorating. Weekends are full of camping, sports, and home improvement. Then when we get 'all stressed out', we take another course—yoga, meditation or stress management.

The person who never relaxes may end up turning to drugs for help, which may be one reason that alcohol, cocaine, marijuana and other illegal substances are such problems. Television (known as the 'boob tube') is another escape and induces a drug-like lethargy almost as effectively as the real drugs.

The family hot tub is a useful antidote to stress. Adapted from Japanese baths, it is a tub full of circulating hot water, in which four or five people can sit. The effectiveness of the hot water is such that nearly anyone can relax in one. (The question on most people's minds when invited to an evening in someone's hot tub is whether or not they will be expected to wear bathing suits. Probably yes. However, if your hosts are nude, you can take your choice as to whether to wear your suit or not. Naturally, you do not stare under any circumstances.)

THE CONTRADICTIONS

The alert visitor will quickly note much that seems contradictory in American life. Freedom of the press has not produced a well-informed public. We're proud of our democracy, but voter turnout is one of the lowest in any democracy. Despite our wealth, we have people sleeping in the streets. Americans are friendly, but neighbors don't stop to chat. Supplied by the world's richest farmlands, America's cuisine leaves much to be desired.

The social commentator Paul Goodman aptly wrote decades ago, 'America has a high standard of living of low average quality.' Despite the luxuries and conveniences Americans enjoy, our lives are not elegant. Even the very rich often do their own shopping, cooking and washing up and afterwards sit down to watch *Jeopardy* on TV. At the same time, the United States also has plenty of high culture, with operas, ballets and symphonies equal to any in the world. There is also an extraordinary variety available, as might be expected of a country of immigrants. Whether you're looking for Armenian Folk Dance or a zither society, it will be going on somewhere.

Expect also to find innumerable exceptions to any of my claims about Americans. Just as not every Japanese is hardworking and deferential to superiors, nor every Chinese devoted to family, not every American is ambitious, patriotic, money-grubbing or even unsophisticated.

THE FAMILY

Nearly all Americans have a family somewhere, but it's often far from evident. The lack of strong family ties is one thing that strikes nearly all visitors to America (with the exception of those from Sweden, where apparently the family is even less demanding).

When an American speaks of 'my family', he probably means his immediate, nuclear family: the group that lives

together in one household—father, mother and children. The 'extended' family—the grandparents, aunts, uncles and cousins—are often far away. Or even if nearby, they can be a small presence in each other's lives, visiting back and forth very little. A quarter of American households consist of one person living alone.

There are plenty of exceptions to this configuration; in rural areas, you'll find extended families that gather together every chance they get. But in the cities and suburbs, each small family is more often floating free of the hometown connections. And to a much greater degree than in many countries, individual members of the family carry on a social life apart from the others.

If you make American friends, you may know them for a long time before you meet their families. Various members of the family with different interests are expected to have different friends. Two women may lunch together or two men might regularly play golf, without ever meeting each other's spouses or children.

"Don't these Americans ever sit down and eat a meal with their families?" asks one Italian woman I know. Yes, many of us do, but according to the statistics, not regularly. Nonetheless, the family remains the entity we fall back on. Holidays, weddings and funerals bring the larger family together, and in times of trouble we turn to our families. But the trail of obligation generally runs only between parents and children. Few people feel much sense of duty to members of the extended family.

Finding a Mate

Marriages are supposed to be between two people who fall in love, and anyone who has seen Hollywood movies will be familiar with the ideal. Of course, anyone who actually insists on a perfect mate becomes sadly disillusioned, either before or after the marriage. So sensible people strive to love someone who is compatible, and then hope for the best. Extensive advice on how to create married happiness fills up books, magazines and workshops.

As in most aspects of American life, single people seeking partners are on their own. They will not be looking to their families for help, nor even for advice; friends may occasionally introduce friends to each other, but even this is uncommon. College is a golden opportunity, but after college there are fewer meeting points. Lacking a community life, single people once felt desperate.

Fortunately, the Internet arose as the modern matchmaker. At one time, advertising in newspapers or searching for love online was considered an embarrassing last resort. No longer. It's the current solution and more productive than hanging around in bars. And it encompasses all age groups and all gender preferences.

The big online services have their own sites; you can also check established sites such as www.match.com, matchmaker. com, and eharmony.com or simply search "personals." Fees for joining are generally moderate. You can find myriad niche sites for Jews, Muslims, Christians, Buddhists, vegetarians, pet lovers, etc. etc. The latest trend is varieties of personality testing, designed to match you with your soul mate.

When you 'meet' someone, you begin by exchanging e-mail correspondence. If that goes well, you advance to a telephone call. Finally, you meet. Online dating keeps many people up late at night, sitting at their computers. One note of caution: Only meet your dates in public places until you know them very well.

The Couple

Once joined, an American couple expects to be happily married, and to a large degree, they are. One obvious reason for this is the prevalence of divorce. If a couple gets along badly, they do not feel they must spend the rest of their lives together. This was not always so: to have 'failed at marriage' was a social stigma thirty years ago, and for this and other reasons more of the unhappily married stayed married. Since then, the American divorce rate has tripled.

The American idea of a well-matched couple (Raymonde Carroll elaborates on this in her brilliant book, *Cultural Misunderstandings*) is one which always presents a united front to the world. Each member of the couple should be highly supportive of the other (in the same manner that 'good' parents are supportive, rather than critical, of their children). They are expected to share a number of interests and activities and should spend vacations and weekend evenings together.

In public, the happy couple demonstrates 'coupleness' with affectionate gestures and solicitude. At parties, they will often be found chatting in the same circle. The suspicion that they might not prefer each other's company to all others is cause for concern.

A good many of those who do divorce never remarry. Thus one out of four American households with children is headed by a single adult. (In some of these, the parent never married.) Any foreigners thinking favorably of the American tendency for divorce should note that recent studies suggest that the children suffer long-term disadvantages. On average, they grow up much poorer than those in two-parent families, have less chance of going to college, and are less likely to have satisfactory marriages themselves. A young Korean exclaimed with astonishment, "Americans don't care when their parents divorce," but actually, they do. They may say it's fine, but many feel that they never really had a family after the divorce.

Homosexuals

Homosexuals were disdained in America for many years, but in the past forty years public opinion has largely changed, thanks to a civil rights movement similar to that of African-Americans and women. The law has now recognized that to discriminate against someone because of 'sexual preference' is akin to discriminating on the basis of color or gender.

While there remain many gays and lesbians (male and female homosexuals) who feel the need to conceal their homosexuality, most often in Southern and rural communities, there are now openly gay and lesbian people in nearly every profession and even in the US Congress. The Episcopalian church has consecrated a gay bishop, and most states allow gays and lesbians to adopt children.

In 2003, the U.S. Supreme Court ruled that gays and lesbians are "entitled to respect for their private lives." Nonetheless, despite increased tolerance for gays, many people, particularly fundamentalists, still believe that homosexuality is a sin and a chosen lifestyle, rather than an inborn trait, There are still many circumstances in which a gay couple cannot great enjoy the same rights and benefits as a heterosexual couple. Homosexuals want the right to marry and are entitled to in the state of Massachusetts, but the majority of Americans oppose gay marriage. It has become a very divisive issue.

Living Together

In the last thirty years, society has ceased to frown on sexual relations between unmarried adults, and many couples live together without getting married. A minority continue to live together indefinitely without getting married, but most of these arrangements conclude either at the altar (i.e., in marriage) or in dissolution. Most people still want their children to have properly married parents.

Single Parents

At some time or other during their childhood, half of American children will be living with only one parent, usually a mother. The child may have another loving parent involved in his or her life, but at least according to statistics, the mother is apt to be the sole support. Consequently, this is commonly a poor household. When the mother is a teenager, the odds become daunting that either mother or child will ever escape poverty.

When both parents remain involved in a child' s life, there is likely to be a court order determining how much time a child spends with each parent. In some cases, the parents have joint custody and thus are supposed to share the care of the child equally.

Blended Families

The 'blended' family occurs when divorced parents remarry, uniting their children into one household. Such families have many inherent problems. The stepparents are often resented and somewhere else the children have another parent, who is frequently on bad terms with his or her former spouse. At best, the children adjust, but the complications of blended families are many.

Housework

The division of housework poses a problem in many American households. Before the Women's Liberation movement, women did nearly all of it while men were expected to take care of the outdoor work—despite the almost total lack of outdoor work in urban households. Now that so many women have jobs, most people agree that housework should be shared. However, old habits die hard. In actual fact, the women still do most of the housework and childcare, although in younger couples the men contribute more than their fathers did.

Friends as Family

You may meet people who claim, 'My friends are my family'. These people very likely have, somewhere, a real family, but they feel much closer to their friends. American life changes greatly between generations. Parents who live in a Boston suburb, attend the Congregational Church and have steak cookouts may not know what to make of a vegetarian daughter living on the West Coast who periodically visits her guru in India.

Less drastic differences than this cause alienation in families. Distance alone may account for loss of contact. Instead of family, groups of friends may get together for Thanksgiving and Christmas, go on trips together, and share joys and sorrows. This is particularly true for those who are single, whether before or after being married.

Despite the appeal of replacing an inconvenient family with carefully selected friends, there is a drawback: Friends cannot be expected to proffer as much aid as family. Those who claim to rely on their friends usually are highly independent, with good health and sound finances. Even the best of friends may be keeping track of favors. Your sorrows are not their sorrows. In catastrophe, you are on your own and will probably turn to your real family. No matter how distant the family in America has become, it has not been replaced.

Babies

Fathers are often present in the delivery room, which has become a more humane place than it used to be. Most people aspire to natural childbirth (that is, with as few drugs as possible), although births still usually take place in hospitals, in case of complications. Some parents now choose to have midwives rather than doctors preside over the delivery.

If all goes well, women leave the hospital very shortly after giving birth. At least half of them breastfeed their babies, feeling that nature's way is best for many reasons. There is no prohibition against women leaving the house in the weeks after childbirth, and they may return quickly to their active lives. Breastfeeding in public is becoming acceptable, although the question of indecent exposure still arises!

The option of unpaid leaves for both parents is required by law in some states, but few people can afford them. Women often return to their jobs far sooner than they would wish.

'The thing that impresses me most about America is the way parents obey their children.'
—King Edward VIII of England

Professional couples may put off having children until they are in their thirties or even forties. They then generally feel that one or two children are enough. The long-awaited baby is much doted on and causes a drastic change in his or her parents' lives. The new parents who formerly went out to dinner nearly every night and saw every new movie now stay home and talk baby talk.

Bringing Up Children

Foreigners are shocked when they first arrive and hear American children say to their parents things like, "It's none of your business" or "Dad, you're really dumb." However, American parents feel their children have many rights, including freedom of speech. Children are also allowed to make many of their own choices—what to wear, what to watch on television, how to spend their free time, what extra-curricular activities to pursue, and even what school to attend.

This degree of freedom may seem ridiculous to non-Americans, but there are reasons why the upbringing of an American child is quite different from that of a Thai, Chinese, French, or Brazilian child. In most other countries in the world, parents feel that their obligation is to raise an obedient child who will fit into society and the family. The little ego must be moulded into that of a person who realizes her many obligations.

Not so here. Although there are many things a child must learn—from eating with a knife and fork to driving a car—the top priority is to raise an individual capable of taking advantage of opportunity. Such a person cannot be overly obedient or hindered by too many family attachments. American life is marked by change and those who thrive are self-sufficient, quick jumpers who can exist, if need be, far from family. Children are taught to be autonomous rather than to fit into the group.

THE ELDERLY
The Youth Cult

The elderly are also the victims of prejudice. The bias towards youth is so prevalent that even young men with a few grey hairs may dye their hair. At the very top, in the executive boardrooms, signs of age are permissible, but in most endeavors, older people—experience notwithstanding—are at a disadvantage.

Distressing as this is, it is not surprising in a country primarily interested in the new. Old people, who represent continuity with the past, have less to offer here than in a culture where tradition is valued. Young people are not attached to the old ways of doing things, and their flexibility is considered an important asset. In new industries, such as Internet technology, young people often do have more experience than their elders.

We have enormous faith in new ideas, new techniques, and new gadgets. If schools aren't trying to solve their problems by imposing new teaching methods, they're trying to solve them by bringing in computers and Internet access. Advertisements will make their entire claim for a product the fact that it is new. They don't even have to add 'better'. To

Old people hope to enjoy their leisure years and many move to the warmer Southern states. such as Florida.

us, 'new' assumes 'better'. If nothing else, young people are newer, and even their unoriginal ideas may look 'new'.

Several hundred screenwriters have brought a lawsuit against a number of major Hollywood studios for not hiring older writers. Many of the plaintiffs had been very successful but by age forty were finding doors closed to them while inexperienced youngsters were hired instead.

Much of the reason for catering to youth, of course, is that they have a great deal of spending money and have not yet developed brand loyalties. So everyone hopes to capture the youth market and in so doing find lifetime customers. It is not an accident that much American entertainment seems juvenile; it is designed for juveniles.

Forever Young

The desperation to look young intensifies yearly. Facelifts, once the province of the very rich, are now undergone by ordinary middle-class people. A range of operations tackle other signs of ageing. Wrinkles are the great enemy, and for their elimination millions of dollars of dubious creams and potions are sold. Hair dye has made grey-haired women scarce.

Although most older women wouldn't wear knee socks and miniskirts, they are not expected to adopt age-appropriate garb. No one would think that bright colors were more suitable for a young woman, or that the woman of years should not be wearing tight blue jeans and a blouse with a plunging neckline.

All people like to hear about how very young they look. One views old age as a stage of life when one is not in demand, when one has nothing to contribute. In a society where achievement is everything, those who are past contributing fall from grace.

Any Roof But the Kids'

Old people tend to spend their days among other old people or alone. The isolation of the old is astounding to many newcomers here. Traditional cultures would never think up such a thing as an old-age home (now called 'assisted living' or a 'retirement home'), an establishment made up entirely of unrelated old people and their caretakers.

However, you should not assume that old people are rejected because they're isolated. Whether or not the relationship is a happy one, grown children feel responsible for the care of ageing parents (or at least for seeing that they get care). But independence is valued as much by the old as it is by the young. 'I never want to be a burden on my children,' is a common phrase on the lips of parents. To have to give up one's own home and go live with a son or daughter, subjected to the moods of badly behaved grandchildren, helpless against loud stereos, ever conscious that one is not a contributing member of the household is an unwanted fate.

Even a retirement home is not always considered such a bad lot. Some are awful, but others are gracious and elegant—but expensive. Paying guests know that they are at least of financial worth to the institution, which is better than being a family dependent. The children may even be financing their parents' stay in the institution, but by not having them under their own roof they are graciously according them some remaining autonomy. Just as their parents encouraged them to be independent at a young age, the children are now allowing the parents to be independent. Having finished with child raising, it is felt that the parents deserve to be around their own peer group—other old people—rather than be bothered by young children.

There are a growing number of 'senior communities', which provide apartments in complexes designed just for old people. Many of these are in the balmier climates of the USA. No children are allowed (except as visitors), a rule set to please the old folks, who obviously do not delight in the pitter-patter of young feet as much as sentimentalists would like to think.

It's the poor (and recent immigrants who haven't acquired American ideas) who are most apt to spend their last years living with family members. The other options appear to be preferable to anyone who can afford them.

There is much talk these days about 'the problem of old people in America'. Part of the problem is that there are so many of them and in a few years there will be many more. Because people are living to be so much older, many 60-year-olds with heart diseases of their own are concerned about parents in their eighties.

Modern medicine has become fairly skilled at keeping very old people alive, but it has not necessarily succeeded at making them healthier. The result is that a large proportion of the country's medical care goes to aged people in their last years of life. Americans are peculiarly averse to dying, so many die in hospitals while trying to prolong life at all costs. An increasing number, though, fill out 'living wills', specifically defining how much medical intervention they do and do not wish to have. It is a good idea to have one of these if you do not wish to bankrupt your family with high medical bills while you're in an extended coma.

One fast-growing trend that is saving seniors from isolation: more and more are working into their sunset years. Between 2000 and 2006, the number of seniors between 65 and 74 in the labor force went from one in five to almost one in four. Although improved health is one reason, a large factor is the rising cost of health care and insufficient income to allow for a long retirement.

THE SPOILT CHILD

Ideally, the American system produces self-confident, capable people. However, it doesn't always, and foreign visitors frequently remark that American children are spoilt. It is true that demanding, tyrannical children are not uncommon.

American parents do not have the confidence they once had regarding child-raising. Therapists, educators, and doctors have become the experts on bringing up children. These experts taught that the child's emotional stability should be the chief goal. The child must be convinced that Mommy and Daddy will love him no matter what.

At the same time, parental ties to community and larger family (and frequently to each other) were breaking down, and so the parents themselves were becoming less secure. They were increasingly unwilling to be authorities, sometimes unpopular ones, in their children's lives. They wanted their children to be their friends. They did not like to say 'no'.

The Foreigner's Despair

To many immigrants to America, the worst part of life here is seeing their children bring home American attitudes of disrespect towards their parents. When the Korean father says to his son, 'Come home right after school,' and the son replies, 'You can't make me,' it is disheartening, particularly as society does not seem to be on the father's side.

In Korea, the son would never have defied his father. Here, immigrant children soon get a taste of the freedom American children enjoy and want the same. Whether or not they insist on it, the different standards nearly always cause family conflict. "We want to have fun, but our parents just want us to stay home," a Cambodian lamented.

It is inevitable that the children will want to be more like Americans than their parents would want them to be. The teenage world here is a demanding one, and the new immigrants are trying to fit in. It is better if the parents are not too rigidly attached to the way things were done back home. Families may have a painful period of adjustment as their children make their own decisions about their futures, yet ultimately the children will probably grow up to appreciate their family's culture and closeness. Parents, meanwhile, do best to trust their teenagers and not to try and manage the details of their lives.

One young Chinese immigrant in a language class, asked if she thought Americans were happy, replied "How could they be happy when they don't have their families around them?" Many of the students in the class nodded agreement. Young people who can combine American opportunities with their own family support structure will be well poised for success in America.

Appliances and urban living have freed children from chores, so schoolwork is their main obligation (and by most standards, there's not much of that). Most parents are loath to impose any hardship on their children. Toys are cheap so in this age of abundance—and smaller families—children have emerged with rooms full of stuff, including computers and personal televisions. If one is inclined to spoil the children, it is very easy to do so, unlike in a society in which the child's labour is needed and toys are few.

TEENAGERS

The teenage years are apt to be difficult for Americans. Delightful as it may seem to be on the threshold of total independence, in fact it can be frightening. Teenagers are aware that they have the task of fulfilling their large potential, but nobody can tell them what this potential is. They have many choices, and although many will be going on to college, they must decide where to go and what to study and, in some sense, who they will choose to be. It is a much more serious time of life for Americans than for some other nationalities, who see it as a last chance for good times before settling down.

Despite their fears—or perhaps because of them—American youngsters frequently cause their parents a lot of trouble during their teenage years. In fact, parents consider themselves very lucky if their teenagers are not extremely difficult. Simply being a teenager is an excuse for antisocial behavior. "It's his hormones," say the parents. There are responsible and mature teens, but they too will probably withdraw a great deal from the family during the teen years. After all, the goal is that the child should grow into an adult who is psychologically separate from his or her family.

Even an unusually family-centred teenager feels he must resist family activities for his own self-respect. Most would prefer not to be seen in public with their family. Parents will joke about this and usually cooperate. They know that this is a phase that will pass. One theory for the distress among American teenagers is that, while they are no longer children, they have no real function or responsibility in society.

Recently there has been a lot of writing about some very miserable children of privilege. These are often the ones who on the surface appear to be on top of everything, but underneath their perfectionistic drive and wish to satisfy their families' high expectations is little sense of basic security. Despite loving and affluent families, they exhibit epidemic rates of depression, anxiety, and substance abuse—even suicide.

Some foreigners may not be surprised to hear this. "Parents in the U.S. are more concerned about making money than spending time with their children," says a man from El Salvador. But sometimes these depressed children were the ones whose mothers gave up careers so that they be perfect at-home mothers. It may be that the children got more help than they needed and lost confidence in their own abilities.

Parents may give up trying to influence their teenage children altogether. It's the peer group that becomes all-important. Both boys and girls spend hours in front of the mirror and adhere to rigid standards of dress that identify them with certain groups. They would spend all their time with their friends if they could. Popularity is terribly important. They identify themselves with their chosen group through music, clothes, slang, and activities—nearly all selected from a world totally alien to the adult world. Nose rings, tattoos, and shaved heads provide the kids with cool ways to horrify their parents.

Not all teenagers, of course, are solely absorbed in teen life. There are a heartening number who give their time to good causes, evidence concern for the larger world, and are ethical, imaginative, and hardworking. Many teenagers have alert social consciences and are quick to challenge injustice.

Teenagers often have jobs, not because their families are unable to support them, but in order to have spending money. Parents are generally happy to have their children work; it's another sign that the kids are becoming independent, it gives them responsibility, and it keeps them out of trouble. Teenagers are usually paid, directly or through a weekly allowance, by their parents for doing chores and often for babysitting younger siblings.

Media

Being home together doesn't mean a family is communicating. TV, Internet, and computer games can be so compelling that direct conversation is rare. American kids are now spending an average of 44.5 hours a week in front of one screen or another. Unfortunately, no matter what the content, interactive or not, watching and clicking does not teach any important tools for life.

Psychologist David Walsh believes that children need to learn self-discipline—the most important ingredient for success—and that means delayed gratification and saying "No" to themselves. The electric screen is based, says Walsh, on a "barrage of Yes messages," a culture of "more, easy, fast and fun," undermining crucial character development.

If children spend many hours per day in these effortless ways, they cannot be expected to be very good at making a rigorous effort on demand. So American children, who can be very bright and intuitive, are often not inclined to apply themselves to the 'hard' stuff, such as learning multiplication tables or studying spelling words or even reading books. This gives a great advantage to immigrant children who are capable of hard work and thus capture a remarkable number of academic prizes.

You won't be alone if you severely limit your children's screen time. There are plenty of studies showing that the less time children spend on TV and video games, the better they do in school. The studies on Internet time aren't in yet, but you can be pretty sure that if your kids are doing what most kids are doing online, it's not helping their grades.

It's wise not to allow kids to have any of this media in their bedrooms. It might be more convenient for you to have the kids absorbed, quiet, and elsewhere, but it's much better for them if you're keeping track of what they're up to. The giant companies that are behind the media are not concerned about your children's character or future, but you are.

Television

Many social analysts think that television's domination of the American home is a major contributor to social problems. Television rivals family and church as the dispenser of values. Repeated thousands of times a day in advertisements is the message that acquiring stuff is a worthy social goal. It is a message that children easily succumb to.

Situation comedies depict children as fearless loudmouths who outsmart their parents, and children often imitate these fictional characters. Even worse, talk shows bring on real people who shamelessly discuss appalling problems.

American television content, with some exceptions, is of poor quality and the amount of violence gives a distorted outlook on the world.

Television interrupts family conversation, and children who watch television are found to have poorer imaginations than those who don't. Little children do not acquire language skills from television; learning to speak requires real people to speak with. On the contrary, actual neurological damage can result from spending the formative years in front of the television rather than in dialogue and play. Nor is the television a good English teacher for adults; conversation, reading and tapes are all far better.

I once asked a roomful of immigrants in an English class, who all objected to the low quality of American television programming, why they did not just get rid of the household television. They laughingly admitted that the whole family had become addicted to it.

Concerned American parents severely restrict their children's television watching. Studies regularly show that the children who watch the least television have the greatest academic and personal success. A small elite in the country have banished television from their homes altogether.

Video Games

The amount of time American children spend on video games competes with television time—13 hours a week for boys and 5.5 for girls (8th grade and younger). As video games are newer on the scene than television, there are fewer studies of their effects. Nonetheless, there is plenty of evidence that the more time spent on video games, the worse the school performance. It appears that video games use very limited parts of the brain; a child's time can be far better spent. Furthermore, recent studies have convincingly demonstrated that the violence in the games lead to more aggression and less helpful behavior.

Nearly every game has a rating on the box—from 'Early Childhood' to 'Adult Only' as well as a suggestion as to its content, such as 'Blood and Gore', 'Strong Language', and 'Fantasy Violence'. As with television, vigilant parents monitor both the contents of the games and the time spent playing them.

Ideally, parents will preview the games their children play, keep the game boxes out of the childrens' bedrooms and find out what goes on at playmates' homes. Unfortunately, in too many homes it's the parents who are playing the games rather than supervising the children. Recently, two starving children were removed from a Las Vegas couple who were too obsessed with video games to feed the children

Internet

At least sixty per cent of children ages 8 to 17 have computers now, and most are connected to the Internet. This great expands parental responsibility. The Internet can be very useful when doing research for term papers, but largely that is not what children use the Internet for. They are more likely to be in chat rooms or shopping. There are a great many sites designed for children, and while these are cleansed of overt sex and violence, many are heavily devoted to consumerism. So kids can be learning what is awesome and cool but not a lot else.

The American Library Association has a list of really wonderful sites for kids (ala.org/great sites) as well as information about how parents can oversee child computer use. At GetNetWise.org, you can learn about software that filters objectionable material, monitors chats, and limits time online. SafeKids.com has parents' and kids' pledges that set safety guidelines. The most important guideline of all is that parents monitor what their children are doing online. Just as you want to know how your kids are spending their time and who they're playing with in the park, you want to know who their web companions are.

Sex

'Dating' is less in vogue than it once was, and young people spend a lot of social time hanging around in groups of friends of both sexes. However, some teenagers begin to date as early as ages thirteen or fourteen. The extent of the date depends on age and parental permissiveness, but most parents see no harm in their youngsters pairing off at a young age—as long as the relationship does not become too serious. Most children have a curfew by which they are to be home.

A side effect of the sexual revolution was that teenagers began to feel that it was their right, if not their duty, to be having sex. The rate of American teen births skyrocketed, and while it is now falling, it remains the highest among Western countries.

However, foreigners should not assume that a date equals sex here in America. The more sensible teenagers are more likely to restrain themselves and see the virtue in doing so, or at least of using condoms and being very discriminating about their partners. And the presence of AIDS and other diseases has given further weight to the arguments against teenage sex. In fact, there is now an abstinence movement (largely spearheaded by Christian evangelicals), which encourages young people to declare their intentions to remain virgins until marriage.

Young foreigners are often pleased to discover the freedom they have to go out with (date) different prospective partners without settling down. We consider it a very good idea to shop around and meet many people before deciding on one.

Drugs

The other great threat on parents' minds is drugs. A variety of illegal drugs are widely available, and many teenagers use them. Whether or not drugs are considered 'cool' varies in different schools and communities. Besides alcohol, the most widely used drug is marijuana. The usual effect of marijuana is to make the user inarticulate and passive. You can sometimes tell if a person is 'high' by the redness of her eyes.

Cocaine (or crack, a cooked form of cocaine), methamphetamine, and heroin are the next three most highly used drugs. Many people are in our jails and prisons solely because they became addicted to these drugs. The War on Drugs has created many criminals, but it hasn't reduced drug use.

It is normal for teenagers to experiment with drugs, but few of those who experiment continue using them. There are a few who become quickly addicted, steal to support their habits and drop out of school, but these were not generally happy and well-adjusted children in the first place. If your children are doing well and have a loving family, it is highly unlikely that they are going to become drug addicts just because the opportunity presents itself.

THE YOUNG ADULT

In the 19th century, there were very few fields of work that required a college degree. A heavy dose of professionalism has now crept into our society, and even people applying for middle-management positions are required to have a college diploma. An advanced degree is required to demonstrate expertise at anything at all. Consequently, parents gear themselves up to make great sacrifices to see that their children are college educated.

Many young people contribute to their expenses while in college by working. There is no disgrace in holding down some menial job while 'getting an education'. As a matter of fact, it is a badge of honour to have worked one's way through college.

Moving Out

For economy, young people may live at home during their college years, but for many the college of their choice is a long way from home. After college, the norm is for them to find apartments of their own, which are often shared with other young people. The fact that their new housing may be far less luxurious than their parents' home is unimportant compared to gaining adult status.

Their careers, or the appeal of a more glittering city, may cause many to move to another city or state, the start of an odyssey that may keep them forevermore at a distance from the family, although they will visit on holidays. Once they have left home and are self-supporting, parents no longer feel much responsibility for them.

Yet, despite the expectation for a young adult to be independent, it's no longer rare for young adults to be living with parents. Often, they have moved back in after living elsewhere for a period. Referred to in the media as 'boomerang kids', they seem to be sensibly reacting to high rents and admitting that they like the comforts of home. As parents rarely regulate their grown children's sex lives any longer, why not? Some parents are pleased to have their children's company and some aren't, but all have probably asked themselves at some time, "Is there something wrong with this kid that he's had to come back home?"

Just the Cash, Please

Many parents do help their grown children with small outlays of cash, but they don't feel obliged to. Once they have provided their offspring with a good upbringing and education, their financial responsibilities are at an end (unless there's a grave emergency, such as severe illness).

Some foreigners find it strange that the tables don't turn at a certain point so that the young people are helping their parents. Unless the children have become immensely rich, there is no social pressure to do so. What's more, on average, today's young adults feel poorer than their parents, who years ago were able to buy houses when they were cheaper and now don't have the expenses of raising children.

THE AMERICAN WOMAN

Just how liberated are American women? In theory, we are the equals of men in every way. Many foreigners think that American women are on top of the world. But in fact, studies show that women, no matter how brilliant, are not taken as seriously as men. Furthermore, the average woman earns 77 cents for every dollar a man makes and still does most of the housework.

As a nation, however, we are committed to the equal rights of women. Jokes about women—as weak, flighty, bad drivers, extravagant, etc.—are considered tasteless. In the legal realm, there has been an enormous surge towards equality in the last 35 years. A woman can aspire to nearly any job or training program, and employers who do not promote women now may get sued.

Women doctors, lawyers, and engineers are far more common than they were a few decades ago. Women are supposedly not combatants in war, but they serve in every branch of the armed services and do everything else that men do.

While women now outnumber men in management and professional fields, they are still thin in the top ranks, and a woman is a rare bird in a corporate executive room. But an increasing number of women have moved to high government jobs, and the idea of a woman president of the USA is not inconceivable.

It is not solely discrimination that holds women back. There is some evidence that when executive women become frustrated and bored in their jobs, they leave to find more interesting work. Also, women remain accountable for the children, and the total commitment required for a high-powered career makes it very difficult to be a satisfactory mother too. Sixty percent of top executive women have no children.

Superwomen

The 'Superwoman Syndrome' refers to the efforts of women to excel as worker, wife, and mother. The well-paid working mother can provide nannies as substitutes for herself, but she may not escape the guilt that comes from not spending more time with her children. The conclusion is always that no one can be Superwoman, although some women give it a jolly good try.

Even the ordinary working woman leads a life of ceaseless motion. She rises early, sees children off to school, and races out of the house to her job. She may commute a long way to work, perhaps dropping off a child on the way. Coming home, she picks up children, then does errands, cooks dinner, supervises play and homework, puts children to bed, and prepares herself for another day's work.

A woman also feels the obligation to remain attractive and youthful, which requires hours devoted to exercise, beauticians, make-up, and shopping. The American woman often seems (or at least feels) less self-confident than her counterparts from other lands. In *Lost in Translation*, Eva Hoffman writes of the time and effort American girls expend on femininity. She herself, a Pole, 'never thought you had to do anything special to be feminine—surely, it's enough to be a woman, isn't it?' Not in the American woman's mind.

When the women's liberation movement accelerated in the 1970s, feminists hoped that good female values would change the world for the better—businesses would become less competitive and more concerned with humane values, men would joyfully take on their share of child-rearing, and women would no longer need to struggle to look like Britney Spears. But on the contrary, women have instead molded themselves to fit into what is still regarded as 'a man's world'. While women's dress is more varied than men's, they must bring the same hardheaded attitude to business to succeed.

The New York Stock Exchange (NYSE) at Wall Street is one of the most important stock exchanges in the world, and about US$ 127 billion worth of shares are being traded each day.

South Beach in Florida is one of the most popular beaches in USA. Colourful lifeguard stations add to the beach's party atmosphere, while the nightclubs and restaurants along the coast ensure an equally vibrant scene after sundown.

MALL

The famed Mall of America in Bloomington, Minnesota, receives 40 million visitors annually and marks the pinnacle of American consumerism. This mega shopping and entertainment centre carries more than 500 stores, a theme park, an underwater aquarium and a museum, among several other facilities.

The Grand Canyon in Arizona is a massive gorge believed to be caused by erosional processes of the Colorado River. Its unique and complex rock formation has made it one of the world's major natural wonders.

In a culture where media fame and stardom are highly-sought after, thousands of youths turn up at the Continental Airlines Arena in Massachusetts to audition for *American Idol*, a reality TV singing competition that allows ordinary citizens a shot at living the 'American Dream'.

SOCIALIZING WITH LOCALS

CHAPTER 4

HAVE YOU GOT A LIGHT MAC?

NO BUT I'VE GOT A PAIR OF DARK TROUSERS

'Good manners will open doors that
the best education cannot.'
—Clarence Thomas, Supreme Court Justice

INTERACTION
The Famous Friendliness
One distinguishing characteristic of Americans is our openness to strangers. Practically everyone agrees that Americans are friendly. Very few Americans care to put on snobbish airs, even if they secretly regard themselves as being far above the crowd. The president of the USA emphasizes what a regular guy he is.

Foreigners may be taken aback when strangers on the street say hello to them. You are expected to smile and reply or at least nod. Says a New Zealander, "Americans are the friendliest people without reserve I have ever met." A Pole observes, "I walk my dog and people say hi to each other. It may not mean much, but I like the sense of being among nice people."

Emotions
Americans do not see the need to hide their emotions. On the contrary, they often seem to be exaggerating them. Enthusiasm, for instance, rises to levels of seeming unbelievability ('It's great to see you, you look fabulous, let's have lunch soon.') These glad sentiments don't mean much more than, 'It is agreeable to be having this exchange on the street corner, and I may or may not be serious about lunch.'

A Vietnamese says, "I tell people they have to be outgoing here. If they are reluctant to be outgoing, they will end up alone."

Happiness here can be loudly proclaimed in big smiles, gestures and statements: "This is marvellous, best news I've ever heard." Unlike many Asians, Americans smile only around good news or happy feelings. An American smiles often, but not when embarrassed or confused, nor would an American delivers bad news with a smile.

Friendly—Not Friends

Saying hello doesn't commit you to anything. It only asserts that you subscribe to our code of democracy. Friendliness should not be confused with friendship. Many foreigners slip up here, and mistakenly think that all that warmth means they're going to have lots of friends. Then they become disillusioned and decide we're terribly superficial and shallow in our friendships. But most of the people we refer to as 'friends' are really acquaintances. True friends are not easier to come by here than anywhere else.

Bad news comes with a sombre, concerned expression. Expressing sadness does not come easily to us. Sorrow interferes with our upbeat, optimistic view of life, and people who are sad do not find ready acceptance. Friends may try to cheer a sad person up but can become quickly frustrated if the sad person doesn't respond.

Foreigners will do best to express themselves in whatever way comes naturally to them. If they try to be as demonstrative as Americans, they will probably only appear insincere.

Touching

Americans are what is known as a 'non-contact people'. Outside of hugs given in greeting and parting, touching, among adults, is generally limited to occasions when its sexual connotations are acceptable. If in a moment of warmth, a Russian man rests his hand on an American man's thigh, the American is stricken. Could this be an untoward advance? Likewise, two American men would never hold hands. Nor would two American women, although they would not be as put off by the whole idea as men would be.

Latin Americans find us cold in this regard; many Americans are envious of people who can reach out freely

Men slap each other on the back, or squeeze another's shoulder, but they avoid any touching that could appear to have sexual connotations.

and affectionately, but our strong sense of private space inhibits us. In conversation, Americans usually stand at least an arm's length apart and are made uncomfortable by people who press closer (unless the relationship is an intimate one). We are careful not to breathe into people's faces.

Children and pets are caressed freely, but the concern about child sexual abuse obliges one to be careful that nothing appears abnormal about one's affection towards children. Teachers must be particularly careful. And if there is evidence of parents sexually molesting their children, Child Protective Services may remove those children and jail the offending parent.

Talking

Because it is important to be assertive, Americans speak fairly loudly, at least compared to Thais or Malaysians, for example. Foreigners sometimes mistake the loudness for anger when an American is only trying to make himself understood.

Anger itself, within limits, is also more acceptable among Americans than in most cultures. If someone thinks he has been wronged, he may feel called upon to show his feelings. This is not to say that we admire people who are out of control—a temper tantrum is not a pretty sight—but a justifiably angry person will not be condemned whereas someone who 'lets people walk all over him' may well be. Some nice guys go far, but you can also become company president despite a reputation for 'blowing your top'!

We are taught to look into people's eyes during conversation. Someone who instead looks around or down appears shifty to us, although in actual fact one doesn't stare continuously at the other person but glances elsewhere every few seconds.

ETIQUETTE

As a low-context culture, we don't have many set routines for particular situations. Formality seems undemocratic to us, and Americans dislike rituals of etiquette that recognise class differences. Our easy manners contribute to the fluidity of our society.

Informal, of course, does not mean 'mannerless'. We would not be any sort of culture if we did not have some agreement as to what nice behavior is. You should refrain from making religious, ethnic, or racial slurs. Don't ignore women or children. Treat people equally. But on the whole, Americans will be very forgiving of awkward manners. We do not have the religious prohibitions that make innocent foreign behavior so shocking in some countries. Nothing but the flag is sacred in our public life and even the right to desecrate it is protected.

Politeness

Visitors usually find most Americans, for all their informality, very polite. This reputation seems to rest largely on the great number of 'Pleases' and 'Thank yous' we deliver, but also on the general recognition given to strangers. One should be considerate of waiters, garage attendants, and household help as well as of doctors and senators. Americans are often shocked to see the peremptory manner in which servants are treated in other countries.

"The way you Americans say 'Thank you' and 'You're welcome' all the time is hypocritical," objected one Chinese man. "You don't really mean it." It's true that we don't mean much by it, but it's an acknowledgement that we don't expect people to do things for us. Even when a service is not optional—such as when receiving change in a store—a person who doesn't give thanks appears rude to an American.

'You're welcome' troubles some newcomers with its suggestion that one has actually done something worthy of thanks. You can always say, 'Oh, it was nothing,' but if it really was nothing, it's best to stick with 'You're welcome.'

Of course, whether you consider Americans polite depends on where you come from. Some Japanese find Americans so rude that they think they are being discriminated against when Americans are only acting normally. Americans are so direct in their speech that they seem rude to peoples who speak in more embroidered styles.

Out in public, manners vary a great deal. A lot of attention has been given lately to a rising lack of public civility, particularly among drivers. And foreigners are often appalled at the behavior of children, who commonly are disruptive

Taboos

There are few taboos for newcomers to think about. Nobody has to worry about using the left hand, showing the soles of the feet, touching someone's head, or any of those prohibitions that seem so mysterious to Americans abroad. There are, however, a few socially unacceptable types of behaviour.

- Do not belch, that is, let gas upward out of the stomach while making an attention-catching noise. Flatulence should be as discreet as humanly possible.
- Do not spit. You may well see someone spit in the street, but you will know from the act that this person

in public. Surprisingly though, many of these same children grow up to behave quite decently.

Etiquette in Theatres, Concerts, Churches

There are countries where chatter by members of the audience does not cause offence, but this isn't one of them. Here, any movement of the lips during a concert or a church service is thought to be too much. Also: no unwrapping of cough drops, excessive coughing (leave if you must), cracking of joints, chewing gum, foot-tapping, jingling jewelry, or undue fidgeting. Or at least this is the ideal. In fact, many people are too restless to sit quietly through anything, to the distress of those who hold to the old standards.

The rules for the movies are slightly less strict than those at high culture events, but still commentary should not extend beyond a whispered, "I'll be right back." Noisy unwrapping of candy bars, etc., will produce dirty looks from those around you.

Extremes

Americans are not traditionalists, and new ideas can spread like wildfire. Since the 1960s, when much formality went out the window, each generation has felt the need to reinvent rules of daily behavior. Sometimes, in the process of ditching

has no class. A gentleman does not spit, even in his own backyard.

- Do not make noise chewing gum. This is lowly behavior, widely indulged in, but objectionable nonetheless. Chewing gum in itself is not charming.
- Do not stare (gaze fixedly at someone you are not talking to).
- It is polite to cover your mouth when you cough, sneeze, or yawn.
- Do not whistle at women.
- Properly, gentlemen should take off their hats indoors.

one way and picking up another, some people can find themselves with little sense of how they are expected to behave. Others have parents who were simply absent or too preoccupied with other things to teach social skills—or didn't know many to teach. The absence of extended families and communities further hampers socializing.

Schools try to substitute, but still, lacking communities and extended families, some people may emerge into adulthood feeling socially awkward. Meanwhile, the pendulum is swinging again, and we are looking favorably at the idea of public civility and predictable rules of etiquette. Thus, with amazement, we now witness etiquette classes for adults as well as for children. Ballroom dancing, with its precise steps, is greatly in vogue.

A newspaper column, Miss Manners, is widely syndicated. We probably will not see gentlemen go back to tipping their hats to the ladies or children leaping to their feet when their elders enter a room, but good manners are appreciated. You may be assured that your own gracious manners will be found delightful.

FRIENDS

It's in disaster or accident that Americans shine. Drive into a snowbank, and someone will pull you out. After the 2004 Asian tsunami, thousands of Americans flew to Southeast Asia to volunteer help. A Polish woman says, "I used to think Americans were selfish, but then I got into all sorts of trouble, and perfect strangers went out of their way to help me out."

She adds, "I've come to like Americans enormously, but they aren't necessarily going to get very close and intimate." The newcomer who takes American friendliness at face value is often disappointed. Americans are indiscriminate with their smiles and their chatter. Foreigners (those who come from places where people don't behave like friends unless they are friends) on arrival may be delighted to find themselves the objects of much enthusiastic attention. They may imagine they may have instantly acquired a bunch of fine friends. "But it doesn't mean anything," says an Indian woman.

"Often the first American we sit down and talk to is at the employment agency, and she's so nice we think we've got this wonderful new friend. Then we find out it was just for profit, and we never hear from her again. We're disillusioned."

However, you shouldn't give up on making friends with Americans; many would be very happy to make new friends and are only waiting for someone else to make the first moves. Just be aware that the mobility of American life has made the term "friend" less profound than elsewhere.

In many countries, most friends date from school days, and it is hard to make new ones thereafter. For Americans it is the exception rather than the rule to remain in one place, and the school friends (who may have changed every year anyhow) are usually left behind. New friends rise up to fill new stages of life. Even when the locale remains the same, new friends step in to match life changes: college friends, work friends, club friends, neighbors, new-hobby friends, sports friends, friends-with-same-age-children.

How to Spot an American

How is it that on any train platform in the world everyone can pick out the Americans? Despite our different heritage, there is a style that marks us. We have shy people and bold, talkative and taciturn and yet the quality of 'Americanness' is unmistakable. The expression, the gestures, and the posture all give us away even before we speak.

Says one Brit who has lived around the world, "Americans have an enthusiastic look. They feel empowered, and the looks on their faces say, 'I can make a difference.' Nobody else has that special kind of confidence."

Frequently, each friend fills a particular niche. There's the friend with whom I discuss certain problems, the one with whom I play tennis, the one with whom I work. When anything changes—my problems go away, I quit tennis, I get a new job—I may stop seeing those particular friends. If I'm lucky, I will have a few lifelong friends, but these could be scattered about the world.

The Rules

Once I've got a friend, I'll be careful not to presume on him or her. That we might be 'bothering' someone is an everlasting concern of Americans, even among good friends.

"Irish people live in each other's pockets," said one woman. "It's completely different here. You keep your distance."

"In Brazil, you move mountains for your friends," says one young woman. "Our boundaries are very blurry."

Here, our boundaries are strict. I will be very hesitant to ask friends for favors—one of my attractions as a friend is that I am not demanding. If I were, my prospective friends would be likely to back off. Neediness scares people. Rather than having to refuse a request, we prefer to have friends we can trust to make their requests rare and reasonable.

We ourselves do not wish to be indebted to anybody else. We like reciprocal arrangements because they keep the scales balanced. This week I drive my friend to the airport; next week she drives me. A Chinese woman related that she tried to join a childcare cooperative, but she found the accounting system so complex (to make sure that no one person did more than anyone else) that it drove her crazy.

Eventually in a friendship one can begin to take small services for granted—the loan of a dress, a phone call to find out vital information—but no one expects a real sacrifice. No matter how desperately my friend might need a babysitter, she would never ask me to miss a day's work to take care of her child. I have sometimes been very confused when foreign friends did remarkable things for me—drove me great distances or took the subway to the airport to meet me. Such things are not in our vocabulary, and I find it difficult to respond.

For the average American, the feeling of being indebted is practically a physical pain. We would rather buy an expensive tool we'll hardly ever use than have to borrow one. When a neighbor had to store some things in my freezer (which was no trouble for me) after hers broke down, she could not rest until she had made me a special dinner. I rescued another neighbor's runaway dog, and she bought me a cake. In point of fact, most of us are human and like to be helpful and would not mind receiving only thanks for a good deed.

But even this constant thanking of others perturbs some foreigners. "Why are you always thanking each other?" says a Palestinian. "At home, I expect my friends to help me. If I'm moving, all I have to do is mention when to my friends and they'll all show up. I would never have to say 'please'. 'Thanks' aren't necessary. I show up when they move. People in the US are very selfish."

Attitudes are different in small towns where people know each other and each other's families well and, besides, don't have the money to buy tools they will use once a year. Here, a great deal of socializing goes on in the name of borrowing and returning things. In the cities, affluence has afforded independence, but it is significant that Americans would rather put their money into independence than into other luxuries.

Best Friends

In the special category of lifelong friends, the favor score card is not so carefully kept. But here the potential for favor-giving must be more or less equal. This is one reason it is difficult to have good friends across economic gaps. If you fly me to your villa in Spain, how can I possibly repay you?

Privacy

"In Malaysia, you don't have to hire a caterer," says one friend of mine. "If we're having a party, our friends all come early to help."

Here, one reason I'm not going to arrive in the morning to help out is that I would be infringing on the party-givers' privacy. They probably don't want to have anyone in their house but family—or hired help—until the first guest arrives, and they don't want me looking inside their cupboards and listening to them bicker about how many bottles of wine to buy.

Furthermore, if I insist on helping, I would seem to be suggesting that they are unable to manage alone. Even when I have a very close friend in need, I will go to lengths to appear not to be inconveniencing myself by helping. Part of my kindness to my friend is to act as if I think she can manage perfectly well without me.

Perhaps she is sick. I will make a casserole dish for her and take it to her house, which is some distance away. I may tell her that the dish was something left over after feeding my family (when in fact I may have shopped and cooked especially to make it for her) and that I happened to be in her area anyhow (highly unlikely). She may suspect the truth but will appreciate my consideration for her feelings.

Big Trouble

All this delicacy is very tough on people who are really in trouble. Middle-class Americans are largely protected against catastrophe, but when big trouble does strike, such as a long illness in the family, it can be disillusioning to discover that one's friends are not going to do very much. The troubled family may be desperate enough to accept any amount of help, but their friends scarcely know how to offer and, besides, are not in the habit of sacrificing much time for others.

A Japanese man told me how terribly isolated he felt when he was going through his divorce here. No support net closed around him as it would have in Japan. American friends wouldn't have wanted to insult him by appearing to think he was needy. Indeed, an American might even feel smothered by too much attention, even though most people would probably appreciate more phone calls than they get.

Some foreigners have observed that Americans prefer to help in an institutionalized way. In the AIDS crisis, many people have volunteered through agencies to help the sick. The sick person feels more comfortable calling the agency than calling his friends; his need is legitimized. The volunteer finds the agency route more straightforward than trying to help a friend who is sick and who would probably endlessly protest, "Oh, please, you've done too much already."

These protests are for the self-esteem of the recipient. You can assume that if someone offers to do something for you, he would genuinely like to do it. Because we don't feel responsible for others, we don't often offer anything we don't want to deliver. And if the offer is turned down, we will also take the refusal at face value.

I do not mean to convince readers that they will find no helpful friends. Many people in America do not live by the 'rules' outlined here, and the country is full of good souls who exist to be of use to others. For true Christians, giving is supposed to be the heart of their religion, so by all means let them practise it.

Neighbors

It can come as a disappointment to foreigners to move into an American community and discover neighbors whose neighborliness ends with saying 'hello'. In many countries, to be a neighbor presumes a relationship. Here, it can be almost the opposite. One reason people move from small towns to big cities is to get away from nosey neighbors, to live in anonymity.

Since early days in America, heterogeneous groups have lived side by side, but living side by side didn't mean they liked each other. When a Scotsman staked out his claim on the frontier, he didn't know who would move in next. It could be a German, a Norwegian, a Jew—someone who wasn't his kind. It was true that people needed each other out in the wild, but they were also suspicious of each other. We remain cautious in approaching our neighbors until we find out what kind of people they are. The neighbor is in a position to be the biggest bother of anyone we know. This is the person who could drop in any time, comment on our comings and goings, do weird things with our children. One might retort that this is also the person who could most conveniently be helpful to us, but help we're not supposed to need.

A factor separating neighbors is that even the inhabitants on a block of identically priced houses may have little in common. Blue-collar workers, computer programmers, doctors, airline pilots, and professors could all be living in adjacent houses. Homogeneous communities are closer. On military compounds or in university housing, you will find groups who reach out readily to the new arrivals in their midst.

The design of houses and the privacy of garages also limit neighborliness. It is possible to live next door to someone and simply never meet him. In the suburbs, whereas people used to pause to chat when they arrived home in the evening, now the automatic garage door opener allows them to glide into their garages and disappear with only a wave. Gardens bring neighbors together, but in the long summer evenings, people are more likely to be indoors watching television than working the earth.

Moving On

Some neighbors do become fast friends, and you shouldn't assume that you won't. What is likely, though, is that you or your neighbors are going to be moving on at some point, and you will have to start all over again making friends with somebody else. Nearly one out of five Americans moves every year.

A person's feeling of community often does not come from the place he lives. Some people's community is the workplace, or their community is made up of a group of people with similar interests. People may spend their spare time communicating with strangers on the Internet and even consider them some sort of a community. Household isolation is exacerbated by the increasingly great distances people live from their work, and the time they spend commuting leaves that much less time for community activities.

THE FOREIGN MAN/THE AMERICAN WOMAN

To foreigners, American women may appear extremely free. The fact that American men help at all with housework shocks some. But the man who openly folds laundry and makes beds is not losing his manhood. He is demonstrating his security in his masculinity and his belief in women's equality.

If you are a man from a country where women don't enter into men's territory, you may need to make an effort to treat women as you would a man. This means not asking the woman of the house about the children and then turning to the husband and saying, "And what do you think of the Mid-east situation?" She will be insulted.

Even American men can have a tough time figuring out the rules for behavior with women. Some feminists take offence when men do things like open car doors for them or pay for them on a date. They think it suggests that they are weak. The younger ones, however, who didn't know a world when few professions were open to women, seem to appreciate the gentlemanly approach.

It is important to understand that many women are not pining for male companionship. A woman traveling alone, eating in a restaurant alone, or doing anything else alone may be very satisfied with her own company and not welcome intrusion (although she may be open to a tactful approach).

Almost half of American women are now single, and a quarter of those have never married. Many of these have discovered that they prefer not to marry. A single American woman has no obligation to stay home and look after ageing parents and other people's children. Instead, she may have a wonderful career and an interesting life and count herself luckier than her married friends. Surveys and statistics of health and happiness prove that on average, compared to the married woman, she is.

Showing Flesh

Foreign men need to realize that the seeming looseness of American women (or girls) does not mean that they are sexually available. Although many young unmarried American women are not virgins, many have no desire to go to bed with someone they do not love, and few wish to have sex with many men.

In some countries, if a woman makes friendly overtures it means she's offering sex. Here, it emphatically does not. A woman may act especially nice because she feels sorry for a poor man alone in a foreign country. When the man misconstrues her kindness as a desire for sex, she is infuriated.

The same is true of skimpily dressed women. Skintight jeans, see-through tops and bikini bathing suits may clothe a girl who hopes to catch a man's eye, but her style of dress should not be taken to indicate that any man will do or that she combines sex and the profit motive.

Men should be aware that not only is rape is a crime here, but so is any harassment of women. Women who are threatened, sexually or physically, should call the police. Men can and do go to prison for abusing their wives. There are hotlines women can call for advice and help.

The woman daringly dressed may hope to suggest that she is a free spirit. Conversely, a Muslim woman who wears a head covering will have difficulty convincing Americans that she is not oppressed. People will assume that she has to take orders from her husband and will be surprised should they discover that she is independent, educated, and an equal partner.

MEETING AND GREETING
- **Introductions:**
  Introductions are casual here and do not signify much (unlike countries where an introduction establishes a relationship). It is more polite to introduce two people than not to, and it places neither under an obligation. If you are with one friend and encounter another, you need only say, "Ralph Scott, this is Mike Phan."

  The more honored party is the one introduced to (in this case, Ralph), but this quaint rule needn't concern you much. Status is of little matter here. Unless there is business at hand, nobody need produce a card (and often not then). When introduced, you only respond with a smile and "Nice to meet you" or "How are you?" (To which the reply is, "Fine, thank you.") If you are seated and the other person is standing, you should rise, unless you are a lady to whom a man is being introduced. Conversation may or may not ensue.

- **Handshakes:**
  People meeting for business and older people greeting each other socially usually shake hands. People who see each other regularly would not ordinarily shake hands. Men shake hands more than women. If two couples are introduced at a party, the men would shake hands and the women may or may not. Shaking hands adds an extra cordiality. Shaking hands on leaving a party is entirely

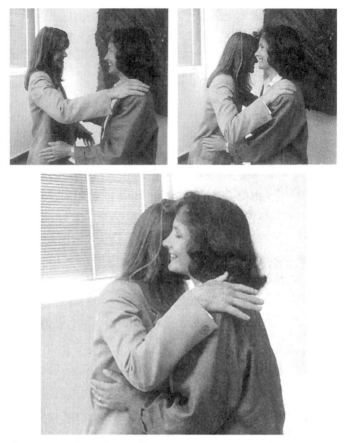

This sequence shows the social kiss as two women greet each other. Note that despite the obvious warmth, the bodily contact is actually quite limited. The kiss itself flies off into the air.

optional. No one will think you rude if you don't, but anybody is glad to shake any hand that is offered.

Do grip the other person's hand firmly (but not so firmly as to crush the bones) and give a couple of springy pumps up and down. The passive extending of a hand, leaving someone else to do the work of shaking, leaves a bad impression. People will think you're either conceited or lazy.

- **The Social Kiss:**

One form of greeting widely replaces the handshake —the pseudo-kiss. To execute this, one leans forward from the waist and presses one's cheek against the other person's, simultaneously kissing the air. One hand usually comes up to simulate a hug, except the hand will stop short of the back and grab the shoulder. While appearing to add warmth, this hand may actually be protecting against too much body contact. Or the hand may pat the other person's back, which is an assertion that what is going on has no sexual meaning. The two people will avoid pressing their bodies together. You go through this routine on one cheek only.

This kind of kissing is routine among sophisticates and even business acquaintances. It means little. Women and women do it; men and women do it. Men and men do not do it; they stick to handshakes.

- **Men's Stuff:**
Back-slapping is acceptable among men. So is a touch or a squeeze of the shoulder. But only ball players in their moments of triumph are certifiably masculine enough to throw their arms around each other.

The New Sensitive Male cropped up in the 1970s in reaction to the too-macho standoffish man of the last generation. This new breed does a lot of self-conscious hugging, but most men limit bodily same-sex contact to throwing an arm around another's shoulders.

Couples in Love

Public displays of affection between couples, disgusting to some Asians, are acceptable here. Deep soulful kissing in broad daylight is not in good taste, but we would not consider it too shocking either. Hand holding, touching, squeezing, and even little kisses are to us are just couples properly demonstrating their mutual happiness. Only if a couple is too wrapped up in each other to notice the others present would we consider it rude and make jokes about it later.

When teenagers 'can't keep their hands off each other', their parents may not be charmed, but they might find some compensation in noting their children's normal sexual adjustment.

WHAT DO I CALL YOU?

It was not so 30 years ago, but first names are now the rule in America. If Ralph meets Mike through Dan, all will immediately call each other by first names. Socially, only in the most formal circles, or when a young person is addressing someone considerably older, need one hesitate before risking the first name.

Friend or Boyfriend?

Women usually have women friends while men have men friends, but it is perfectly possible for friendships to cross gender lines. Women like to feel that a man's interest in them needn't be sexual. But partly because there is often some confusion about whether it is or isn't, close male-female friendships are in the minority. However, sometimes a woman's best friend is a gay man.

The first name is the given name. Most babies also get a middle name, which is less used. The last name is the family name and is inherited from the father. Forty years ago, women universally took their husbands' family names upon marriage, sometimes keeping their former last name as a middle name. A woman might then become Harriet Beecher (her father's name) Stowe (her husband's name). She would be known widely as Mrs. (which denotes a married woman) Stowe, and letters would arrive addressed to Mrs. Calvin Stowe. Her husband would remain forever Mr. Calvin Stowe.

Times have changed, and the women's movement has made many women reluctant to change their names for the sake of a husband. Thus Catherine Zeta-Jones does not become Catherine Douglas when she marries Michael Douglas. She might occasionally be called Mrs Douglas but could not properly be called Mrs Zeta-Jones because that would make her the Mrs. of someone named Zeta-Jones, which she is not.

That leaves her with two possible titles: Miss Zeta-Jones, which is the usual title for an unmarried woman or girl but is proper for married women retaining their own last names, or else Ms Zeta-Jones—pronounced **mizz**—which is the feminist alternative to Mr. and does not denote a marital state. Ms. is widely used in newspapers and on business letters but is less often spoken.

These complications and the fact that so many women have divorced and remarried make it much easier just to call everyone by first name. This only leaves the problem that using a first name connotes a familiarity that not everybody likes. An older person, in particular, may much prefer that people with whom she does business call her Mrs. Stevens rather than Mary.

Your friend's friends will expect you to use their first names, but if in other situations you have any doubts as to whether a first name is appropriate, start with the more formal address (i.e., Mr. Smith) and wait for the other party to insist that you call him Fred.

If somebody calls you by your first name, then you are free to use his or hers (unless you are very young or talking to a doctor who is nearly always called 'Dr'). Even children regularly call adults by first name, to the dismay of many foreigners. Teachers, however, should be addressed formally, unless they insist on being called by another name.

Few people are called by title. Exceptions are doctors and people in the military, whose rank confers a title, e.g.. 'General Powell'. Police are addressed as 'Officer'. One might address a college professor as 'Professor Harries' but a teacher is just Mr, Mrs, Miss, or Ms, like nearly everyone else.

In offices nearly everybody is now on a first-name basis, including the Chief Executive Officer. But if instant familiarity makes you uncomfortable, stick to your own way. I am charmed to be called Miss Wanning.

Nicknames

Some people are universally known by their nicknames, which may or may not relate to their actual first names. Many are hold-overs from childhood. Such names as Tinky, Buzz, Butch, and Muffie are rarely on a birth certificate. A Robert is often called Bob, a William called Bill, and a Richard called Dick. A John is called Jack, a James, Jim. Other names are simple diminutives—Mike from Michael; Dan from Daniel; Liz from Elizabeth; Art from Arthur. Then there's Hal from Harold; Steve from Stephen; Sally from Sarah.

However, many Roberts are just called Robert. You may need to ask, "Do you go by Robert, Rob or Bob?"

The latest crop of children seem to be known by nicknames much less than former generations. Presumably this is because there are fewer of them and so each one has assumed an importance too great to be reduced to a nickname. An Alexander in his crib is called Alexander; a little Benjamin is no longer known as Benny; Katherines aren't Kathy. This may also be because people are more inclined now to choose a favorite name, rather than name the child after a revered relative. So little Benjamin is not going to be confused with Uncle Benjamin, nor does he need to fill his shoes.

SPECIAL OCCASIONS
New Babies

It is customary for a friend to give a 'baby shower' for an expectant mother. Traditionally, only other women are invited, and each arrives with a present for the baby, prettily wrapped. The usual routine is for the party to begin with refreshments and chat, followed by the opening of the presents. The women sit in a circle and the mother-to-be opens the presents one by one amidst 'oohs' and 'aahs'. Baby books, bonnets, little stretch suits, toys, blankets, and anything else a baby might want are all appropriate. A handmade item is especially appreciated.

Christening

A ceremony at which a baby is named and received into the Church, usually as part of Sunday morning services. If you're invited to one of these, just do what everyone else does, and don' t be insulted if you're not invited—usually only relatives are.

There is no particular custom for visiting after the baby is born. Good friends might arrange to stop in a week or more after the birth, bearing a present if they haven't already contributed one at the shower. As new parents are harried and have little time to cook, they will be grateful if you bring them something for their dinner.

Birthdays

Except for children's birthday parties, most birthday celebrations are kept within the family. Usually each family member gives a present to the birthday person. Children count on birthdays and Christmas as the times to get the big things they really want, such as new bicycles.

A home celebration consists of a special dinner, ending with ice cream and cake. For children, each candle on the cake represents one year of life, and everyone sings, 'Happy birthday to you', when the cake appears with candles lit. The honoree then makes a wish and tries to blow out all the candles at once.

Weddings

The traditional American wedding was rocked by the sixties and emerged in a variety of new forms. It became popular for couples to write their own vows and to add a variety of personal touches to the proceedings. Nonetheless, many of the old customs survive, even if in an updated form, and some couplings are more tradition-bound than ever before.

Six months before a wedding, you may receive a "Save the Date" card. You don't need to respond to this; it is only to warn you not to make other plans. A proper invitation will follow, perhaps six weeks before the wedding. This you must respond to as soon as possible, saying exactly who among

the invitees are coming; if children are not on the invitation, they are not invited. And you should certainly not show up at a wedding bringing anybody not on the guest list.

The most important thing to know about weddings is that you must arrive on time to a wedding. This is an occasion when the guests should appear before the hosts; it is most embarrassing to arrive after the bride has already walked down the aisle. As wedding ceremonies should start on time and are usually very short, you may could miss the main event entirely by being late.

The Classic Church Wedding

When the American girl dreams of her wedding, she probably sees herself wafting down a church aisle on her father's arm, radiant in a long white dress.

You as a guest are occupying a pew in the church. When the processional music begins and the first members of the wedding party are visible, the congregation rises to its feet. Ushers, bridesmaids, and flower girls lead the procession, and the bride and her father bring up the rear. The groom, best man, and minister slip in quietly to their positions in front.

The minister begins, "Dearly beloved, we are gathered here together to join this man and woman in matrimony..." After his opening, the groom steps in to the father's place. (Modern variations remove the implication that the bride is a piece of livestock being given from the father to the husband.) Rings are exchanged—to be worn on the fourth finger of the left hand—and the ritual questions asked, "Do you take this man to be your husband/wife, to have and to hold, to love and to cherish, in sickness and in health, till death do you part?"

By this time many in the audience are becoming weepy and getting out their handkerchiefs. The minister concludes with, "I now pronounce you husband and wife," the organist breaks into Mendelssohn's *Wedding March* and the happy couple sweeps joyfully back down the aisle, with the wedding party trailing afterwards.

The congregation departs, falling into the arms of long-lost relatives on the way out, and all go off to the reception.

The Variations:

The above describes the standard Protestant ceremony. A Jewish service is somewhat different, and a Catholic Mass a great deal longer. Very often the wedding is not in a house of worship at all, but in a hired hall, clubhouse, hotel, home, or garden. Often a justice of the peace presides, removing the religious factor.

The simplest wedding of all is the City Hall version: the couple and a few witnesses or two appear before a judge and are married.

The Reception:

Here's where the money goes. There are means of spending lavish sums on a wedding reception. The caterers get the largest share, followed by expenditures for reception rooms, champagne, flowers, photographers, orchestra, printed napkins, and countless other little touches. Some families go into debt for years to pay off their daughters' weddings. (Tradition has it that the bride's family pays for the wedding, although increasingly—now that people wait longer to get married—couples finance and arrange their own.)

There is no disgrace, however, in a party at home with food supplied by the relatives. There are those who consider the small home garden party more charming than the no-holds-barred hotel affairs usually directed by a bossy photographer.

If there is a receiving line, etiquette demands that you pass through it. You kiss the bride (if you know her) and tell her she looks beautiful, and you shake the groom's hand and tell him he's a lucky man. You tell the bride's mother how moved you were by the ceremony, and you make a little joke to the bride's father about not having to pay his daughter's bills any more.

You have now done your duty and may drink champagne and circulate and join in the festivities, which usually start with food and drink and move on to dancing. When the orchestra strikes up, protocol demands that the bride and groom dance the first dance alone and the second with their parents. After the parents have danced, the rest of the guests may join in. When the word goes around that the bride and groom are going to cut the cake, everyone pulls close for a look at their first cooperative married venture. You must eat at least a bit of the cake for good luck.

Properly speaking, you should not leave before the bridal couple does. The old standard is for the bride to disappear somewhere, then to reappear in her travelling clothes. Preferably from some balcony or staircase she throws her bouquet to a young unmarried woman—who may expect to be the next to be wed—and departs on the arm of her groom, amid showers of rice (a fertility rite). Today, however, many couples prefer to enjoy their parties to the end, and you may leave at your convenience.

Presents:

An old-fashioned custom was to display wedding presents received before the wedding at the reception, but most people no longer consider showing off 'the loot' tasteful. You may bring your present to the wedding (it won't be opened until later), but most couples would prefer you mailed it to their home address.

Theoretically, one is allotted a year after the wedding in which to send a present, although most people don't wait that long. Cash is not quite as frequently given here as in some countries, although it is often most welcome. If you are uncertain, you might inquire from relatives as to the couple's wishes. Should the couple already have a house groaning with toasters and china, it may be that there is nothing they would like better than money.

But cash (make it a cheque) should not be your first thought. The traditional wedding present is a handsome household item—anything from a good frying pan to a crystal punch bowl. Most couples register list their desires at a prominent local store and/or places like Macy's, Williams-Sonoma, and even Home Depot and Target. Having found out where the bride is registered, (If such facts are not noted on the wedding invitation, as they sometimes are, you can e-mail or call the couple or a relative and ask where they are registered.) you can often go to the store's website and, you then need only appear there and pick out whatever is in your price range. Shopping at prominent stores in general has the advantage that the couple may easily return your present if they don't like it or if it's a duplicate.

Price should not be affected by the lavishness of the wedding reception—but often you can't help but feel that you should at least cover the cost of your dinner. The real determinants of price should be your fondness and goodwill towards the couple, their needs, and how much you have to spend. A well-chosen gift of low cost will arouse delight among decent people. And if your own resources are small, the couple would feel badly should you spend more than you can afford.

If you are invited to a wedding and cannot attend, you are not obligated to send a present—although you may wish to. (You must, however, mail your regrets as soon as possible.) Likewise, if you receive an announcement after the fact of the wedding, a gift is entirely optional.

Quite promptly after sending your present, you should receive a thank-you note, giving specific and personal reasons as to why the couple was so delighted with your present. To not acknowledge a wedding present is unforgivable.

Funerals

These too come in a variety of forms. Most frequently, they are held in churches or funeral homes. Properly, You should wear sombre, proper clothes (such as a dark suit with a sober tie for men and a prim dress or suit for women) and arrive looking reasonably solemn.

An usher will should guide you to a seat. The service will probably be between a half-hour and an hour long. Many funerals now include testimonials from friends, but unless you have been solicited beforehand, you will not be required to speak, although you may be given the opportunity.

American funerals sometimes display an open casket and provide an opportunity for the attendees to file by and pay their last respects to the departed. You may find your friend remarkably changed in death, probably due to the morticians, who go to such lengths to make the dead face look serene that he or she may be unrecognizable.

During the funeral, you may sob all you like but you should not lose control or cry out loud. Unless you are next of kin, you do not wish to draw attention to yourself and your grief.

You may have an opportunity to greet family members after the funeral, whereupon you convey how sorry you are and how greatly the deceased will be missed. Sometimes there has also been an opportunity to call in at the funeral home on preceding evenings to console the family. There may be a graveside ceremony after the church service, which usually includes only family and close friends. Unless you are specifically invited, you should go home.

There may instead be a reception or a wake, likewise by special invitation. This may turn into a very jolly party, but you should try to do your part in keeping the focus on the departed—with stories and reminiscences of his or her uniqueness. It is sometimes hard to remember the sadness of the occasion when a number of long-lost friends and relatives gather together, and a certain amount of mirth is excused.

Dying

If you should suffer a death in your own family while in this country, be very wary of funeral homes, which are famous for charging astronomically for unnecessary services. Although it is not a time when one cares to be thinking about finances, it is unlikely that your loved one would wish you to bankrupt yourself for something he or she will not enjoy. So think twice about whether you really need a mahogany, velvet-lined coffin or a silver-covered guest book.

Death is not an occasion for monetary contributions to the family. Close friends and relatives may send flowers and wreaths for display at the funeral; often the family requests contributions to a certain charity instead.

If someone you know dies and you do not have an opportunity to speak to the bereaved family, you should write a note or send a sympathy card. Even if you attend the funeral, a note to family members reiterating your sorrow is thoughtful.

Banquets

All kinds of clubs and civic organizations find excuses to have banquets so you may well find yourself at one sooner or later. A banquet is usually held in a restaurant, but there the resemblance to a restaurant dinner ends. At a banquet, you're in someone else's hands and you do what you're told.

A cocktail hour nearly always precedes dinner, which gives everyone a chance to gather together. 'No-Host Bar' means you pay for your own drinks. An 'Open Bar' provides free drinks. If you don't attend the cocktail reception, you probably won't be missed, but you should be on time for the dinner. Restaurant management sees to it that banquets begin on time.

Numerous, large round tables fill most banquet halls. Your place at one may be designated by a place-card (which you will have to search for) or you may have to find a seat of your own. If you don't know anyone, you want to cast your eye quickly around for people who at least look compatible, and then present yourself at that table and inquire if there is an empty chair. You will be expected to converse with your tablemates.

Sometimes the tablemates join in ordering bottles of wine, each person paying for a share. You will not have a choice of foods and don't expect any personal service. The group rate the organization is paying for the dinner is based on efficiency. Servers are capable of sweeping the meal on and off very quickly and hope you will not linger too long over your plate. The speech-making usually begins as soon as the coffee has come around, and any further clanking of cups and spoons should be subdued. Banquet speakers are generally forced to contain their remarks within strict time guidelines, but the social hour may go on after the meeting has officially adjourned.

If you are the honored guest, you will probably sit at the head table and not have to pay for your drinks. If you make a speech and people applaud, don't applaud back. You would then appear to be clapping for yourself. Just look gracious, allow a small smile to upturn your lips and nod your head in acknowledgement.

GIFTS
Giving

Except for a few special occasions, Americans are not big gift-givers. Although a salesman may pass out free samples, there is no ritual exchange of presents among executives. In fact, if one American businessman were to give another a nicely-wrapped present that had no bearing on the company's business, the recipient would consider the gift quite inexplicable, unless the object were valuable. Then the move could look like an embarrassing attempt at bribery. Even an inexpensive present could be taken as a slightly crass attempt to win somebody's consideration.

Americans have learned something of the role that gift-giving plays in certain other cultures, and when an American businessman goes to Tokyo, he goes equipped. But among ourselves, we don't see that we need presents. Presents cement the blossoming friendship among business partners, but as we don't need friendship to do business, we don't need presents either. We have contracts instead.

Even friends may never exchange presents. When I go abroad, I try to bring back little mementoes for close friends, but nobody would feel slighted if I didn't. I may occasionally buy a copy of a book for a friend, but I rarely remember a friend's birthday, and few people outside of family remember mine. If someone gave me presents too often I would think it tiresome, and I would feel the burden of having to reciprocate. Besides, like most Americans, I have plenty of stuff already.

However, a gift from a foreigner—suitably typical of his or her homeland—has greater dimensions than anything my fellow American could give me and won't go wrong, except to government employees who are prohibited from accepting gifts. Otherwise, don't hesitate to give small tokens to personal or business friends if you want to. But don't be insulted if you get nothing in exchange.

Receiving

One usually opens a present immediately and in front of the donor. (Exceptions: Christmas and birthday presents may be saved for the day, and wedding presents, as mentioned, are not opened at the wedding.) The best reaction is outright pleasure and delight at receiving something so lovely/indispensable/thoughtful. Show as much enthusiasm as possible and return to the subject periodically thereafter.

The donor will be particularly pleased if you emphasize that the gift shows his or her unusual sensitivity to you and your tastes. ('How did you know that my old sugar bowl broke and that I collect Scottish china?' or 'Peonies are my favorite flowers!') It is not necessary to go on much about how the donor shouldn't have gone to all the trouble, etc. Too much of that and we begin to think maybe indeed we shouldn't have and become embarrassed that we did.

The Guest

You may want to bring a bottle of wine or flowers to a dinner party, but the practice varies in different social sets and you are never expected to. In more formal houses, the flowers may already be magnificently arranged, and your hosts do not at the moment of your arrival wish to go poking around looking for the right vase. Nobody will mind if you bring a nice wine, but your host is not obliged to serve it that evening. The grander the house, the less appropriate a present is. After all, you wouldn't show up at the White House with a bottle of wine under your arm.

It is customary (although not obligatory) to bring something if you are going to be an overnight guest in someone's house. Some gourmet item, a good cheese, a present for the children—any little thing that shows your appreciation. It needn't be wrapped. You might instead send a gift afterwards.

Christmas

Christmas accounts for most of the necessary gift-giving in this country. Children in many families receive presents only at Christmas and on their birthdays—but then frequently in great quantity. Some people give all their relatives presents; others only give to their immediate family. Children are expected to give as well as to get presents.

Some friends exchange presents at Christmas and some don't. Some instead give presents to the small children of friends. I usually keep a few spare presents on hand around Christmas of the generic type—candles, fruitcake—wrapped under the Christmas tree so that if people unexpectedly produce presents for me, I have something for them.

Christmas is the time to settle the score with anyone who has been helpful throughout the year. There are certain required cash outlays—to doormen, babysitters, house cleaners, newspaper deliverers—for anyone who has served you regularly (*see 'Tipping' in the* Resource Guide *for details*). You might want to give a little something (not money!) to your children's teachers or to those among them who have especially extended themselves.

There is a considerable flow of liquor bottles during the holiday season. In business, Christmas presents are often a one-way street where the buyer gets the present. If a company has been favoring you with their business, you give. They don't need to give you anything; it's enough that they pay their bills.

Within the company, bosses may hand around gifts to their subordinates—or they may not. Many companies give a small Christmas bonus to all personnel. A hard-working secretary is often rewarded with something rather nice, and if the secretary is particularly fond of his or her boss, the boss may get a present too. It is unlikely that you need to provide presents for all your co-workers, though if you work in a small group, everyone may give each other presents. Some departments have lotteries; a hat goes around with everyone's name in it, and you bring a small present to the Christmas party for the person whose name you drew.

LONELINESS

"America is the loneliest country in the world," said Mother Teresa. Loneliness is the price we pay for individuality.

A Peruvian concludes that Americans watch television so much because they have no neighbors to talk to. An Arab immigrant finds life very empty here: "I just go to work and come home, eat dinner, and go to bed. Life here is just for making money. My soul aches."

A friend from El Salvador tells me that there people start coming to your house at 9:00 am in the morning. She says, "The good part is you're never alone, and the bad part is that everybody knows your life." She works with immigrants and says, "People who are used to that life feel very isolated here."

"There is a lot of intrusiveness in Brazil," says one immigrant to the USA. "But there are fewer problems of self-identity. You always have a safe harbor. Even if your own family would disappear, friends would make you part of theirs. Nobody is alone."

Not only are there people actually alone here, there are many who feel alone even when with friends. Says an Iranian, "With some people here, even when I'm talking to them, I feel that some part of them is always lonely. They are emotionally hungry."

"I like Americans very much," says a Polish women. "But I have a very hard time making friends. One step doesn't lead to the next. You have an important conversation and just leave it at that. I used to be bitter about it. Now I don't think people here really make deep, meaningful friendships, but still there is this kindness and pleasantness, which I appreciate, even if it is superficial."

In fact, many Americans cherish their time alone. Says a Chilean, "The fun is different here. In Chile, people have fun traveling in a group; here, people have fun traveling alone."

SETTLING IN

CHAPTER 5

'Eighty percent of success is showing up.'
—Woody Allen

IMMIGRATION AND VISAS

Sadly, since the attacks of 9/11, getting into the USA has become more difficult, although if you qualify for the Visa Waiver Program (VWP), you won't need a visa. Citizens of 27 countries qualify for the VWP—if they are coming for business or tourism and are not staying more than 90 days; have a round-trip ticket; fly on one of the main carriers; and have a machine-readable passport.

Documents Needed

According to the State Department, all visitor visa applicants must have:

- Non-immigrant Visa Application, Form DS-156, completed and signed (use recent form or fill out outline)
- Current, valid passport or travel document
- Photograph (2x2 inches, passport type)
- Application fees and or issuance fee
- Evidence of funds to cover expenses in the United States
- Evidence of compelling social and economic ties abroad
- Supplemental Non-immigrant Visa Application, Form DS-157, for men between 16–45 years of age and for all applicants age 16 and over who are from Cuba, Iran, North Korea, Sudan, and Syria. Note that a consular officer may ask any applicant to complete this form.

Everyone else needs to apply for a visa, which may mean a personal appearance at the U.S. embassy or consulate in their country. The U.S. Dept. of State maintains a webpage with specific information for each country.

Nearly all visitors must have passports that meet certain requirements, which are described at the State Dept. website. You can also get information from your local consulate.

U.S. Visa Policy

For complete information about United States visa policy and procedures, refer to http://www.travel.state.gov/visa, the U.S. Department of State's web page.

For information on becoming an American citizen, contact the United States Citizenship and Immigration Services (USCIS) through the Department of Homeland Security (formerly the Immigration and Naturalisation Service or INS) at http://www.uscis.gov or (1-800) 375-5283.

For a referral for an immigration attorney, contact the American Immigration Lawyers Association (http://www.aila.org) at 1-800-954-0254 to speak with a representative or send an email to ilrs@aila.org.

If you hope to stay longer than six months, you can apply to join the 33 million foreign-born people living in the USA. In general, in order to be eligible to apply for a permanent immigrant visa (a green card), a foreign citizen must be sponsored by relatives who are U.S. citizens or by a prospective employer. The Diversity Visa Program also provides a certain number of permanent resident visas annually, drawn from countries with low rates of immigration to the U.S.

It's a complex process, and applicants are encouraged to apply for their visas as early as possible in order to build in time to submit the appropriate forms and photographs, schedule interviews and wait for the paperwork to be processed. Hiring an immigration lawyer may be a good option, since he or she can help you fill out the appropriate forms, explain the laws and legalities that might either assist or complicate your case and represent you at hearings. (Immigration 'consultants' and 'notarios' should be avoided, as few have any legal training and many are corrupt.)

Since 11 September, 2001, heightened security and intensified scrutiny has frustrated the process further, but the U.S. Department of State has made a goal of delivering all accepted visa applications within 30 days; however, it's best to err on the side of caution and plan far in advance of your departure.

FINDING YOUR NEW HOME

Once you're here, your biggest initial challenge is likely to be finding a satisfactory place to live. It is particularly hard in or near cities such as NYC, Boston, San Francisco, LA, and Washington DC, where there are housing shortages. In other areas, apartment complexes are offering a month's free rent to newcomers, so the level of difficulty all depends on where you're trying to settle. If you're lucky, you'll have friends or relatives you can stay with until you find your own place.

Finding the "right" neighborhood is key. Consider proximity to your work, public transportation, safety, stores, and entertainment, the quality of the local schools (*See 'Education' on page 122*) and how safe the neighborhood is.— and then enlist the help of friends or a realtor to recommend areas that may be right for you. There are two options for securing a home: renting or buying. Both involve money up front.

Renting usually entails a monthly payment that allows you (the 'tenant') to live in a place owned by another person or a company (the 'landlord'). Generally, landlords get to decide the terms of the contract (or 'lease') that allows you live in their place, such as the length of the lease (generally a year, with an option of extending at the end of the term), the amount of monthly rent, any requirements for upkeep, and the amount of the security deposit (usually a month's rent), and cleaning deposit, if any.

Landlords often ask for references from former landlords and want to do a credit check. If as a foreigner, you don't have either references or a credit record, you will need to be able to prove adequate income or bring an "offer letter"

from your employer. Sometimes an employer will even co-sign for the apartment.

It is illegal to refuse to rent to anyone on the basis of race, gender, age, or having children. Landlords can refuse pets, however, and often do.

The landlord is supposed to maintain the property and provide you with working appliances. You, however, will probably be paying your own electricity, heating, and water bills.

The security deposit is supposed to be returned to you when you move out, minus the cost of any damage done to the home beyond 'normal wear and tear'. It is a good idea to walk through the place with the landlord before moving in, noting pre-existing flaws so that you won't be held responsible for them. Check whether doors and window close properly, if there are spots on carpets and walls or chips on cabinets, if blinds are clean, if toilets flush well and water flow is good. If you decide to paint the walls another color, be aware that you will have to pay for repainting when you move.

If you have a dispute with your landlord, you may find a housing rights group in your area to assist you. And in

This typical ranch home can be found anywhere in the USA.

the case of fire or theft, it is wise to take out a renters' insurance policy, an inexpensive but important precaution that will repair or replace your belongings should anything be damaged or stolen. AAA and other insurance companies offer these but note that 'Acts of God' are usually not covered. Where I live, earthquake damage comes at considerable additional cost.

Purchasing a Home

Between 1995 and 2007, housing prices increased by more than 70 percent (adjusted for inflation), fantastically more than the normal rate of growth. By nearly any definition, this has been a bubble fueled by speculation. Buyers have been over-extending themselves to get in on the market, confident that when they get out, they will profit. Many homeowners have been using their houses as ATM machines, using the increased value of their house as collateral and taking out second mortgages. In addition to that, lending companies eagerly expanded their markets by making loans to unqualified buyers who have been defaulting in large numbers.

The exuberance is now over, and prices have fallen in many areas. The big question is whether they will continue to fall and by how much. According to some economists, a real burst of the bubble would lower house values from 25 to 40 percent.

You may still want to buy a house here, but you do want to be cautious, particularly in the most expensive markets. However, owning a house affords many pleasures, not the least of which is a tax deduction for the interest paid on your mortgage.

There are three basic kinds of properties you can buy—condos, coops, and houses.

A housing cooperative ("coop") is a corporation that owns a building; this form of ownership is most prevalent in the NYC area. If you buy into a coop, you buy a share in the corporation and the right to live in one of the units. Technically, you don't own your unit at all, but you do have the right to vote in the housing association and to take part in managing the building, as well as in deciding who can move in and who can't. You will pay monthly maintenance fees, as well as the price of buying in.

A condominium (or "condo") is also a shared form of ownership, except that you will own your own unit yourself—which may be an apartment or a town house—and will have joint ownership of the common areas. In a condo, a homeowners association will manage the common areas—which can include club houses and swimming pools—and make assessments when there are extra expenses, such as for a new roof. There are rules about anything visible on the outside and monthly fees for maintenance.

Lastly, there is the single-family home, which you own individually and for which you make all the decisions, pay all the taxes, take care of the yard, and finance all the repairs. Some people prefer condos because many of the tasks of home ownership are taken care of for them, and they can go away without worrying about such matters as having the driveway ploughed if it snows.

Unless you are an experienced real estate buyer, you will probably want to use a real estate agent, whose job it is to steer you toward homes in your price range, help you negotiate a fair purchase price, coordinate with housing inspectors to ensure you are buying a solid home, and help you through the paperwork. In exchange, the realtor gets around 6 percent of the seller's proceeds—but this is negotiable. If buyer and seller each have an agent, they would split the commission, which should cover expenses, such as ads and listings.

While a good agent can be extremely helpful, you must remain aware that the agent above all wants to make a deal. So if the agent is more enthusiastic than you are about certain properties, remember that you're the one who will live in the house, and it's your money. Studies have shown that when agents are buying or selling their own houses, they are not in nearly as great a hurry.

To buy a house, unless you plan to pay for it entirely outright, you will need to qualify for a mortgage The mortgage company will require extensive information on your salary, any savings or investment income, your credit rating, and outstanding debt. Based on the information, the mortgage company will decide how much they are willing to loan you. A thirty-year mortgage is common.

You will probably need to make a down payment, rather than financing the entire cost of the house, and you will have other costs to consider—attorney, inspection and appraisal fees, title searches, taxes, and perhaps prepaid interest And don't forget to budget for property taxes, general repairs, and maintenance.

Buying a house can keep you on pins and needles while you wait to see whether your offer has been accepted. Another function of your agent is to hold your hand and cheer you up, whatever happens.

Moving

Once you've found a place to live, you have to arrange to move into it. The method you employ generally reflects the stage of life you're in: if you're a student, you can offer a friend a six-pack of beer to help you move your two boxes and a futon. If you're newlyweds, you can coerce several of your friends to help load up your rented van in exchange for unlimited pizza. If you're at a phase in life where your time is worth more than money, you hire somebody to pack and/ or move your things while you sit and drink beer.

Moving companies often provide a variety of options, ranging from one-day truck rentals to coast-to-coast, full-service relocation packages complete with insurance coverage for any items broken or lost in transit. When researching potential moving companies, try to get referrals and be sure to get several detailed estimates—disreputable moving companies will provide a low estimate at first and then later tack on additional charges based on distance travelled, weight of cargo, or number of burly fellows doing the lifting. One friend was charged extra for 'expenses related to using an elevator'. Check the Better Business Bureau for any complaints just to be on the safe side and be skeptical of ultra-low estimates. You don't want Mo's Moving Co. to pack up your stuff in their van, never to be seen again.

THE AMERICAN HOME

The most typical American home is a one-storey 'ranch' house built sometime in the last sixty years. It is on a suburban street where there is no public transportation because there is so little demand for it. A school bus may pick up the children, but families usually have two cars and spend a lot of time driving the children to their various activities.

Should you come to visit, you will enter via a walk leading to the front door. On either side of the path is an expanse of green lawn, usually maintained by the man of the house or by a garden service. This lawn is part of the great lawn that spreads across America, cultivated on deserts, mountains, and seashores— a triumph over the wilderness. Few crops are more unnatural or more difficult to grow than a velvety green lawn, which must be planted, weeded, fertilized, watered, and cut regularly. But by our lawns are we judged. Your neighbor may know nothing about you, but he will note the condition of your lawn.

House Tour

Foreigners often think it strange that Americans will show them every room of the house. "No wonder they don't want people dropping in," says an Irish woman, "when it means cleaning the entire house." But our hosts expect that we are curious to see everything, and they are rather proud of the size and decor of the bedrooms and of the pretty wallpaper in the bathrooms.

Houses are usually spacious and comfortable. Very often there is an "open" plan so that one room flows into another. There may be a "family" room with a big television in addition to a more formal living room. The kitchen is likely to be in the back, often with a door leading out to a back yard. Children often each have their own rooms, crammed with stuff. There will probably be a couple of bathrooms, and the more luxurious houses have many, very large closets.

Houses are generally kept very clean; all those ads for cleansers on TV have had their effect. The houses tend to be tidy as well. Often they seem strangely anonymous to people from other countries, as if interchangeable people could be living in each one.

Across the country, houses have been built to similar plans, with little attempt made to make the house suit the landscape or the climate. To many Europeans, these houses are not well-built. The walls are not thick and sturdy, the doors are hollow, and the ceilings are low. There is no wood trim or extra décor, no hidden nooks or crannies, no secret places, no signs of wear. The furniture is new; there are few family heirlooms and little that indicates the personalities of the owners.

After all, the people who live in these houses do not imagine living in one place all their lives. They certainly don't expect that their children will grow up and stay in the same place. When people plan improvements, they often think more about what will increase the resale cost than about what they themselves would most like.

Electricity and Utilities

The U.S. electricity supply is very good and steady; there is rarely a power outage. You may not see any power lines because they're buried underground. If there were a power outage, many household essentials would stop working: the water pump, the heating system, the refrigerator, the freezer, the microwave oven, the televisions and stereo, the computers, the telephone answering machine, the various rechargers, the doorbell, the garage door opener, the dishwasher, the clothes washer and dryer, the lights, the electric toothbrush, the sprinkler system controller, and the air-conditioner. Burglar alarms have battery backups so a thief cannot disconnect them by cutting the electrical wires to the house.

Communications

Once upon a time, AT&T provided most of the phone service across the nation, which made decisions very simple when you moved—where did you want the family phone installed? With deregulation, everything changed. Now there are a great number of both local and long distance companies to choose from, although only one company in an area maintains the network of wires connecting the whole system. Many people just continue to use this one company for phone service—and for high-speed or dial-up Internet service—but you can explore packages offered by other companies by searching the Internet. To install or repair wires in the house, you can do the work yourself, hire someone from the network provider, or hire any other phone installer.

When it comes to television, you can get your reception from a cable service; a satellite provider; or an antenna. Cable companies have area monopolies, so you'll have to go with the local provider. It will offer you different packages, varying with the choice of channels. The company may not be eager to tell you about the lowest-priced, basic choice, so be sure to ask. Cable TV has the advantage of secure reception, generally undisturbed by weather. You can also get broadband Internet service from your cable company.

There are two main satellite companies: Dish TV and DirecTV, along with assorted specialized services. You'll get the greatest choice of channels through satellite; your choice may be based on which provides the most access to TV stations from your homeland. You can also get DSL high-speed Internet along with your satellite connection.

After February 17, 2009, all television broadcasts must be in a digital rather than analog format. This will not affect cable and satellite viewers, but antenna users with analog TVs with will need to get a converter box.

Another change currently under way is to High-Definition TV (HDTV). This provides a much improved picture and Dolby sound but requires both a TV with an HD tuner and HDTV broadcasts. An HD tuner box may be required for an older TV

Climate Control

On hot days, the American family may close the windows and doors and turn on the central air-conditioner. Cold air circulates throughout the house. Less modern houses have window air-conditioners, which only cool one room apiece. Some old houses and apartment buildings do not have adequate wiring to run air-conditioners, and a few people don't like them anyhow because of their noise and the artificial chill they produce. In the summer, open windows have screens in them, which keep flies and mosquitoes out.

In the winter, the central heating in most houses can be counted on to heat all the rooms equally. In cold areas, storm windows are put up in the fall for insulation. The furnace is probably in the basement, and vents in each room distribute the heat. Not driven together to heat themselves by a stove, family members may spend much of their time in the privacy of their own rooms. When the family is away, they turn down the heat but leave it on. Otherwise, the pipes would freeze—a disaster

Managing Stuff

Americans are consumers, not collectors. What happens to all the stuff they buy? Drive around on a Saturday or a Sunday, and you will find garage sales. The family puts prices on their excess goods and sets them out in front of the garage. Everything from shoes that pinched to the old couch can be found for sale in a festive atmosphere, and if you like to bargain, this is your chance. Garage sales are a reasonable way for newcomers to furnish their houses.

You might also want to investigate resale shops, to which some people donate their used goods. Goodwill Industries and Salvation Army thrift stores can be found in almost every town. These organizations collect donated clothing and household goods, then sell the items in their retail stores throughout North America and abroad. The revenues are funneled back into community programs and social services.

Another clearinghouse for those who are emptying their houses or looking to fill theirs up is Ebay, a confusing but engrossing online auction house that lists at least one of every single item you will ever need or desire, including cars, antiques, new and slightly used apparel and shoes, artwork, and kitschy collectibles. Craig's list (http://www.craigslist.com), covering individual cities, is another good buying and selling site.

The stuff that people neither want to use nor to get rid of may be down in their basements, up in their attics, or in storage. Storage units rent for US$ 50/month and up, and a surprising number of people spend large amounts of money to keep things that they readily admit are junk.

HOUSEHOLD HELPERS

We rarely use the term 'servants', a word that offends our ideas of democracy. They are house cleaners or housekeepers or babysitters or cooks—terms that imply some specialty other than being subservient.

American women have been lamenting the household help problem ever since World War II, when the household helpers went off to work in the factories and afterwards never wanted to work in other ladies' houses again. And no wonder—the pay is bad, the employer can be difficult and there are few benefits.

Even well-to-do families became accustomed to doing most of the household work themselves. Now, thanks largely to the enormous influx of workers from south of the border, many people have house cleaners who come periodically. But only very wealthy people still have cooks, gardeners, and daily housekeepers.

Consequently, families have found many short cuts to make up for the fact that with both Mom and Dad at jobs, there's nobody spending the day looking after the household. Breakfast may be a bowl of cereal, no one comes home for lunch, and dinner is often pizza or Chinese take-out food. There are numerous time-saving services, from pick-up-and-deliver dry cleaners to hired dog walkers.

Americans are mad for time-saving devices, no matter how minuscule the time saved. Power mowers, electric knives, microwave-ready meals, robot vacuum cleaners, automatic watering systems, and power-nap software that puts you to sleep and wakes you up all give Americans the illusion that they may someday get time under control.

Nonetheless, the real work remains. The weekend for the typical hard-working family consists of shopping, cleaning, fixing things around the house, gardening, and an overall attempt to get ready for the next frantic week. Few people socialize much. Besides the various reasons taken up in Chapter 6, there just isn't time.

PETS

It sometimes seems that the most popular member of a family is the family dog. Considering how loyal, polite, and

Dogs are important members of many households.

affectionate dogs are, this is not surprising. (Americans find the thought of eating dogs repugnant.) Cats are also full-fledged members of many families. When the pet dies, the family is genuinely grief-stricken.

Some foreigners consider it rather a dirty habit to have pets around the house. Indeed, animals do shed hair and bring dirt in on their feet, but they do not carry life-threatening diseases to humans. Most of us (excepting farmers) consider that our cats and dogs belong inside the house with the rest of the family. And a sure way to infuriate your neighbors is to leave a dog barking outside. Not only will this make you unpopular, you may soon have the sheriff at your door. In most communities, there are laws against barking dogs.

In cities and even suburbs, when you walk your dogs, you need to scoop up their poop and throw it in the trash. Dog walkers usually keep bags in their pockets for this purpose.

DRIVING

In order to get around, you can take public transportation if you live in an urban area, or you can drive. Many employers today offer a public transportation stipend to employees who take the bus or subway to work. Some athletic types might walk or ride their bikes whenever possible—undoubtedly the most reliable and responsible method for a wide gamut of reasons—but when you go to the hardware store to buy lumber, you'll want wheels. America has more cars on the road, parked in garages, or on blocks in the front yard than there are drivers, and the car culture has in many respects become the 'fuel' for epidemics such as road rage, smog, and obesity.

If you're going to drive, you must have a driver's license and the car must be registered. These are two separate processes but are usually done at the same place: the state Department of Motor Vehicles (DMV) or the Motor Vehicle Administration. Mere mention of the DMV can elicit groans in memory of the long lines and short tempers, but there's little escape (although AAA can register your car). The licence helps the government keeps track of you as the driver, and the registration helps keeps track of the car.

An international driver's licence, available at AAA offices, is a desirable item to have, but not absolutely required for visitors. However, the police would much rather deal with one than something in, say, Arabic, and so would rental car companies. Besides that, a driver's licence is the primary form of identification requested during almost every transaction—from opening a bank account, making a purchase with a credit card, writing checks, boarding a plane, buying a drink, or getting a senior discount at the movie theatre. You must get an American driver's licence after a year's residence here, which requires passing both a written and a driver's test. Even if your stay won't be that long, it's a good idea to pick up a booklet on driving rules at the DMV.

Owning a car requires money, a licence, and auto insurance. In exchange, you acquire the dearest American freedom—not having to take the bus. However, a new car is not strictly speaking a good investment, since it depreciates in value the minute you drive it off the lot.

There are alternatives to a new car. You lose less by buying a used or 'previously owned' car, although you can't be entirely certain of the condition or life expectancy of the car; you may be able to buy it a warranty, which guarantees that anything that breaks will be repaired or replaced. New car dealers offer some options, such as leasing, which is more like a long-term rental and cash-back offers. You can also buy a car directly from an individual, who signs the car title over to you.

There are multiple companies that will rent you a car for a daily, weekly, or monthly term, provided that you have a valid driver's licence and a good driving record. Deals and discounts for car rentals can be found on the Internet or through travel agencies and credit card companies.

Rules of the Road

Traffic laws are taken seriously here. While it's true that on some highways marked at 55 mph the traffic may be moving at 65 mph, the argument that 'everybody was doing it' will not help you in court. You must come to a complete stop at red lights and stop signs, even if there isn't another car in sight (the one you don't see may be a police car). If a police car wants to stop you, he will follow you flashing his overhead lights. Even if you can't imagine what's on his mind, pull over. You should remain in your car, with your driver's licence and car registration ready. You may also need to produce proof of car insurance.

Parking regulations are enforced as well, and fines can be high. It is particularly dispiriting to find that one's car has been towed away and can only be retrieved at great cost. You will have to find out what the various curb colors and signs in different communities indicate. Never park in front of a fire hydrant or at a bus stop. In most states, you may make a right turn on a red light, traffic permitting.

In some states, you may not talk on a cell phone unless you have a device that allows you to keep both hands on the steering wheel. You must fasten your seat belt. Children/babies must be in car seats and/or in the back seat; the ages and types vary by state; http://www.iihs.org/laws/ChildRestraint.aspx is a web site that lists the laws state by state.

Do not attempt to bribe a policeman. The gesture will not be appreciated, and happily, corruption among them in most regions is low. You might do better trying to persuade one that your foreignness accounted for your confusion. If you feel you have been unfairly cited, you may appear in traffic court and argue your case.

OPENING A BANK ACCOUNT

In order to open a bank account, you must first determine what sort of bank you'd like to use. There are super-mega nationwide financial institutions like Citibank, which offer online banking as well as a multitude of local branches and automatic teller machines (also known as cash dispensers or ATMs). There are smaller local or regional banks that generally offer good customer service, and then there are 'virtual' banks, where you make all of your transactions through the Internet. It's a matter of personal preference and convenience, but be sure to inquire about any fees for 'services' such as ATM usage fee, minimum balance fees, check processing and rejection fees, etc.

To open your account, you will need a driver's license or passport to prove that you are age 18, have an address, and are who you say you are. You will also need to produce a recent piece of mail, such as a phone bill, with your name and address, giving further evidence that you are legitimate.

EDUCATION

It is largely by passing through our public school system that immigrant families from all over the world have come to identify themselves as thoroughly American, absorbing American values, culture, and folklore. Without this educational filter, it's doubtful if the American experiment could have worked. When and where the system operates as it should, it provides the means for someone from the poorest home to advance in society to any height.

The American school system provides free schooling to every child from age 5 to 18—or from kindergarten through 12th grade. The object is to bestow a broad education on every youngster. Few students are expected to become intellectuals or scholars, but, theoretically, anyone who

completes the academic course in high school can go on to college.

Traditionally, attendance is mandatory until age 16, but there is a trend now towards raising that age to induce more students to graduate. Because each of the fifty states runs its own schools, school requirements vary across the nation, and there is no federal testing of students. However, since 2002, when the No Child Left Behind Act (NCLB) was signed into law, all states have been required to provide standardized testing. Low-scoring schools that do not improve on schedule are penalized. NCLB has been highly controversial, mainly because the focus on test-passing can leave little time for anything that isn't on the tests.

Problems

Despite the latest reforms and many years of schooling, far too many youngsters remain profoundly ignorant of basic facts when they graduate. Few know what the Bill of Rights is, when World War II was fought, who Thomas Jefferson was, or even what countries are north and south of the USA.

In math and science tests comparing American youngsters with those of other nations, Americans do fairly well in elementary grades, but their performances worsen in higher grades. Among 15-year-olds Americans rate 24th in math and 19th in science when compared to 37 other countries. In reading, this same cohort ranks 12th, and in problem-solving they rank 26th.

The top 10 per cent of American students, while short on facts, are probably as able and skilled as the best students anywhere. But the bottom 50 per cent is barely literate. Whether this is solely the fault of the schools or whether families and communities are equally to blame is the subject of hot debate.

Concern about the educational system is nearly always couched in terms of national needs. If the next generation can't read, who will run the businesses? If they can't compute, how will we compete with the rest of the world? Education for its own sake, for the sheer love of knowledge, does not get much press.

Educational Philosophy

American schools are blown around a lot by changing pedagogical theories, and the latest method for teaching math or reading sometimes leaves parents lost when facing their children's homework. However, while methods change, the belief remains that students should be active agents in their own educations, enlivened by their studies, rather than passive receptacles for facts. Students and teachers both regard pure memorization as uncreative and somewhat vulgar, although dismal test scores have led to something of a backlash. Lessons today are likely to contain more pure drill than they did a few years ago.

The amount of time spent on music, art, physical education, and such secondary subjects has greatly diminished in recent years. Part of the reason is that the budgets of schools are so stretched that they can't afford to pay the special teachers, but largely it's because so much time is now spent on the 'core subjects'—reading, math, and science.

Also, schools are expected to instill 'life skills'—logical thinking, analysis, problem solving. Schools must also address the ever growing stock of social problems. Racism, teenage pregnancy, alcoholism, drug use, reckless driving, and suicide are just a few that have appeared on the school curriculum. This all contributes to a high degree of social awareness in American youngsters but takes time from an already short day.

Structure

At the age of five, children start kindergarten, where they concentrate on getting ready for the heavier burdens of grade school by singing songs, painting pictures, learning to hang up their coats, and identifying numbers and letters. Grades 1 through 5 or 6 are known as elementary or grade school and concentrate on teaching reading, writing, and arithmetic, with some science and social studies, along with varying degrees of health, art, music, gym (sports), and computer skills.

The curriculum usually broadens in middle school/junior high (which is usually 6th through 8th grades) to include foreign languages and by high school (which traditionally begins with 9th grade) a wide choice of elective courses may be offered—academic as well as subjects like auto-tech, band, computer programming, business education, journalism, photography, and drama. Offerings vary greatly from school to school.

Those in their first year of high school, 9th grade, are called freshmen; 10th graders are sophomores; 11th graders are juniors; and 12th graders are seniors. (This terminology repeats itself in college when first-year students are freshmen; second-year students are sophomores, etc.)

In high school, students get to decide whether they wish to take a college preparatory or a vocational curriculum. Students are also often further separated between regular classes and the more challenging 'honors' classes.

Throughout school, from 1st to 12th grades, there are also 'special education' classes, which separate out those students who have extra difficulties—whether from behavioral, academic, emotional, or physical problems. Schools are mandated to provide a free public and appropriate education to all students, no matter what problems they might have. As some disabled students require very expensive services, this can be a considerable drain on the school budget.

Large urban schools often have some version of bilingual classes as well, most often in Spanish. There is a lot of controversy over bilingual education and its value. The emphasis is now on 'transitional' bilingual education, which teaches in the student's native tongue but with instruction in English and the goal of transitioning into regular classes. Another version is 'dual-language', which splits the class between native English-speakers, who learn a second language, and speakers of the minority language, who learn English.

Student Life

For many students, school is a happy experience. But it can also be anguishing. Overall, public schools are not nurturing places, and the competition for grades is minor compared to the competition for being cool, wearing the right clothes,

Enrolling Your Child in School

Your child should be guaranteed placement at your local public school, provided you have proper documentation of your address. To find your local school, contact your realtor, the state board of education, or your county office of education. The documents needed for enrollment vary, but may include:

Proof of age of student: birth certificate, passport, or other legal or notarised identification

- Proof of immunisations—3 DPT, 3 Polio, 2 Measles/Mumps/Rubella (MMR)
- Proof of identity of person enrolling student—if you are not the parent or legal guardian, you should contact the local school board for instructions on how to proceed
- Social security card or number
- Withdrawal papers from previous school and current report card or transcript
- Proof of residency, including a recent property tax bill, current lease, and a current utility bill, or a notarised Shared Housing Form AND either a current property tax bill of homeowner or copy of lease of renter
- Three additional supporting documents, which may include current pay stub, income tax form, two bank statements, medical bills, car registration, current utility bills, or a car insurance policy or bill.

The better the school, the harder they make it for you to enroll your child because so many desperate but well-meaning parents will try anything, including faking an address, to get their kid into one of the 'better' public schools, meaning a school with higher graduation rates, better teachers and more funding. If you were hoping to enroll your child in a private or alternative school, contact the school itself to determine enrollment periods and necessary documentation.

and having the right friends. The harassment of a child who is a little peculiar, unathletic, or unpopular can be serious, and the anonymity of websites has paved the way to vicious attacks. A spotlight has been on bullying lately, which can be extremely traumatic to the victims, and most schools are now taking it seriously.

Kids dress extremely casually for school. There are dress codes, but the difficulties in enforcement and social pressure to wear the 'right' clothes have caused even some public schools to turn to uniforms. Whether students should be forced to wear them has been the subject of a number of lawsuits; the Supreme Courts has ruled that students are entitled to 'freedom of expression'. However, this is sometimes overridden by sheer danger. Where gangs are strong, just wearing the wrong colors can create trouble, and in some schools, neither red nor blue may be worn.

Schools have various cliques—jocks, brains, nerds, Goths— but there isn't a place for everyone. However, many of those who suffer miserably through high school find grown-up life rich and rewarding, while for some popular high school jocks, life afterwards is never as bright again.

To the students, the most notable difference between elementary school and the higher levels is that in junior high they start 'changing classes.' This means that rather than spending the day in one classroom, they switch classrooms to meet their different teachers. This gives them three or four minutes between classes in the hallways, where a great deal of the important social action of high school traditionally takes place.

Society overall does not take the business of studying very seriously. Once foreign children have learned English, they may find their studies too easy and be bored. Schoolchildren generally have plenty of free time, which they are encouraged to fill with extracurricular activities—sports, clubs, cheerleading, scouts—supposed to inculcate such qualities as leadership, sportsmanship, ability to organize, etc. Those who don't become engaged in such activities or have after-school jobs have plenty of opportunity to 'hang out,' listen to teenage music, and play video games.

Compared to many other nations, most American students do not have much homework. Studies also suggest that American parents have lower expectations for their children's success in school than other nationalities do. (Historically, there has not been much correlation between American school success and success in later life.) "He's just not a scholar," the American parents might say, content that their son is on the swim team and doesn't take drugs.

However, there are affluent areas where attitudes are very different. Instead, students study furiously through high school, desperate to get into the best colleges, driven by their equally desperate parents who are convinced that the road to success must go through Harvard or Cal Berkeley. These students engage in volunteer work, take extra credits, and play instruments—hoping that their college applications will demonstrate their versatility. Stress levels at these schools are very high, as are anorexia, drug use, anxiety, and depression.

Competition is omnipresent in American schools, and in innumerable ways children are pitted against each other —whether in classroom discussion, spelling bees, reading groups, or tests. Every classroom is expected to produce a scattering of A's and F's (A = excellent; B = good; C = average; D = poor; and F = failed). A teacher who gives all A's looks too soft—so students are aware that they are competing for the limited number of top marks.

Cheating by students is a growing problem. A recent study showed that 75 percent of students admit to having cheated—and that doesn't even count copying homework from others. Students also download papers from the Internet and submit them as their own; text message answers to test questions; get test answers to questions from students who have already taken the test; and smuggle answers into a test room. Students seem to consider that if it is their job to get good grades, they have to do it by any means possible. What's more, if everyone cheats, and they don't, they're at a disadvantage.

The Ever-Blowing Winds of Change

Sadly, the current school situation caps 40 years of well-intentioned reform. The progressivism of the 1970s was successful in making school curriculums more sensitive to the cultures of students not of the white, Christian majority. Most of the old textbooks were thrown out for being too sexist and ethnocentric and were replaced by textbooks that attempted to tell the stories of every minority group. There was a massive and largely unsuccessful attempt to integrate the school system so that Black, Hispanic, and Asian students would have equal opportunity to attend better schools. The term 'busing' referred to the practice of transporting students by bus out of their neighborhoods to a school lacking in minority students.

Unfortunately, one response to busing was for many white people to move to suburban towns or to send their children to private schools. Today, many urban schools don't have very many white students left to add to the racial mix.

The recognition of the rights of minorities and women led to the discovery of students' rights. Consequently, dress codes were thrown out, students' opinions became much more important, students got more choices, and a teacher's word was no longer law. Freedom, unfortunately, did not always lead to responsibility. Unfortunately, in the ensuing years, test scores sank, behavior problems worsened, and students' own interests led too often in the direction of drugs rather than towards intellectual endeavour. The wind is blowing the other way now, with an emphasis on discipline and standards.

Teacher Respect

Teaching is not a high-status occupation in the United States. This is in keeping with the pay scale, which is poor compared to other professions. (In another country, one could be respected and poor, but rarely in America.) Furthermore, teaching has traditionally been a woman's field, another strike against it. And, in all truth, many teachers are not very learned themselves.

Teachers are heavily burdened both inside and outside the classroom. They are the foot soldiers who must carry out a constant flow of orders descending from school boards, politicians, and principals. Students' rights remain paramount, and parents are quick to call teachers to account, as are the students themselves.

Many foreigners have rather simplistically concluded that it's the absence of corporal punishment (which is illegal in many states) in the schools that causes all the problems. No evidence bears this out. More likely, numerous social issues are inevitably reflected in the schools.

School Choices

American schools vary enormously. Some do poorly. There are also sterling schools, safe and orderly, from which students get top grades in nationwide exams. In many schools, even when the average standard is low, an excellent education is available to those who take advantage. "You could learn an awful lot here if you listened," said a visiting Swedish student of her suburban high school.

However, if you are packing your child off to the local school, you cannot assume that it will be satisfactory. You must investigate, preferably before deciding where to live. Many Americans consider a good local school one of the most important criteria in choosing a neighbourhood.

Better schools are generally in better areas, but there are scattered success stories everywhere. Big cities may have so-called 'magnet' schools, which emphasise particular studies—such as art or science—and attract students from all over the city. 'Charter' schools are exempted from many state requirements so that they may offer an innovative program—such as an emphasis on the arts or a particular teaching method, such as Montessori. Some large cities also have at least one select high school, which requires high grades and test scores for admission. These schools are as high-pressure and prestigious as any private school.

Beating the System

Overall, unless you're living in a small, one-school town, the school set-up is complicated. Your address determines your child's school assignment, but often it is possible to change that assignment. You can probably read about local schools and access their test scores on the Internet; many have websites of their own, so you can see what their offerings are. Still, the best way to learn the ins and outs of your local school system is to talk to neighborhood experts. It's from them that you'll discover that you have a good chance of getting into School A if you come from a certain ethnic group, or that if you are really keen on entering School B, you must line up very early in the morning on a certain day.

Or Escaping

You may instead decide to follow many Americans (of all colors) to the suburbs. Nice suburbs have fairly safe, homogeneous schools. Another alternative, one chosen by one in eleven American children, is a private school. (Private schools are ones to which parents pay tuition; public schools are supported by taxes.)

Gaining entrance to the well-known schools is highly competitive. In large cities, there are private schools for every need— from the intellectually advanced to the learning disabled. There are also religious schools and schools adhering to particular educational philosophies. But bear in mind that some affluent city-dwellers send their children to public schools merely because they want their children to have the broader social experience of a public school.

Lastly, there are boarding schools, mostly for 9th through 12th grades. Some of the old New England boarding schools have educated generations of families. Happily, in recent years these 'snob' schools have made considerable efforts to recruit students from varied backgrounds. Simply being a foreigner may make your child a desirable candidate from the school's point of view.

Private school costs might run from US$ 3,600 a year for a religious school (and you don't have to be a Catholic to go to a Catholic school) to US$ 29,000 a year for an exclusive high school. Nearly all private schools have some scholarships, and the oldest ones have endowments large enough for them to accept anyone they want—regardless of ability to pay.

Some parents send their children to a religious school such as this one for the Lubavitch community in Brooklyn, New York, as these schools provide a better quality of education.

Universities

Over half of high school graduates ultimately go on to some kind of advanced study, so there is nothing exclusive about a college education. At last count, there were more than 3,000 institutions of higher learning in the United States. This includes everything from two-year colleges with a few hundred students to state universities (a university offers both a four-year undergraduate program and advanced degrees from its various graduate schools) with 35,000 students on one campus.

Nearly every college charges tuition. State universities are much cheaper than private ones, where total costs including room and board can be as much as US$ 35,000 a year without books, which can add nearly another US$ 1,000. While this sounds staggering, at many colleges as many as two-thirds of the students are receiving scholarships.

Despite the plethora of colleges, every year tension mounts as high school seniors wait to find out if the colleges they want have accepted them. The criteria for acceptance include high school grades, personal recommendations, achievements outside school, and test scores. These tests consist of nationwide, though private, exams known as SATs (Scholastic Aptitude Tests), which test both mathematics and verbal skills, and SAT2s, which test knowledge in particular subjects and are usually only required by private colleges. There are alternate tests called the CATs (College Aptitude Tests), which are less used. Although important, these tests do not inspire the suicidal impulses that the big exams in some other countries do.

A status education is available only from a relatively few high-profile colleges, although an excellent education is actually available at most schools. It is conversely possible to go to one of the 'best' schools and emerge with a dim education. The standards for completing the course may not be as demanding as those for entrance, and students often find they have a great deal of time to party.

Some colleges are best known for such qualities as the regular drunkenness of their students or the excellent nearby skiing. Sports teams, especially the football team, may be a college's greatest claim to fame. Colleges often recruit players who are potentially professional athletes but have few academic skills. The football coach is likely to be the highest paid person on campus, and millions are spent on maintaining sports programs. The hope is that successful teams will induce alumni to donate generously.

In the last thirty years, universities have relinquished their parental role. Most colleges do very little to regulate the lives of students, other than to dismiss those who fail too many courses and to offer counselling to the troubled. Teachers do not assume parental roles. Families who want supervision for their young might have to find a Christian college.

A Tanzanian who arrived here to attend Corning Community College says he'll never forget the first day's registration: "It was terrible, overwhelming. I had never had to choose my courses before. This would never happen in Africa." American colleges require certain basic courses (varying with each college), but beyond these leave students free to pursue their own interests. Consequently, nearly every institution has a fat catalogue with a giant smorgasbord of courses—from social relations among the Inuit to nuclear physics.

Graduate Schools

Beyond the parties, remedial courses, and football teams, there is a higher level at which the American university is manifestly successful. It is in the graduate schools that the American academic system shines, where intelligent inquiry and the analytic tradition pay off.

The serious student who reaches the advanced levels will be as well-trained as at any university in the world. Professors from around the world flock to American universities as much for the intellectual excitement as for the handsome salaries. (Professors are held in much higher esteem than schoolteachers, which is reflected in their salaries as well as in a much greater degree of autonomy in their teaching.) Increasingly, foreigners occupy a large number of places in American graduate schools, particularly in the sciences.

The College Classroom

The participatory classroom is the American ideal. Teachers want evidence that the students are interested, listening, and excited. Usually, this comes in the form of questions, and students are sometimes graded on 'classroom participation.' Foreigners are often surprised that the teacher wants to hear what they think and what they don't understand. Teachers even welcome disagreement.

There is, however, in nearly every class one student who talks too much and bores everybody. You should not become so carried away with the American system that you become this student.

Teachers may want very much for their students to learn, but they do not feel insulted if a student does not understand or responsible if a student fails. The ultimate effort is up to the student.

The Licensing of America

A century ago, very few occupations required licensing. Doctors, lawyers, and accountants learned their trades through apprenticeships. Today, those who want to go into these reliably lucrative fields need years of postgraduate training. Even many service occupations, such as beautician, electrician, and plumber, have training requirements that restrict membership.

Until World War II, many successful businessmen had little schooling; now most prospective managers need college degrees, and those with an MBA (Master of Business Administration) are most in demand. A degree from one of the prestigious schools commands a high starting salary. Teachers and social workers, besides acquiring a bachelor's degree (conferred on completing the undergraduate course) must submit to specialised training.

Because of the length of training and expense for a particular career, there are not as many open doors in America as there once were, and many people of talent are limited in their pursuits. However, those who know what they want to do can probably find a way to get the necessary degree.

Adult Education

After complaining about many aspects of American life, a 40-year-old woman from Hong Kong concluded, "But where else could someone my age go back to school and get a degree in social work? Here you can change your whole life, start a new business, do what you really want to do."

To millions of others, adult education is the path to a new career, or if not to a new career, to a new outlook. Schools generally encourage the older person who wants to start anew, and besides regular classes, schedule evening classes in special programs. Today there are so many people of retirement age in college that it is no longer remarkable.

CHILDREN
Daycare

Half of American mothers with children under five years old have jobs. As only a quarter of these have mothers, husbands, or other relatives able and willing to look after the baby during the day, finding good childcare has become giant problem.

The government operates very few day care centres, and these are reserved for low-income families. There are numerous private day care centres, but the staff is often underpaid and weary from looking after too many children. Few of these accept infants or toddlers who aren't toilet-trained. Cooperative day care centres have the advantage of high parent supervision, but parents must be able to contribute a certain amount of time each week.

Some parents arrange work schedules so that one parent is nearly always home. Quite a few telecommute from home. Parents who can afford to will try to hire someone to come into their home and look after the baby, but good caretakers are hard to find and keep. Live-in nannies usually come from foreign countries as such work is not popular among Americans. Sometimes two sets of parents will share one caretaker. Alternatively, the parents may take their child to the home of someone who takes in several children during the day. Some progressive employers—not nearly enough—actually provide day care centres at or near the workplace, recognizing that a happy parent is ultimately a good worker.

How to Choose a Daycare Centre

Before choosing a day care environment, parents should be familiar with the state licensure regulations for childcare. They should also check references and observe the caregivers with the child. Parents should look for day care centres that provide:

- a high proportion of adults to children
- individual attention
- long-term staff, who enjoy and understand children
- opportunities for creative work, imaginative play, and physical activity,
- lots of drawing and coloring materials and toys, as well as equipment such as swings, wagons, jungle gyms, etc.
- no reliance on television or videos
- trained, experienced teachers for children over three

There is little public supervision of most day care centres, and occasional reports appear of physical and even sexual abuse. Parents should be extremely careful in selecting a centre. The chances that your child will suffer overt abuse are low, but it is quite possible that your child will receive less loving attention than you would wish. You should be very suspicious of any centre that does not welcome unexpected parental visits or tries to keep the parents at an arm's length from the classrooms.

After-school Care

Seventy-two percent of mothers with school-age children now have jobs outside the home. Some consider this a travesty and blame working mothers for the erosion of family values, while others insist this is a productive outgrowth of the women's movement, which encouraged women to pursue careers. Where the truth lies is generally irrelevant to the working mother, who works because she needs the money.

Some children stay at school for after-school care or go elsewhere and their parents pick them up after work. But

Children too young for school whose parents work often spend their days in daycare centres where they are cared for by paid workers.

many cannot afford care. The sad result is the latch-key child, a term for the preponderance of children who come home from school and spend the afternoon waiting for the sound of their mother or father's briefcase in the front entry hall at 6:00 or 7:00 pm.

Parents agonize over childcare, and there are those who are lucky enough to have relatives who will look after their children. Some women relinquish promising careers to be with their children. Others actually seem to have found a balance between work, school, soccer, and the babysitter, and manage to raise secure, well-adjusted kids. Too often, children grow up with dominant memories of parents who are always in a hurry.

Babysitters

The whole concept of evening babysitters is a novelty to many foreigners, to whom the thought of leaving children in the care of a stranger is appalling. What would actually be appalling to us is the thought of never being able to get away from the kids. Lacking a supply of relatives to look after our children, we hire someone, which has the added benefit of allowing us to pay for the service and not have to build up any social obligations.

The babysitter might be the older child of neighbors, someone recommended by friends, or a student from a nearby college. If the first time went well, we would try to hire the same babysitter, so he or she won't remain a stranger long. But as long as the person is reliably recommended, we don't worry overly about the stranger aspect, as American children are supposed to learn to relate to many different people.

The usual routine with the babysitter is to, first of all, leave a phone number where you can be reached in case of an emergency, then oral or written instructions for children's bedtime, and other rules relating to television, video games, meals, and an invitation to 'help yourself to anything in the refrigerator'. You should have established when you first spoke how much you pay per hour (you'll have to find out what local terms usually are). You are responsible for seeing that the babysitter gets home safely—meaning that you either drive him or her home or provide taxi fare.

One other alternative is a live-in *au pair*. This is a young man or woman from another country, who gets room, board, and modest pay in exchange for childcare. Such a person is often studying and is not expected to work full-time; he or she is treated much more as a member of the family than most hired help. This can be a very happy arrangement for both parties.

Self Discovery

The child must get the chance to find his or her niche. This means leaving him or her free to experiment, to try one thing and then another. We (at least in theory) resist the kind of tracking that in many countries directs children along career paths from a young age. If you're going to fulfil your potential—the object in life here—you can't settle down too early.

We also consider it important not to break a child's spirit. A child who is too demure and obedient will not have the audacity to go far in this society. It takes self-confidence to start your own company, to think of new ways to split atoms, to play in a rock band. So parents try to emphasise the positive. Rather than pointing out to a three-year-old that his picture of a house ought to have a roof, we declare it the most magnificent picture of a house ever and tape it to the refrigerator. We want each child to feel that he is a very special child, with unique, notable abilities. After all, self-promotion goes a long way, even in lieu of talent. America's great humorist Mark Twain wrote with some truth, "All you need in life is ignorance and confidence, and then success is sure".

Privacy and private property are both considered sacrosanct. A child may refuse to allow anyone into his room. It is considered poor behavior on the part of a parent to read a child's diary or mail without permission. Parents shouldn't be too nosy. It is taken for granted that children will have secrets from their parents.

Many parents do not believe in spanking and use other means of discipline. Contrary to some rumors, it is not illegal to hit your children in the USA, but it is illegal to seriously hurt them or to molest them in any way sexually. If you beat them badly, you may hear from the police. Neglect and emotional abuse, although harder to prove, are also against the law.

Some parents do seem to give their children more freedom and decision-making power than the child actually wants. Sensible parents modulate decision-making according to age, but the attitude that 'it's up to you' is much more prevalent here than elsewhere. Learning through failure is the

American way. Abraham Lincoln failed at many enterprises before becoming a president revered by history.

The Reinvention of Discipline

On the positive side, many people of all ages have good relationships with their parents, far friendlier than in cultures in which the parents, often fathers in particular, are remote authorities. But there are 'spoilt' children—undisciplined, self-centred, and unhappy. Recently, the experts have turned around and discovered 'limits', concluding that children are happier when they have parents who act like parents and give them rules and structure, along with love and attention.

Newcomers to the United States should take heart that more Americans are rejecting total indulgence. If you are 'strict', you may be in the minority, but you are not alone. So do not let your children persuade you that all American parents let their children do anything they want.

MEDICAL CARE

Says a New Zealander: "One of the biggest failures of my second favorite country in the world, the USA, is its failure to guarantee medical treatment for all its citizens, so millions go without care." Unlike all other developed countries, there is no national health plan in the USA, and the cost of medical care is staggering. Consequently, you must have private medical insurance or be sure that your home-country insurance will pay for you. Insurance here is costly, but without it illness could ruin you financially. An overnight hospital stay could easily cost you US$ 25,000. (Insurance companies can negotiate lower rates, so uninsured individuals pay the most.)

You could be refused admission to a hospital if you don't have insurance, (unless your situation is life-threatening in which case the nearest hospital has to take you) and be forced to go to the overcrowded public hospital—where you will still have to pay, unless you have no money whatsoever.

The medical profession charges up and down the line for each separate service—for X-rays, tests, medicines, and office visits; in addition to your hospital bill you may owe money to surgeons, anesthesiologists, private nurses, respiratory therapists, pharmacists, and people you scarcely realized existed. You will discover a separate charge for each time your doctor popped into your room.

Health Maintenance Organizations (HMOs) are the big trend in healthcare now. In an HMO, you pay a monthly membership and receive whatever services you need at little or no additional cost, but you must use only the services covered by the HMO. Consequently, the HMO, which is usually a profitable corporation, has a strong interest in limiting the amount of treatment you get. If the company decides you truly need a certain treatment, you will get it, but the HMO does the deciding—not you.

Getting Insurance

If you are working for a company here, your employer is likely to at least partially pay for your health insurance, but note that policies rarely cover all medical expenses. If you don't have employee insurance, you will have to find a private plan and your insurance agent should be able to advise you on short-term insurance. Colleges have health plans for students.

The poor aren't completely without resources. Medicare, a national plan, provides coverage for the old and disabled. Seniors buy MediGap policies in addition to cover fees Medicare doesn't pay for. Medicaid and various state plans cover the indigent. Still, 47 million Americans have no health insurance at all. Prices for health insurance have risen so much that only 63 percent of employers now provide it, and employees often pay a large share of their premiums, as well as co-pays and deductibles.

Quality of Care

At its best, American medical care is excellent, but the fragmented care and proportion of resources going to billing lead to errors. In most hospitals your care will be adequate, although nurses are extremely busy and rarely linger by your bedside. Many people acquire hospital infections; it's just as well that stays are short.

As in most countries, it's helpful to have family or friends around to assist with your more mundane needs. However, you will find American hospital wards very quiet. The presumption here is that the sick person needs to rest and to rest he or she has to be alone. So large gatherings at the bedside are rare. Friends arrive with flowers, but make their visits very brief. An alternative to visiting is to send a get-well card or to have a florist make up and deliver a bouquet of flowers to the hospital.

You may find that for a simple ailment you are offered much more extensive and high-technology care than you would get in your own country. This is partly because doctors get sued if they don't consider every possible permutation of a problem. You can refuse treatment that you don't want; if some test or treatment seems extreme, talk over the alternatives with the doctor.

Up-to-date American doctors are encouraged not to be too bossy or domineering and should be happy to discuss your problems at length. However, doctors are under pressure to see a high volume of patients, and your visit will probably be short. So write down your questions and ask them fast. A Canadian living here tells me that when she was seriously ill at home in Montreal, the doctors were very proactive, calling her to check on her and make suggestions. Here, she must instead pursue the doctors and make the suggestions herself.

Very few doctors make house calls; no matter how sick you are you will be expected to appear in their offices unless you are in the hospital. A recognized problem is that in this world of specialists there may be nobody who is in charge of your case. Filling this gap are internists or family doctors, who treat the basics and coordinate the specialists

It's a good idea to line up a doctor—if not a 'family' specialist, perhaps an internist—as soon as you arrive if you're staying for an extended period. If anything bad happens, you will need a doctor to admit you to a hospital. Furthermore, most effective drugs, antibiotics for instance, must be prescribed by doctors. So there's a good chance you'll need a doctor sooner or later. Your choices may be limited due to whatever medical plan you're on. If not, try to get recommendations from people you know.

Mainstream Alternatives

A segment of the population has become increasingly sceptical about modern medicine, which often seems to have lost touch with human and spiritual forces. Occasionally the treatment is worse than the disease, and the reluctance on the part of both doctors and patients to let nature take its course leads to over-medication.

In reaction, people have started both to look after themselves (through diet, exercise, etc.) and to turn to 'alternative' health practitioners: acupuncturists, homeopaths, chiropractors (who do not consider themselves 'alternative'), nutritionists, Chinese herbalists, and other healers. Time-honored native remedies are much in vogue among New Age types. Most of the aforementioned healers have the advantage of being at least fairly harmless. But do not assume that because they operate legally there is reason to believe that their cures work. It's strictly *caveat emptor* (Latin for 'let the buyer beware') in this department—which admittedly is the case no matter what kind of doctor is treating you.

AIDS and Hepatitis C

New treatments have greatly reduced the death rate from AIDS, but the disease remains incurable and tragic. The majority of the sufferers are either homosexual men or drug addicts who have shared needles. Also tragic is the epidemic of Hepatitis C (Hep C), a disease that transmits in ways similar to that of AIDS and often results in chronic liver disease and even death.

You need not worry about contracting AIDS or Hep C unless you have sexual relations with someone who carries the virus, you shoot drugs with dirty needles, or you receive infected blood in a blood transfusion. However, all blood donations are tested, and the odds of getting either disease from a transfusion are very, very low.

If you feel you must have sexual relations with someone who could carry a disease, you should use a latex condom. But condoms can fail. Drug addicts and homosexuals are the likeliest transmitters of both diseases, but heterosexuals are not exempt. The days of exuberant free love in America are long over.

Chastity will also protect the visitor from a few other venereal diseases—herpes, syphilis, gonorrhoea—that would be unpleasant to take home.

Do not take up with prostitutes—male or female. Other than in a few counties in the state of Nevada, prostitution is illegal. Consequently, prostitutes are not subject to disease checks, and many are drug addicts. Furthermore, you could end up being beaten and robbed. The sexual underworld is a dangerous place.

HEALTH
Dieting
Mother Nature, in protecting humans from famine, made fattening foods appealing and American industry has made fattening foods quick and cheap. People from many cultures get fat here, including ones that have little obesity back in their homelands. According to the Surgeon General, 61 percent of America's adults and 16 percent of the children are overweight.

Yet it is fashionable to be very thin. (Whatever you do, don't tell people they look fat.) The effort to be thin while constantly tempted by fattening foods has put many people (usually women) on recurrent cycles of weight loss and regain.

Despite evidence that at least 95 percent of the weight lost in dieting is regained, Americans remain irresistibly attracted to new diets and weight-loss gimmicks. The top selling books in this country are cookbooks and diet books.

There is an unfortunate prejudice against fat people, which comes from the viewpoint that the fat person is a person lacking in self-control, rather than the victim of metabolic or other problem. Foreigners in particular, surprised to see so much obesity, often suffer from this prejudice.

Self-Improvement
It is doubtful whether there is another place in the world where people are so intent on improving themselves. Americans' nearly unique belief in progress includes the proposition that individuals can change their natures—or at

the very least, their bodies. Our Constitution guarantees us 'life, liberty, and the pursuit of happiness.' Not to be happy is not just a misfortune; it is a failure. We want inner peace and contentment, and duty to family is not a good excuse for unhappiness. We believe you should renounce the family if necessary in order to strive for individual fulfillment.

Psychologists say we must love ourselves before we can love other people. So we are trying to. Foreigners usually think that Americans are quite good at loving themselves already, but they may mistake the outer bluster for the real thing. Actually, the competitive atmosphere in which we live makes people very critical of themselves. Depression is a major problem. Furthermore, the belief in progress suggests that life ought to be constantly getting better and better. As it usually isn't, we must find what's wrong and repair it.

Modes of Repair

Popular psychology has lined the bookshelves with volumes promising to bring happiness into individual lives. Most of them have to do with modes of right thinking. They teach how to be more assertive and to get the things out of life one deserves. Rather incredibly to the foreigners who feel that we're already the most selfish people in the world, many of these 'philosophies' train people how to say 'no' when other people make demands on them. A few popular favorites are: *Self Matters* (by the ubiquitous Dr. Phil); *Codependent No More*, *Boundaries,* and *Stand Up For Your Life*.

A perennial favorite for the past 65 years has been *How to Win Friends and Influence People* by Dale Carnegie. It's the basic textbook for popularity, and Dale Carnegie courses, which teach the techniques, are flourishing.

Weekend workshops cover all the same subjects that the books do, at much greater cost but promising a nearly instant new self. The past decades saw an emphasis on books and courses that straightforwardly promised to make a person rich. There is instruction in time management, negotiation, sex, and many words have been written on making relationships work and on raising children.

Therapists

When troubles get too big, many Americans go off to see a therapist. There's a broad selection of them: doctors trained in psychoanalysis, psychologists, people with master's degrees in family therapy and in social work. The range of methods used is likewise broad, and the necessary credentials to practice vary by state.

Usually a person visits their therapist once a week for fifty minutes, and the course of therapy can last between a few weeks and a decade, depending on the method and the goals. At best, therapy helps people overcome depression, anxiety, phobias, substance-abuse problems, and to deal successfully with work, family, and relationship issues. At the least, one can expect a therapist to listen intently and give you a sense of being understood. The price is high—US$ 80 an hour and up—although many therapists and clinics will adjust the rate according to income, and there are clinics providing lower rates.

Most Americans do not consider it shameful to go see 'a shrink' (short for 'headshrinker'). It's a quintessentially American way of dealing with problems. Foreigners are often aghast and say, "Why don't they talk to their families or their friends?" but therapists are trained to look at the big picture and find the mysteries behind people's irrational behavior; this in itself is an intriguing undertaking. If you do decide to go in for therapy, be particular about which one you choose. Some therapists are much more effective than others.

Prozac and Ritalin

In the last twenty years, antidepressants have been replacing therapy for many. Medical plans appreciate that they're cheaper than therapy. These drugs, of which Prozac is the best known, have become the subject of much debate. Should we really be covering over our social problems by prescribing drugs to a large proportion of the population? Some of the Prozac-takers aren't even particularly depressed but find that the drug enables them to be more successful in life.

Prozac is also prescribed for children and even dogs. And children who are having trouble in school are frequently diagnosed with ADHD (Attention Deficit Hyperactivity Disorder) for which they are given medications such as Ritalin. These help them quiet down and concentrate, but many wonder if drugging children is the best solution to a problem with broader implications.

Exercise

A lot of people have concluded that exercise works even better than therapy. It doesn't seem surprising that after several generations of riding around in cars and watching television hour after hour, Americans would discover that they have lost a sense of physical wellbeing.

Doctors have been telling us for years that the post-industrial age has produced physically well cared for but sadly unfit bodies. Furthermore, they said, the American heart was in as bad shape as the rest of the muscles. The American male, it seemed, was inclined to drop dead before men in the rest of the Westernized world.

One of the answers, we were told, was aerobic exercise. (Aerobic exercise is the kind that raises the pulse to a certain

Joggers can be seen on city streets from early morning until late at night.

level for a certain period of time, thus giving the heart itself a workout. It is also said to increase the brain's production of norepinephrines—natural tranquilizers.) Jogging was the first great craze. Then came stationary bicycles, rowing machines, the stairmaster, and roller blades. Swimming has always been in style. Aerobic dance, in which a roomful of sweating men and women run and kick and jump to loud, throbbing music, has many followers. 'Pilates' is a new kind of workout that many swear by.

Most experts concede that brisk walking provides fitness enough and that 10,000 steps a day should keep you in the pink. (You can buy a pedometer to count them for you.) The most recent studies suggest that an hour's exercise nearly daily is required to maintain health and fitness.

Health clubs, usually equipped with workout machines, swimming pools, and saunas, can be found almost everywhere. Read the agreement carefully if you're thinking of joining one. Many use high-pressure tactics to sign newcomers up for extended periods. Some have initiation fees, large or small. Nearly all have some scheme whereby you can try out the club before joining.

FREEDOM FROM DIRT
Home and Person

"Cleanliness is next to godliness," my grandmother used to say. Americans are almost religious in their devotion to eliminating dirt. Daily baths or showers are the norm, underwear and socks are changed daily and men head out the door each morning in a fresh shirt.

In fact, it has been shown that the American housewife spends more time doing housework than she did fifty years ago. One reason is that standards of cleanliness have risen to meet the time saved by washing machines and vacuum cleaners. A great deal of effort can go into making kitchen floors and counters shine; supermarkets fill entire aisles with cleaning formulas and devices.

Above all, the American person does not wish to smell dirty. The matter is so sensitive that it is unmentionable. An enormous industry produces deodorants, aftershave lotions, powders and colognes guaranteed to fend off any hint of body odor. A person who vigorously exercises will want to shower immediately afterwards. Houses now often have as many or more bathrooms as occupants, each a sparkling temple to cleanliness.

The Streets

On a world scale, even if not up to the standard of Copenhagen or Tokyo, American cities are pretty clean. We frown on garbage-strewn streets, and the better suburbs are immaculate, with perfectly cut lawns and not an ice cream wrapper in sight. In some poor city neighborhoods, on the other hand, trash blows around freely and graffiti defeats fresh-paint efforts.

Under no circumstances should you drop waste, be it ever so small, on the ground. Practically every community has some sort of public trash collection, but we are a civic-minded people and consider everyone responsible for keeping the outdoors tidy. If there is no trash can in sight, you may have to fill your pockets with empty bottles and candy wrappers until you get home. Good citizens go so far as to pick up other people's refuse when they're in a park or garden.

The rule goes for the middle of the desert, the national parks, zoos and mountaintops as well. Those who offend nature by leaving refuse behind are considered to have had poor upbringings. Alas, there are many of them, despite fines for littering. In a country like ours, which generates such mountains of waste, one considers with horror where general littering would lead.

Homelessness

Most immigrants no longer arrive thinking the streets of America will be paved with gold, but neither do they expect to find people sleeping in the streets. This is still the world's richest country. But people live on the streets, by the hundreds, in all the major cities. Thousands more spend nights in temporary shelters, not knowing where they're going to spend the following nights.

America has a housing problem. In the last 35 years, little low-cost housing has been built, and rents and house prices have climbed dizzyingly. What used to be cheap housing is now expensive. It is a much greater struggle than it used to be for a reasonably successful family to afford a house; for marginal people it becomes impossible.

A proportion of the people living on the streets are beyond helping themselves. But a substantial proportion of the homeless are families or single mothers with children. Some of these have just had a run of bad luck, and others have problems exacerbated by drugs, alcohol, or mental instability. (These often only get off the streets by going to jail.) Clearly, the laxity of family ties is a factor—otherwise more of those down on their luck would have a relative to stay with. There are teenagers living on the streets because they have run away or been kicked out of an abusive home.

Foreigners find the homeless situation difficult to comprehend because often in their own countries—no matter how poor—everybody still has a place to stay even if shared with many others. Here, both city governments and private charities try to provide shelters for the homeless, but there is never enough money. The homeless situation is a shameful one for America.

CRIME

Few people arrive here unaware of American crime. It is so well publicized that many foreigners are surprised to find that there isn't a bandit behind every tree. Although there is indeed a high crime rate—which inhibits us all—the odds are that the visitor will not have any personal experience with it.

In fact, the US murder rate has been sharply declining since 1991, most of the murders take place in very poor neighborhoods or in criminal circles. Unless you're smuggling drugs, your odds of getting murdered are slight. Nonetheless, Americans are cautious walking in certain areas; there are districts of some cities that I would never set foot in.

Robbery rates have also declined, but people still bolt their doors and set up burglar alarms—even in safe suburbs. We are a rather fearful people and don't care to take chances with our health or safety.

The Problem

A large proportion of crime is in some way related to illegal drugs. Drug use is widespread; users may be successful professionals, the alienated offspring of middle class families, or poor people, enviously watching on television the ritzy lives of the successful.

Although drug use is widespread in affluent areas, it is most visible in the ghettos (city areas of much crime, little family stability, and high unemployment) among disillusioned young people. Drug use dissolves moral inhibitions and drugs are high-profit, so brutal crimes result.

The crime problem is exacerbated by the millions of guns floating around the country. It is an amazing fact that almost anyone can go into a store and buy a handgun—or a semi-automatic machine gun. A phrase in the United States Constitution granting the 'right to bear arms' causes the National Rifle Association to insist that any limitation on gun sales is unconstitutional. Actually, the founding fathers were providing protection against unpopular tyrants and probably would have considered the free sales of hand guns as crazy as most foreigners do.

Drugs

Illegal drugs have been a problem for a long time among the have-nots of America. Heroin (made from the poppy and imported from Asia and Latin America) has created drug addicts and caused crime for years. Marijuana has been long available in some inner city neighborhoods, but it was not until the 1960s that college students widely indulged in smoking marijuana. Since then, marijuana has become much stronger and its use has spread around the country; many people think smoking marijuana should not be a crime.

The use of a wide variety of other illegal drugs has spread into every level of society. Heroin addiction is now a major problem among middle-class youth.

Crime Precautions

Foreigners are automatically more vulnerable to crime than natives because they're on unfamiliar territory. They are less aware of what trouble feels like, less wary of the suspicious character. They pause when they should be walking briskly and stare at the tops of buildings when they should be looking at doorways.

Here are a few precautions:

- Keep your wits about you. When you're on city streets, don't ever get so lost in rapture that you are not conscious of your surroundings. People who look lost in any manner are easy targets.

- In American cities, bad areas and good ones can be intermixed in a manner perilous to the stroller. If you're a visitor, have someone tell you which areas to avoid. If you suddenly find yourself in an uncomfortable area, leave, hailing a taxi if necessary.

- Don't ever become separated from your pocketbook. You should have body contact with it at all times in public. Even in a restaurant, be sure you've stowed it where no one can snatch it.

- Men's wallets are best in a sealed pocket. Lacking that, the front pants pocket or inside jacket pocket is best. Be on the lookout for anyone who jostles you in a crowd. (Sometimes he's just distracting you while his accomplice picks your pocket.)

- Don't carry around any more cash than you need. Nearly every purchase can be made with a credit card, and travelers' checks can provide cash reserves. The Japanese, who are not accustomed to paying for meals with credit cards and often carry large amounts of cash, are known to thieves as fine targets.

- Always lock your car. Put possessions in the trunk rather than visibly on car seats. If you're traveling with a carload of stuff, be careful where you park. At night, bring bags into your motel or hotel. In some areas you don't ever want to leave things in the trunk. People in New York City go so far as to put signs in their car windows, saying, 'Thieves, don't bother. Radio already stolen.'

- In hotels, have your valuables locked in the safe.
- Keep your eyes on your luggage at the airport. Airports are well worked by thieves, and foreigners are first-choice victims.
- Don't go to a park at night—unless there's some sort of event going on or many other people are there.
- If someone does 'mug' you (threaten you with harm unless you turn over your money), give him your money. Far better to lose your money than to be hurt.
- Always lock hotel rooms, apartments, and house doors. Do not open the door unless you know who is on the other side. Many doors have a peephole so you can look through and see for yourself.
- If you open a window, check to make sure it doesn't provide easy access to an intruder. Close windows before going out.
- Have your keys ready before you walk into your building. If you are entering a locked apartment building, do not allow anyone to slip in with you. If you are entering the foyer of your building and think someone is following you, walk on down the street until you've lost the person.
- If you are robbed, call 911, the police emergency number. You do not need to pay for police services.
- Obey the police and don't make sudden moves around them. They have guns and will shoot if threatened.

Marijuana, which comes from an easily grown plant, makes the user feel dreamy and confused, passive rather than violent. For people who are 'stoned' a lot, problems don't get solved, the laundry doesn't get washed, appointments aren't met. Its use is particularly unfortunate among young people who don't face the problems of growing up. It is a dangerous drug for a worker who must be alert. Fortunately, not everybody likes the effects of marijuana. Some people feel paranoid when they smoke it or unpleasantly weird.

Methamphetamines ('meth' or 'speed') is a synthetic stimulant that can be made up in home laboratories. Meth inspires tremendous energy and euphoria; users may stay awake for days at a time without eating. Continued use leads to bizarre behavior and even psychosis, sometimes lasting. Withdrawal brings round-the-clock sleeping and depression. Meth is very addictive and currently very popular, taking many of its victims to jail.

Cocaine is popular among young, urban professionals because besides producing a fine feeling of well-being, it makes the user feel creative and energetic. However, the euphoria lasts but a short time, it's expensive, and people who become addicted are subject to some unpleasant physical side effects. Clinics are now full of people trying to kick the cocaine habit.

Cocaine comes from leaves of the coca plant, which is grown primarily in South America. It can be further refined into crack, which is sold in small doses cheaply on the street, and when smoked provides a very fast intense sense of exhilaration. Crack addicts are often the most desperate of all drug users. Babies born to crack or cocaine-addicted mothers often have multiple, and perhaps permanent, problems.

'Ecstasy', or MDMA, produces euphoria and loving feelings for others. It's the drug of choice at 'raves'—huge, all-night music and dance gatherings of young people. Sniffing glue and solvents is a particularly unhealthy addiction. It produces a high but can also stop the heart. LSD is a synthetic drug that induces hallucinations and thought disorders.

None of these drugs are easy to buy unless you happen to know the right people. People who mistakenly hand money to an undercover narcotics agent can spend a long time in prison.

Just Say No

Every elected or appointed official is conscious of the monumental drug problem in America. The cure is elusive. Many drug addicts are locked up, often for long terms because of mandatory sentencing, and the prison business is a growth industry. There are not nearly enough places in drug rehabilitation programs for the people who want them. Federal attempts to intercept drugs before they reach the street have been so unsuccessful that the price of heroin has remained stably low for years.

Alcohol

The most used drug is the legal one—alcohol. The first settlers were very heavy drinkers, and this has long been a hard-drinking country. Recently the consumption of alcohol has dropped, but alcohol still (it is estimated) contributes to over half the crimes committed and most certainly creates a great deal of unhappiness. Many families have at least one member who drinks too much, complete with neglected children and lost jobs.

Alcoholics rarely stop drinking without help, which is available through Alcoholics Anonymous (AA), a worldwide group of sober alcoholics who give up drinking and stay sober by meeting together and helping each other. A listing for AA can be found in nearly every phone book in the country. There are also many treatment programs for alcoholics. Cities have residences, usually very basic, where addicts can go for a few days to sober up.

Americans once considered drunk driving inevitable, but attitudes have changed. Drunk driving laws have become quite strict; in many states you automatically lose your license if convicted. If you cause harm, you could go to jail for a long period of time.

If you are stopped by the police and accused of driving 'under the influence', you must take the sobriety test offered, or you will be automatically convicted. The test will be of your breath, blood, or urine.

HAZARDS
Noise Pollution

As might be expected in a country settled by Pilgrims, Puritans and Quakers, we don't like unnecessary noise. We can stand the sounds of progress such as jackhammers and chainsaws, but we do not feel our neighbor has the right to disturb our peace.

At any rate, this is the opinion of the old guard. Unfortunately, our neighbor now has the means at his disposal—namely stereos with incredible decibel levels—to disturb us from blocks away. Since popular music has come to rely on volume to impose its message, a generation has grown up that seems to equate silence with death. But it should not be thought that because some excuse for music is everywhere, filling elevators and offices, that everybody loves it.

Despite the inroads of the noisy, the law is generally on the side of the peaceful. Each community has its own

noise code, regulating volumes at certain times of day and night. If your neighbors continuously disturb you with noisy parties, you can probably get satisfaction by calling the police—and many people do (to the horror of my friend from El Salvador who can't imagine doing such a thing to one's neighbors). Driving around blasting a car stereo is strictly illegal in most cities, although police are usually more preoccupied with other matters. Working car mufflers are also required.

If you have neighbors whose television or stereo disturbs you, you should not be embarrassed to ask them to turn it down. You will be performing a community service. One is often successful in requesting a reduction of musical volume in restaurants.

Some suburban areas have banned the use of leaf blowers because their roar filled every weekend. If you find yourself in a back yard community, you might consider what you can do to preserve the quiet. The soothing click-click of a manual lawn mower is much more pleasant than the roar of a gas-powered one.

Suing

The practice of dragging one's neighbor, doctor, spouse, host, and employer into court causes shock among newcomers to this country. We are a most litigious people, and we prefer to believe that there is always a responsible party for every event in life.

People have sued for: injuries attained while breaking into houses, losing a spelling bee, being fired, loss of pleasure when injured, emotional distress, tripping on sidewalks, and choking in restaurants. The list of seemingly ridiculous suits provides great mirth and, rarely, large awards.

To some degree, the pattern of suing has led to safer places and practices, but to a greater extent it has created high insurance rates and the sacrifice of services. Towns have gone bankrupt when held responsible for accidents on public property. Schools have lost play yards because they can't afford liability insurance. Some churches won't shelter the homeless because they lack the necessary insurance.

Bad as the situation is, some foreigners have picked up an exaggerated idea of it. It is not true that no doctor will ever stop if there's an accident. In many states, a 'good Samaritan' law forbids suing a doctor under such circumstances. Families still take friends' children camping. Usually if your friend falls off your garden wall and plans to sue you, he will find out what your insurance is first, and the suit can be worked out amicably without much damage to you. Nonetheless, if someone could break a leg falling through the hole on your front porch, fix it.

Should you decide to do a little suing yourself, bear in mind that it's one thing to sue and win, another to collect. It's not worth the bother of going to court unless you have a realistic chance of seeing the money. Much of the proceeds of a case often end up in the lawyers' hands. Cases drag on for years, and your time will be unpleasantly spent. The two parties to the dispute usually, in one way or another, both lose.

Smoking

Smoking is very much out of fashion in the United States. As soon as smoke from other people's cigarettes ('second-hand smoke') was proven unhealthy, the non-smokers drew battle lines. There is now a ban on radio and television advertising of cigarettes. Smoking is prohibited on all airline flights within—and most flights to and from—the continental United States. Smoking lounges in airports are few.

Ordinances have passed in many locales banning all smoking in public buildings. In some states, workplace safety ordinances prohibit smoking nearly everywhere, including in bars. In other states, restaurants must have smoking and nonsmoking sections. Some companies don't allow smoking, and a few won't hire smokers. Even some beaches, particularly in California and Hawaii, prohibit smoking.

A smoker may reach for a cigarette with some embarrassment. It is generally assumed that he is someone who has tried to quit and failed; by smoking he reveals some flaw in his personality. If you wish nonetheless to smoke, first make sure you're doing it in a place where smoking is allowed. Do not ever light up in an elevator (fire regulations prohibit it).

If you're in someone's home or office and feel a craving for a cigarette, you might ask, "Is there anywhere I can smoke?" Your hosts will either tell you to go ahead and light up and will find you an ashtray or will point to the street or backyard. House guests of nonsmokers may spend a good deal of time shivering in the garden.

Pipe smoking is slightly more acceptable than cigarette smoking, but pipe smokers should still inquire before lighting up. Outside of the new cigar clubs, cigar smoking is wholly unacceptable—unless you and your host are alone smoking cigars.

UNCLE SAM, TAXES AND YOU

There is an old saying that 'There are only two sure things in life: death and taxes'. Whether you're working here or just visiting, you'll be paying taxes through sales tax, annual income tax, or property taxes. Avoidance of taxes is punishable by large fines and/or jail time, so it's best to pay on time and in full if you owe anything.

Filing your income taxes involves getting the right federal and state tax forms, which you can pick up at the post office; your Form W-2 or Wages and Earning Statement from your employer; all statements from your financial institutions, disclosing interest earned or financial losses; and paperwork showing deductible expenses.

If you have a regular job and no other income, figuring out what you owe is fairly simple. A certain amount is withheld from each paycheck by your employer, and when the year is over, you receive a W-2, stating how much you paid in taxes during the past year. If you don't have excessive tax-deductible expenses, you fill out a simple form and take the 'standard deduction.' It should be easy to calculate whether you owe the government money or the government owes you. You must mail your return in by April 15, enclosing a check if you owe more money. If it's the other way around, you will quite promptly get a refund check from the IRS (Internal Revenue Service).

If, however, yours is a more complicated case, you might want to enlist the expertise of an accountant or a certified tax preparer to file your taxes. There are also several computer programs that will lighten the burden if you don't want to pay someone else, and the Internal Revenue Service (IRS) makes an effort to provide the public with tax preparation assistance by maintaining a fairly comprehensive website (http://www.irs.gov) and offering a Taxpayer Advocate Service (1-877-777-4778) to call if you have an ongoing dispute with the IRS. Local IRS offices can also offer personal assistance; quality of service varies.

FOOD AND ENTERTAINING

CHAPTER 6

'Never eat more than you can lift.'
—Miss Piggy

AMERICAN CUISINE IN ITSELF IS NOT BAD. Our cooks have an abundance of fresh ingredients and a heritage of wonderful regional dishes: apple pie, clam chowder, southern fried chicken, Louisiana gumbo, barbecued oysters, fresh buttered corn, buttermilk biscuits, strawberry shortcake, and hundreds of other fine dishes. As many guidebooks lamely say, it is possible to eat very well in America.

It is also possible to eat very badly, and many Americans do—by choice rather than necessity. A lot of supermarket food, while cheap and plentiful, is produced to provide the most sugar and fat with the longest shelf life and the shortest preparation time. The result is frozen dinners, packaged sweets, instant puddings, bottled salad dressings, and canned sauces. Manufacturers are working night and day to invent new products that will captivate the public. Almost any conceivable meal is available ready-made.

The problem is that most of this stuff isn't much good. It supplies calories, but in real satisfaction it doesn't measure up to anything fresh or home-cooked. Even fruits and vegetables are raised to survive long shipping or storage periods, rather than for taste. Meats are tender and good (unless you like a gamey taste), but very fatty and distressingly laden with hormones and antibiotics. Also, most supermarket food is wrapped, canned, frozen, jarred, or packaged in such a way that you can't examine it until you take it home. (Many are so well sealed that they're maddeningly difficult to open even at home!) If you do try to open jars or poke into packages at the supermarket, the management will be distressed.

If you come from a country with severe food shortages, you won't complain, but most foreigners find that American food takes some getting used to. And some searching for the gold among the dross is required.

SWEET AND BLAND BUT LOTS OF IT
A Tanzanian said he found American food so bland he nearly starved when he first came. "Back then, I couldn't even find a bottle of Tabasco [(a hot sauce]) in my little town." Then he discovered pizza and survived. The American palate has become braver than it used to be, but in the average household you won't find much seasoning in use beyond salt and pepper.

And sugar. There seems to be no end to the march on sweetness. One food writer swears that at a banquet he attended he was served a cup of M&M's (little chocolate candies) as an appetizer. Americans are stuck on sugar, and sugar of some kind (such as fructose or sucrose) is added to most packaged foods. It's hard to find a snack that isn't sweet, and even some main course dishes are served with a sweet, such as pancakes with maple syrup and lamb with mint jelly. American pastries are very sweet, and Americans eat sweet desserts much more regularly than most other peoples.

A lot of sodium (an element in salt) is regularly added to packaged foods, which has caused such an outcry among doctors (too much raises blood pressure) that new lines of foods are coming out advertising themselves as "sodium-free." There are also a lot of sugar-free foods, but you have to read labels carefully to make sure you aren't just getting honey or corn syrup or an awful-tasting artificial sweetener.

A law requires the contents of foodstuffs to be listed on the package, in the order of the greatest to the least quantity. It's enlightening reading. However, there is no requirement, as in many other countries, to label genetically modified organisms (GMOs)—foods with genes from other organisms added to their DNA. If you want to avoid these, you must search for 'organic' foods.

Foreigners often comment on the huge portions that are served to them here. "Everything on the plate is one and a half times the amount we would have at a home," says a Spaniard. Visitors observe too that Americans look as if they eat too much. A popular book, *French Women Don't Get Fat*, has a lot to say about the American penchant for quantity over quality.

EATING HABITS

The first two meals of the day eaten by an American are generally quick. The classic American breakfast of bacon and eggs is seen more on weekends than when the whole family is rushing to school or work. Cereal with milk and a cup of coffee is probably the usual morning sustenance of the average American. Lunch consists of a sandwich, soup or salad. Dinner is the large meal of the day. (When the lunchtime meal is the big one it can also be called 'dinner', and when the evening meal is simple, it may be called 'supper'.)

The American dinner has fallen under medical disapproval due to its high cholesterol content. The traditional version consists of a large piece of meat, ketchup, vegetables with butter, potatoes (fried or with butter and sour cream), and a sweet dessert. It might also be an equally fatty frozen meal, heated in the microwave oven, a high-calorie pizza, or a bucket of Kentucky Fried Chicken.

A large proportion of Americans report that they would like to change their diets, but habits are hard to break. The beans, vegetables, and whole grains that doctors keep urging us to eat require time to cook, which we haven't got. Take-out Chinese food is many people's idea of a low-calorie, low-cholesterol meal, but actually our Chinese restaurants use a lot of fat in their dishes.

Snacking

There appear to be people who rarely eat a whole meal at once. Instead, they just grab a snack when hungry—a hot dog, a doughnut, a container of sweetened yogurt. At home, they snack while standing in front of the open door of the refrigerator.

What seems to distress our foreign visitors about snacking is the lack of seriousness about food. For people who invest a great deal of time thinking about mouth-watering dishes shared with friends and family, the life of a snacker hardly seems worth living. To us, it's a life rich in efficiency, pared down to the essential elements. If only we could speed up sleeping.

Good Eating

There is, thankfully, another side to this story. Dismayed by a landscape of tasteless and unhealthy fast foods, a reaction has sprung up. It began with the appearance of health food stores, which stock foods in as close to their natural states as possible—whole wheat flour and breads, brown rice, organic produce (fruits and vegetables grown without chemical fertilizers, pesticides or GMOs), and wide assortments of nuts, beans, and grains. Prices for these select foods can be quite high. A Peruvian here was surprised to discover that brown rice costs more than white. To us, it's a health food rather than sustenance for poor people.

For those not on a tight budget, Whole Foods is a chain store with wonderful foods of every kind, mainly organic. The health food trend has also come to supermarkets and now some large chains carry eggs from uncaged chickens, peanut butter without additives, organic vegetables, etc. Once the customers materialized, speciality farms started to produce lovingly grown, tasty vegetables, and even 'organic' cattle and pigs. (Most American meats come from factory farms, in which tens of thousands of animals are cruelly crammed into cages and eat unnatural foods that fatten them quickly. The crowding and stress lead to heavy use of antibiotics. Fish too are now crammed into aquatic 'farms', fed, and dosed with drugs.)

Asian and Middle-Eastern immigrants have improved the quality of produce markets and gourmet food stores and fresh fish markets have proliferated. Major cities have grocery stores selling staples for every kind of cuisine. It is possible to find excellent ingredients in most (though not all) parts of the country, although it may take extra effort and money.

Foodies

There have always been some American gourmets, who take great pleasure in good food. The most demanding of all are the 'foodies', who are exacting about everything that passes their lips. Cheeses alone absorb vast quantities of their attention. They are on a voyage of discovery, constantly on the lookout for new and exotic foods: Périgord truffle cannelloni, sesame seed corniches, thyme ice cream, heirloom new potatoes, sweet red onion crème fraîche, to name a few from the menu of The French Laundry in Napa Valley, thought by some to be America's best restaurant. Foodies watch famous chefs on television, cook and hasten to new restaurants. They do not touch fast food.

Because of the time and financial investment required of foodies, most are Yuppies (Young Upwardly Mobile Professionals) or Dinks (Double Income No Kids). Foodies are exceptions to most of the rules about American eating. They are an influential minority.

DINING OUT

Restaurant dining is not the natural heritage of the American, and constant eating out strikes us as somewhat lazy and thriftless. Nonetheless, as kitchen time disappears, restaurants are increasingly where Americans eat. In large cities you can partake of nearly any cuisine in the world; a small town may have a single diner.

The following categories start with the cheap and end with the high-priced.

Fast Food

Fast food establishments, such as McDonald's, Burger King, Wendy's, Kentucky Fried Chicken, Subway, Panda Express, Pizza Hut, and Taco Bell purvey their specialties from coast to coast (and around the globe), totalling more than 300,000 fast-food restaurants nationwide. Their foods are convenient, predictable, cheap, fattening, and according to a recent lawsuit, addictive. (The argument is that their heavy doses of fats and sugars work on the opiate centers of the brain in much the same way drugs do.) A lawsuit is attempting to hold the fast-food corporations responsible for diseases of obesity.

Each item in a fast-food restaurant is mass-produced according to an exact prescription. No alcohol is served. You throw out all your serving containers and cutlery after eating. You should specify if you want your order to take out. No tipping is expected. American fast-food restaurants are expensive and exotic places to eat in some other countries, but here they are the cheapest and least exotic places to eat. Only under very peculiar conditions would business people meet at a fast-food restaurant.

Coffee Shops

A coffee shop is easily identifiable, however, by its seating arrangements (a counter, booths and possibly some tables) and bright lighting. You needn't wait to be seated. In the classic coffee shop, waitresses call you "Honey," and pies and doughnuts are displayed in glass cases behind the counter.

Sandwiches are the mainstay of the menu, although a short-order cook stands over the grill and turns out eggs, pancakes, burgers, and fries. Occasionally a coffee shop will have a dinner menu, but most aren't even open for dinner. The breakfasts are usually an excellent bargain. (Americans like going out for breakfast, especially on weekends.)

A waitress will often offer coffee as soon as you sit down. In the hospitable Western part of the country, she will refill your coffee cup as fast as you can empty it. On the East Coast (where 'regular' means with cream), you will have to pay for your second and third cups of coffee. However, you may find that one cup is more than enough as the coffee may be barely drinkable.

You might be able to order beer or wine in a coffee shop, but rarely hard liquor. Often, you pay a cashier on the way out. You should leave a tip of about 15 percent on the table as it won't be included on the bill.

For really good coffee, you go to a café, such as Starbucks. These serve expensive espresso drinks and usually fancy pastries and delicacies rather than hearty food.

A modern American-style eatery with booth seating is one of many options available when eating out.

Distinctive little eateries such as this may be well worth stopping at. You are likely to find real people and real food. This particular one, in the state of Maine, features seafood and blueberry dishes.

Diners

Diners are the rural version of the coffee shop. They do their best to look like railroad passenger cars, and you should not shun one merely because it looks a little rundown on the outside. The food may be excellent, unlike the fast-food franchise that always looks newly minted. Legend has it that you tell a good diner by the number of big trucks parked in front of it—truck drivers are supposed to know where they'll get their money's worth, although it may be that their choice is based on the size of the parking lot instead. Still, a truck stop may be colorful and probably will be cheap.

Family Restaurants

This is an amorphous category, so-called because you can bring the kiddies, usually meaning the place is fairly casual, the bar, if any, is out of sight, a high chair is available for the baby and the food is of the familiar American kind—chops, steaks, fried fish, salads and potatoes. (The 'family', however, does not include your dog, which is barred from all restaurants by sanitary codes.) Many family restaurants are Italian and pizza and spaghetti now seem as American as apple pie.

On entering, you should wait to be seated. No matter how crowded the restaurant is, you won't be asked to share a table with another party, even if you're alone. If you spy a table you prefer to the one you're led to, feel free to speak up.

You'll probably get a basket of bread and a glass of water without asking. Menus are frequently large and elaborate, describing the food in superlatives ('cooked-to-perfection chicken breasts in Bèchamel cream sauce with fresh seasonal vegetables'), but you should ignore the adjectives when deciding what to order.

You may have a choice of ordering a dinner or à la carte. If you order à la carte, you will be paying separately for the various components of your meal, such as the salad and dessert. The dinner, which costs more, includes the extra courses. Read the small print to find out what comes with what.

At this level of dining you may run into the kind of waiter who appears at your table and says, "Hello. How are you tonight? My name is Steve. I'm going to be your waiter. I'd like to tell you about our specials." (If he doesn't tell you the price of the specials, feel free to ask.) You are not expected to introduce yourselves to him. After his speech is over, he will behave much more like a real waiter—disappearing when you want him most—than a friend. When you want to call him, you do not hiss or snap your fingers as in some countries. You must try and catch his eye; you may delicately wave to do so.

Your soup or salad will be served before the main course. This is to keep you happy while you're waiting. The drawback is that after bread and salad one is often too full to eat the rest of the meal. As large servings are a feature of family-style restaurants, you may want to ask for a 'doggie bag' to take your leftovers home in. The waiter will whisk your plate away and bring back your dinner wrapped up for your next day's lunch.

Family restaurants have a pleasant lack of pretension and reasonable prices but do not attract gourmet eaters. A 15 percent tip is sufficient, as in most restaurants.

The Ethnic Restaurants

In the big cities, you have your choice, from Afghani to Zimbabwean, with prices big and little. The Asian selection has particularly exploded in recent years, and in many of these a little money goes a long way. In the Southwest and California, there are also many wonderful Mexican and other south-of-the-border restaurants. In Middle America, Chinese may be your only choice when the urge for something foreign comes over you.

Regional Restaurants

Keep your eye out for regional specialities when you're travelling around the country. In the South you can hope to find hominy grits, black-eyed peas, mustard greens, southern fried chicken, sweet potato pie, okra soup, and numerous other specialties. (The South has some wonderful cafeterias you might want to try; most cafeterias in the North are of low quality.)

New England is known for corn, clam and fish chowder, New England Boiled Dinner (corned beef and boiled vegetables),

Boston baked beans, and blueberry pie. In Louisiana, Creole specialties are blackened fish, shrimp gumbo, and Creole pralines. The West goes in for barbecued meats of any kind, corn-on-the-cob, baked trout, and bean soup. However, don't expect to automatically find New England specialities in New England restaurants, western specialities in the West, etc. You will probably have to search them out.

Bar Restaurants

Some of the better food is found in places where much drinking is done. It won't be fancy, but simple steaks and large sandwiches are often excellent and not overpriced. You may find, though, that the noise level interferes with conversation.

Trendy Restaurants

Trendy restaurants are the ones talked about, and 'foodies' hasten to every new one. In many of these places, the chef dreams up original dishes, often marrying unexpected cuisines together. Novelty is often what makes a restaurant trendy. Certain regional cuisines periodically rise in favor. Down-home comfort foods—such as meatloaf, stuffed cabbage, and mashed potatoes—have enjoyed a renaissance. Often notable for stunning, expensive décor, very trendy restaurants may play alarmingly loud and awful music by way of suggesting that they are fun places.

Haute Cuisine

The peak dining experiences in America are often in the French restaurants. This is also where you'll find the most intimidating level of service—captains, tuxedoed waiters, sommeliers, busboys, and so on. It is best to have an expense account and to know bits of French in order to read the menu.

You will need to make a reservation, by phone, in advance. If you don't arrive reasonably on time (within 15 minutes or so), you may not get a table. Some restaurants enjoy such popularity that they are booked weeks in advance.

There is a lot of rigmarole to eating in these places, and many Americans feel a bit insecure about protocol in them.

When the waiter uncorks the wine, he will pour a little bit into the glass of whoever ordered it. This person is to taste it, and then nod approvingly, perhaps adding 'very good', whereupon the waiter will serve the other members of the party.

You are only supposed to refuse the wine if it's actually not fit to drink—not because you have just discovered that you don't like that particular wine. This will only expose you as ignorant.

When the check comes, you should study the items and addition before paying. This is a very respectable thing to do, and you may be sure that even Rockefellers (the legendary rich American family) take care that they are not being overcharged.

Waiters in these grand places expect 20 percent tips (very rarely is a tip already added to the bill); there's a place on the credit card receipt for adding a tip. Calculate the tip on the pre-tax charge. Do not worry about tipping the many different individuals who served you, unless you had some special service, such as a maître d' who found you a table when you hadn't reserved one. A cloakroom attendant should be tipped a dollar per coat.

Not every French restaurant is so formal, and there are now plenty of other kinds of restaurants vying with the French ones for the top dollars; high-class Italian and 'continental' (eclectic European) achieve similar degrees of elegance and price.

DRINKING

Although Americans are consuming less alcohol than ever before, drinking still occupies a large role on the social stage. 'Let's meet for a drink' usually means let's get together at a bar after work and before dinner, although such a thing can also be done after dinner.

Some bars serve food, but their primary stock is alcohol. The price of a drink could vary from US$ 2 in a down-and-out saloon to US$ 14 in a mahogany-panelled room with a view. You won't get a menu, but the bartender is supposed to know how to make almost any concoction you order. Mixed drinks (known as cocktails when consumed before dinner) have ringing names that suggest little about the ingredients: Martinis, Margaritas, Cosmopolitans, Bloody Mary's, Cement Mixers, B-52s, Between the Sheets. Many of them pack a wallop so it's wise to find out what you're imbibing. You may also order whisky neat (no ice), on the rocks (with ice), or in a highball (with ice and water in a tall glass).

Don't let it worry you if you don't happen to drink. Many people do not and go right on 'meeting for drinks'. Soda water or tonic with lime are non-drinker standards, and every bartender can make a Virgin Mary—spicy tomato juice without the vodka of a Bloody Mary.

In some bars, you pay for your first round with a large bill, and then leave the change on the bar. The bartender will remove the correct amount from the pile for each subsequent round. You pocket what's left when you've finished, leaving a tip.

After a few drinks, you do not wish to casually wander the streets of any large American city late at night. Be sure you know where you are and how you're getting home. And don't accept a ride from a friend who has had one drink too many.

TABLE MANNERS
When to Eat

Back on the farm, where the day started at 4:00 am, dinner was at 5:00 pm. Our dinner hour remains quite early, although family dinners have gotten later since Mom got a job.

You might meet someone at a restaurant any time between 6:00 and 8:00 pm, but rarely later, unless traveling in very sophisticated circles. The East Coast operates at somewhat later hours than the West, partly because people on the West Coast have to get up early in the morning to call people on the East Coast.

Breakfast takes place before the day's work begins, whenever that is. Noon is the classic lunch hour, although many people eat earlier or later—largely to escape the crowds. Few people take more than an hour for lunch, and many take less, unless there's a business excuse for it.

The Mechanics of Eating

Correctly, no one should start eating until everyone has been served. However, if some people are served before others, those not yet served should turn to the served and say, 'Don't wait; please start'. The served pretend to do so, but pick slowly at their food until everyone can eat.

The array of silverware at a classy dinner can be formidable, but the rule is simple—use it from the outside in. That is, you use the outside spoon for your soup, the middle one for dessert and the inner one for your coffee. The truth is, though, that nobody will notice or care if you use the salad fork for your cake.

We eat nearly everything with a fork, which most right-handed people hold in the right hand. If something has to be cut up, you switch your knife to the right hand, do your cutting (holding the item in place with the fork in the left hand), then lay down the knife (on the side of the plate), switch the fork back to the right hand, stab the bite-sized piece with the fork and eat. Got it? There are those (English people in particular) who ridicule our mode, preferring the efficiency of keeping the fork in the left hand and the knife in the right.

You use the fork even when facing a number of foods that easily could be eaten with the fingers. Generally, if something could grease up your fingers, don't touch it. The exception is fried chicken, which may be seized between both hands. Bread, bacon, artichokes, pizza, olives, corn-on-the-cob, and raw vegetables may be eaten with the fingers. With rolls and muffins, we break off and butter one small piece at a time, having first transferred an adequate supply of butter from the general butter plate to our own butter plate. Never stick your hand or your fork into a serving dish. If you want the last cherry tomato left in the salad bowl, remove it to your plate with the salad tongs.

When the knife is not in action, it is most pleasing to have the free hand resting in the lap, although few people will look askance at a forearm on the table. The eating arm should rise off the table when carrying food to the mouth; the mouth must not be lowered to meet the fork or spoon.

One leans forward slightly to avoid drips in one's lap. Elbows are properly kept off the table, at least until the plates are cleared. Implements should not be waved around in the air to punctuate conversation.

Foods too liquid to be eaten with a fork are eaten with a spoon: soup, ice cream, puddings. It is bad form to drink from your soup bowl, which should not be lifted from the table. The soup spoon is slightly larger than a dessert or coffee spoon and you pour its contents into your mouth from its side, not from the tip. When you're finished, lay the spoon on the plate under the soup bowl. You indicate that you've finished your main course by laying the knife and fork side-by-side on the right-hand side of the plate.

You should not burp or slurp at the table, although blowing one's nose is perfectly all right. (Persistent sniffling is irritating.) Do not pick your teeth. Food should slide into your mouth as quietly as possible and be chewed with the mouth closed. Most Americans are put off by the sight of the food in someone else's mouth—you must swallow your food before speaking or at least give the appearance of having done so. Should someone suddenly ask if you realize that your wife is having an affair, you must still finish chewing before replying.

The Check

My Chinese friend was dumbfounded to hear of a father and two brothers who went out to dinner and split the check three ways. I assured him that this was most unusual in a family, but among friends, splitting the check is common. Unless it was made very clear to you that someone else is paying—or you are—you should expect to pay your share of the check. A friend may propose both the lunch and the locale but not mean to pay for you.

If you're with friends, and someone else grabs the check and says, "Here, I'll get this," you might protest, but you can assume the other person genuinely means to pay. If you really don't want him or her to, you can try to force a bill over, saying, "Here, at least take this."

A frequent question is whether to simply split the check in equal shares or have each person pay for precisely what he or she ate. The person who says, "Let's just split it, shall we?" should not be the one who consumed most extravagantly. So if you ordered filet mignon and insisted on champagne, you should pay more.

This exactitude horrifies many foreigners, but it represents not so much stinginess on our part as our fondness for self-reliance and our idea of fairness. If you don't owe me and I don't owe you, we have a nice even relationship (which I may be willing to sacrifice in favour of a free meal, but if I really doubt that you can afford to pick up the check, I will be embarrassed if you insist on paying).

Smoking Sections

In many places, smoking in restaurants is banned. In others, restaurants are required to provide both smoking and non-smoking sections, and the hostess will ask you which you would prefer. When this question comes up, smokers do not automatically defer to non-smokers. If yours is a mixed party, you will just have to try to work out your seating in the way that will cause the least all-round suffering.

ENTERTAINING

Some Americans carry on immensely busy social lives, and others live in virtual isolation. Some spend most of their time with their families, and others see almost everybody except their families. Some people love parties, and some hate them.

Social class is one determinant here. The upper classes, having more time and money at their disposal than most, entertain and visit a great deal. The lower classes, less mobile and lacking space for large parties, are more apt to limit their social lives to church suppers and their families.

It's the middle classes that get headaches over entertaining. It's for them that magazines run endless articles about party food, serving, decorating and manners. The articles serve only to fuel middle class American anxiety over being hosts and hostesses. We have the impression that the good life involves lots of gay parties, but entertaining doesn't come naturally to many of us. It's not only a lot of work, it's stressful.

Corn being harvested from a field in the State of Iowa. The USA is the world's largest producer of corn and soybeans, although agriculture makes up just 1 per cent of the country's GDP.

Chinatown in San Francisco, California, has a history that goes back to 1848 when the first Chinese immigrants settled into the area. This place has since developed into the largest Chinatown outside of Asia, and is now a well-loved tourist haunt.

湖 興 戲 院

院 南 又 一 村

HUNAN HOME'S

湖 南 又 一 村

大
DA

花旗蔘

AMERICAN
HEALTH FO

GREAT STA
THEATER

明 興 戲 院

吳 興 仁

大 壽 工 程

TEL:415-982-0618

Pho Binh Cafe

興 隆 小 章 兄 弟 有 限 公 司
Hing Lung Foreign Exchange Corp.

外 匯 兌 換

Mo

Fo

大 安 承 醫 公 司

DAAN ACUPUNCTURE & HERBS CENTER
P.A JACKSON ST.

Professional American football is a favourite spectator sport in the country. Super-Bowl, the yearly championship game that concludes the regular National Football League (NFL) season, is the USA's biggest event on the sports calendar, and generates a phenomenal national following.

The Yellowstone National Park, primarily located in the state of Wyoming, is a World Heritage Site where one can find a spectacular variety of wildlife, waterfalls and geothermal activity. Here in the Midway Basin, a herd of buffalo walk beside the Firehole River as a jet of steam is seen gushing out from the ground.

The Macy's Thanksgiving Day Parade held in New York City has been run annually since 1924 by Macy's, a chain of department stores. Thanksgiving is a significant holiday in the USA. Popular American cultural symbols such as McDonald's, Walt Disney and Coca-Cola are prominently visible at the parade.

The magazines and TV cooking shows have convinced us that 'an informal dinner' requires very out-of-the-ordinary preparations—elegant foods, special wines, flower arrangements, a clean house. This is a lot of work (if you have no servants) just in order to sit around and talk.

Some people love to cook, but many are acutely aware that they have nothing in their repertoires that will do for parties. We are at a disadvantage because the dishes we were brought up on (roast beef, fried chicken) are neither healthy nor gourmet. So we must pore over cookbooks making up the menu, shop at speciality markets and arduously follow the small print of the recipes. Lining up the guests can be a challenge too as many people have their Saturday evenings, the most usual night for a dinner party, scheduled weeks in advance.

The truth is many Americans really don't enjoy this form of socializing. It can be strained, it's time-consuming and perhaps our friends are not such brilliant conversationalists that it seems worth the bother.

Why a Party?

Nonetheless, entertain we must. It's a requirement of middle-class life, and people who don't fulfil it feel guilty and are constantly muttering, 'We must have the so-and-so's over'. A party may be given in celebration of an occasion (birthday, wedding, graduation) or to honor a visitor, but more commonly takes place for no other reason than 'the fun of it'.

A generation or two ago, company wives were expected to entertain in order to boost their husbands' careers; now that many wives are more interested in their own careers, the business dinner is likely to take place in a restaurant. Business gatherings have an advantage in that people are doing what they really like best: working. But aside from business, there are still many reasons for throwing a party.

If nothing else, one wants to show off the house. The average American is are obsessed with home decorating and after having spent a large amount of time and money in fixing up the place, it's nice to have people come and admire the results (do say nice things about people's homes when you visit). After all, we discourage people from dropping in (partly because we don't like to be caught with a messy house) so what is the large living room for?

Another motivation for having parties is that our families are often either physically far apart or spiritually distant. A gathering of friends is an attempt to fill the empty place left by the dispersal of the clan. No one wants to feel alone in the universe. We may not want friends to take up too much of our time, but we do want to have them. A big party is an efficient way to keep in touch with scattered acquaintances. And of course, party obligations and social debts must be returned if one wishes to continue to have a social life.

The Guests

Visitors from afar may be surprised at how homogeneous the guests are at even a large gathering—no old mothers or dotty uncles or children. People tend to socialize with their own age groups. Children have children's parties; old people have old people's parties. If you find otherwise, you have probably happened in on a family party, or have arrived in rural circles.

This homogeneity of age, however, does not necessarily assist the conversational flow. Because Americans move around and change jobs so much, many of them do not belong to any particular social circle and their various friends often do not know each other. In fact, the hosts themselves sometimes barely know their guests. They round up their disparate acquaintances in the optimistic hope that some party magic will take over and make the fun.

Too often, conversation falls flat or becomes hard work. We have all at one time or another found ourselves in a room full of strangers looking desperately for a friendly face to talk to. Few hosts find time to do a proper job of introducing people to each other. Under such circumstances, don't hesitate to bluntly introduce yourself. "Hello, I'm Lakshmi Karna," followed by "How do you know the hosts?" are acceptable opening lines from which further conversation can usually be developed.

You may find people's office mates mixed among the crowd, but it is not necessary to entertain work colleagues. People who are inseparable in the office may have never been to each other's homes. An Indian confided, "When I first came here, I was terribly offended that the people I met at work didn't invite me home. Later, I was glad because I wanted to have time to myself too." For better or worse, our busy lives tend to be compartmentalized.

Once you've accepted an invitation to a party, you must attend. If something happens to prevent you, telephone with your excuses as soon as possible. People work hard to give a party; you must remember that it's nearly always your hosts, not the servants, who have spent the day cooking and cleaning, and they could be very upset if you don't show up. Furthermore, other guests may have been invited specifically to meet you.

Having Fun?

A Chinese man says that what strikes him about American parties is that people rarely seem to be having an awfully good time. I think this is a fair observation. There's a lot of onus involved in being an American—that is, in being individually responsible for one's fate, and it doesn't fly away at a party. We don't arrive surrounded by a family or a culture that makes us feel secure and the party itself may seem like another test—new people to meet and impress. Some people use alcohol to remove their inhibitions, but many prefer to cope without both the high spirits and the hangover. My Irish friend thinks that American parties are simply too civilised. This is not to say that all American parties are grim. Most are quite pleasant and some are positively jubilant.

Actually, despite any generalizations I may make, there's a large element of surprise in an American party. The old rules for entertaining have been thrown out and new ones haven't replaced them. Americans may be as bemused as you are at the form the evening takes. Will the meal be served as soon as one walks in the door or hours later? Will loud music substitute for conversation? Will the other guests be fascinating and friendly or otherwise? Who knows? Perhaps the hosts will arrive home with the bags of groceries while you're standing on the doorstep. On the other hand, there may be a caterer. Visitors from abroad, at least, can chalk it all up to cultural experience.

More and more people have just given up on the whole effort and meet friends at restaurants. This is a very acceptable option.

The Dinner Party

When invited to a dinner party, you should respond as soon as possible. If you are married, you can assume that your spouse is invited; unless specified, your children are not. If you are living with a 'significant other,' that person is usually invited, but it's up to you to make sure that your host knows that the person exists. What you should not do is show up with an unexpected guest—no matter how informal the occasion.

The dress code for a dinner party can be unpredictable, and it's not only foreigners who are puzzled by it. The problem is that there are very few conventions remaining. People who wear a white starched shirt and tie to work every day may greet you at the door in jeans. Party wear often consists of looking as if you made an effort for your hosts' sake without forsaking the casual look altogether.

In the an Eastern city, if your hosts are older or the occasion is formal, men might be wearing suits or jackets and ties. In a younger group, a man should be safe wearing a 'dress shirt' (one with a collar and buttons down the front), tan or gray pants, and a blue blazer or other jacket. If he's insecure, he could fold a tie in the pocket of the jacket and put it on if ties are prevalent.

In the suburbs or the West, you can go a little more casual—maybe khakis or jeans instead of the pants, and a fleece vest or lightweight sweater instead of the blazer. Even with jeans, so, good shoes, probably of leather (nicely shined) are best. Jeans and sneakers are okay for an informal dinner (a potluck or barbecue) among people who are already friends. Among young people, jeans are very acceptable—almost mandatory—dinner wear.

Women often dress up much more than men—perhaps because there are few opportunities left to wear a pretty dress. At any rate, a woman can always wear dressy pants with a blouse and fit in anywhere. In America, a skirt is more elegant, and more formal, than pants. If you are suffering any doubts as to what to wear, simply ask your hosts, "Is it dressy?"

Protocol

You don't need to walk in the door on the dot of the time you were invited for, but you should arrive within 10 to 20 minutes afterwards. If you're much later, your hosts may grow anxious. American dinner food is usually ready at a particular time and gets overcooked or cold with waiting. At some houses, though, it doesn't matter when you arrive because a long cocktail hour will precede dinner. However, as one rarely knows which houses these are, if you are going to be more than half an hour late you should telephone and say so. Whatever you do, don't arrive early.

The old etiquette was to serve dinner 45 minutes after the time of the invitation, and this is still a good rule of thumb. It is customary to offer people a drink as soon as they arrive. "What'll you have to drink?" says the host. "What have you got?" is the usual answer. There is no need for the hosts to provide everything anyone might want. They may reasonably offer only wine, beer and soft drinks. Some people put out elaborate hors d'oeuvres (appetizers), while others prefer that their guests save their appetites for dinner.

At the Table

If the dinner is the least bit formal, guests will be ushered to a dining table to eat. They should hesitate before grabbing seats and ask the hostess where she would like them to sit. If she is a very vigilant hostess she will have calculated places in advance, probably putting men between women. There is also a fading custom that the place of honor for a man is on the hostess's right and that of a woman on the host's right. Your hosts may say, "Oh, sit anywhere," in which case you may be able to manipulate yourself into a seat next to someone you think you would like to talk to. At any rate, men should not all huddle at one end of the table, leaving the women at the other end.

Don't start eating until everyone has been served. A few families say grace before meals, which is a thank you to God for the food (such as: 'Lord, we ask you to bless this food to our use and ourselves to thy service. Amen.') It is embarrassing to be caught with your spoon in your mouth when grace is being said and your head should be bowed. It is nice to repeat 'Amen' at the end of the grace.

You may or may not have soup to start, followed by a main course (fish, meat, or perhaps pasta or a casserole) with vegetables. Salad may come before, with, or after the main course. A fattening dessert and coffee generally ends the meal. (*See 'Table Manners' on page 175 for details on using the silverware.*)

Asians and Middle-Easterners sometimes go away hungry from American tables because they consider it polite to refuse food when it is first offered. Here, if you say you do not want more, your hosts will believe you and probably will not urge you further. When hosts offer more food, they like their guests to immediately say, "Yes, please. It's delicious." They also like guests who eat everything on their plates. If you fail to, you should explain that good as the food is, you are too full to finish.

Dinner party conversation is often punctuated with exclamations about how delicious the food is. We do not take for granted that someone can cook and tend to rhapsodise whether they do it very well or not. The rest of the conversation may be wide-ranging. It's important to keep it going and your efforts will be appreciated. Nothing is worse than a dinner at which the party eats in silence. Be sure to address your remarks equally to the men and women at the table. Women are as educated and well-read as men and resent not being considered equal conversationalists.

Departing

You should not leave immediately after dinner; doing so would suggest that you could hardly wait to leave. You must let a certain conversational period elapse, and then you should make excuses for going at all. You may, for instance, suddenly look at your watch and say, 'Good heavens, look at the time. We really must leave.' Or, 'Whew, past my bedtime. Early game of golf tomorrow.' You should do this before your hosts begin to yawn visibly and look threateningly at you. Staying too late is almost as bad as leaving too early. Your hosts still have the dishes to do. If you are not out by 11:00 pm, they probably have cause for complaint, and many parties break up earlier. Should your hosts object vigorously when you start to leave and beg you to stay longer, do—but only if you want to. Before departing, say good night to the other guests, expressing your pleasure at having seen or met them.

It is excellent manners to telephone the next day and offer further thanks for the fine time you had, but not everybody does. If you prefer, a note of thanks (even a postcard) is just as good as a phone call—or even better as it takes very little of your time and none of the host's.

Some people may enjoy your company enough to ask you repeatedly to dinner without a return move on your part, but usually you are expected to return the hospitality before being invited back again. This is a convenient custom because if you are not anxious to continue the relationship, you can simply fail to reciprocate. However, if you want to pay them back in some other way, you can send flowers, or invite your friends to a restaurant or to the theatre.

Cocktail Parties

This drinking institution was lagging in popularity a short time ago but is now rumored to be making a comeback. The cocktail party does have a solid contribution to make to social life as it allows the hosts to entertain a large number of people in a small amount of time. It's largely a stand- up institution so you can invite as many people as you can pack vertically into your house. Very often an invitation will give both start and finish times, for instance 5–7 pm. In reality, unless the hosts are rushing off to the theatre, a 5–7 party would probably go on until at least 8, but guests should arrive by 6:30 pm anyhow. Cocktail parties are apt to be a bit dressier than other kinds of parties, perhaps because they've survived mainly in old-fashioned circles and because people come directly from work.

Some cocktail parties will offer only a few potato chips and olives to eat. Others have lavish, delectable displays that substitute nicely for dinner. At a buffet table, you help yourself without waiting for an invitation from your hosts.

Americans are demonstrably drinking less than formerly, and most of your guests will probably drink wine, beer, or soft drinks. A hot, non-alcoholic punch I once made was surprisingly popular. But you should still have hard liquor on hand at a cocktail party (unless you have religious or moral objections to alcohol in which case you might better give a tea party)—gin, bourbon, scotch, and vodka along with the so-called set-ups (tonic, soda, lime, and plenty of ice). Some people add pizazz to their parties by mixing fancy cocktails.

You should know that if someone drinks too much at your house and has a car accident on the way home, you could be held responsible. If any of your guests do get drunk (and it should certainly not be because you forced drinks upon them), do not allow them to drive. Either keep them with you, drive them home yourself, get someone else to drive them home, or send for a taxi.

The Potluck

This bring-your-own-dish party is an old American custom. Its origins lie in the church social, when a large group would gather for an informal supper, each family bringing a dish. Organizations often have potlucks, and some individuals do too; you may be invited to bring your share of the food to anything from a brunch to a wedding. Such a gathering is usually extremely informal, and you needn't be as precise about whether or not you're attending as for a dinner party (unless it is a wedding).

Some potlucks are so casual that the invitation does not even require a reply. But usually there's an RSVP (which is French for "answer please"), and it would be rude not to reply. Increasingly people are using the web service using a Evite to send invitations, which while neither elegant nor personal, is efficient and practical.

For a potluck, you may be instructed in the kind of dish to bring, but if not it is polite, though not obligatory, to ask. If you haven't been told, it is helpful if you announce beforehand what you plan to bring. Some people arrive with just a bottle or two of wine, but obviously it would not be a good thing if everybody did that.

The drawback of potlucks, besides having to bring a dish that nobody may eat, is their unpredictability. Most have far too much food (your dish need only be large enough for one course for four people—or the equivalent of one person eating four courses), but I've been to a few where the table was practically bare or the choice was limited to varieties of pasta salad. Some potlucks, however, garner a wonderful array of delectable dishes.

A potluck is much looser in terms of arrival and departure time than the dinner party. Usually eating goes on throughout the party so your dish may be consumed even if you arrive late. It's good to bring something relatively simple from the eating point of view. You can count on plates and forks being available, but if you're bringing soup you'd better bring the bowls too. The casualness of potlucks extends also to dress. It's a rare potluck that requires a suit.

Some foreigners are appalled by the very idea of potlucks. "What's the point," asks a Chinese man, "to invite people to dinner and to tell them to bring the food?" Potlucks are more often than not thrown by people who are genuinely sociable, but who don't want to spend days cooking for a large crowd. They would say that eating isn't the point of a party anyhow, it's the company.

The Barbecue

A barbecue is where American hosts come into their own. All you need is a back yard and a grill; the informality suits us well. There's nothing President Bush likes better than to have his guests down to a real Texas barbecue at his ranch. Barbecue meats vary greatly by region, and in the South the barbecue sauce makes or breaks the cook's reputation. However, at the standard suburban barbecue, any kind of meat that can be cooked on a grill will do.

Barbecuing is a manly art, and it's your host who you will find behind the grill. Your hostess will bring out the side dishes—salads and bread. Dessert may be pie, cake, or ice cream.

The Brunch

Brunch is a Sunday morning affair that combines breakfast and lunch, held anywhere between 10:00 am and 2:00 pm. The meal imitates breakfast, usually featuring juice, fruit salad, pastries, and eggs, but anything is possible. Champagne or Bloody Marys (tomato juice and vodka) are often on the menu.

Dress is usually casual/pretty. It is Sunday morning (church-going time) so you want to look nice. But degree of dressiness depends on the place and the hosts. An attractive jogging suit could be the thing.

The After-Dinner Party

This is apt to be an anything-goes party. Dress up or dress down, come early or late. The party probably won't be in full swing until quite late in the evening. Loud music may inspire dancing. There will certainly be drinks; food may be scarce, or it may be abundant. Try to find your hosts to thank before going home.

Birthday Parties

An adult birthday, unless it's one of some significance, such as 21, 40, 50, 60, or 75, is usually just an excuse for having a party and doesn't need special recognition. You could bring a little present, but you don't have to.

For a children's birthday, however, you must come with a present. The price category is tricky. A bag of balloons would look cheap next to other presents, but a remote-control car would be far too extravagant. Parents have an unspoken agreement not to go broke on kids' birthday presents and look with displeasure at those parents who overspend. We like to think that children don't love presents according to their price tags.

Where parents often try to outdo each other is in laying on the entertainment for Junior's party. There are those who hire clowns and ponies and caterers and magicians or else sweep the children away to fancy clubs, theatre matinees, etc. While this is all very nice (if ostentatious), children still enjoy playing the traditional party games—pin-the-tail-on-the-donkey, spider's web, blind man's bluff, musical chairs, etc.—followed by ice cream and cake. The Latin influence from south of the border has brought the piñata to North America; any games you can introduce from your culture will add a memorable note. In fact, a birthday party just like the one you would give back home would doubtlessly be fine. If you're intent on the American kind, greeting card shops or big drugstores often sell booklets that tell how to run a traditional children's birthday party.

ENJOYING THE CULTURE

CHAPTER 7

'America has colonized our minds.'
—Wim Wenders

Nobody needs to be introduced to certain aspects of American culture. It has spread around the world: Jazz, Darth Vader, *The Wizard of Oz*, Will Smith, Brad Pitt, Mickey Mouse, *The Sopranos*, Rock n' Roll, rap, hip-hop, Disneyland, *Dallas*, *Desperate Housewives*, Paris Hilton, Harrison Ford, Cameron Diaz. Even McDonald's and Coca-Cola are cultural icons that an American may be dismayed to encounter when traveling to exotic, faraway places.

Despite the glories of days gone by of the past, it must be admitted that current American mass culture is largely canned, homogenized, insipid and, often, trashy. A few evenings watching commercial television, including the scores of ads that constantly interrupt each show, may be more than enough for my more high-minded readers.

"What struck me most about the United States when I first came was sex and money," said a Japanese man. He meant by that the importance assigned to both—the bombardment of sexual imagery in advertising and the lust for money.

In the midst of this unrefined landscape, you would not expect much high culture, but in fact the USA shines in many of the arts. There is, however, a great gulf between high culture (classical music, ballet, opera, museum art) and mass culture (movies, television, popular music, hotel art). Only a small proportion of the public support the museums, opera houses, symphonies, chamber groups, and dance companies.

Nonetheless, the arts are thriving and the calibre of performances high, despite little government support. Most of the financial backing comes from private individuals and foundations, and fund-raising for the arts never ceases. In the past decade, many of the Western and Southern cities, which were long considered cultural wastelands, have developed top-flight artistic programs. Recent immigrants contribute greatly to the pool of talent.

A discriminating viewer can find good shows even on television (look for PBS channels), and the FM band on the radio carries National Public Broadcasting (NPR), which presents some of the most thoughtful programs. AM talk radio covers the spectrum from the sublime to the ridiculous and is a good introduction to the extremes of America—from Al Franken and Randi Rhodes on the left to Bill O'Reilly on the right. The more we commute, the more we listen to the radio.

And how do Americans actually spend their idle hours? Certainly, most leisure activities are of the passive sort. There are large audiences for daytime 'soap operas' as well as for the evening lineup of TV shows. Other people rent a couple of movies almost nightly. But probably nobody's time is as fully occupied as that of the true sports fan.

SPECTATOR SPORTS

Many American men are deeply involved with sports. This does not necessarily mean that they play any of them. What they do is watch national teams on television. There are men who follow baseball, football, basketball, hockey, golf, and tennis—which requires them to be in front of the television set for the better part of any weekend. If they are sociable, their buddies may be watching with them. There are plenty of female sports fans too, but not many women feel as free as men to give up their weekends to watching sports.

Baseball is the great American unifier and has followers in all income and ethnic groups. Nearly every major city has a team, and as each team plays 162 games a year, following baseball can be time-consuming. The season occupies spring and summer and culminates in the fall World Series, during which the two leading teams play each other. The first to win four games wins the Series. Although called the 'World' Series, Canada is the only other country to participate.

Football, played in fall and winter, also has a powerful hold on the country. It should not be confused with the game called 'football' elsewhere, which we call 'soccer'. There is very little kicking in our football, which has more to do with running with the ball and knocking people down. Serious injuries are common in football. Each team only plays 16 games during the regular season, and these take place on Sunday afternoons and Monday evenings.

Super-Bowl Sunday, the final football play-off in January, finds half the country glued to the television set, although if the local team is not in the finals, the passion is muted. Friends gather together in front of the largest television in the crowd. Quantities of beer are swilled, and platefuls of food passed around. The food is of the easily eaten variety—hot dogs, potato chips, cold cuts, bread, salads—so that people can fix, eat and watch all at once.

Professional teams, which include basketball and ice hockey teams, are expected to be profitable for their owners, and they certainly are for the television networks. The games allow plenty of time for commercials.

Soccer is of growing importance among schoolchildren in America and is also now played on the national level. A professional league is well-established and although game attendance remains comparatively low, cable channels (particularly Spanish stations) find it worthwhile to provide coverage. Still, people who follow world soccer are good candidates to buy satellite dishes.

College sports occupy the television screens when nothing else does. Christmas and New Year's Day are devoted to college football. The big state universities, which avidly recruit promising players from high schools, are invariably the winners. Whether college players should be intellectually capable is an ongoing debate in the sports world. Many colleges feel that if they want their alumni to donate generously to their old school, they need a winning football team. Curiously enough, this seems to be true.

Some adults continue to play baseball after high school and college on amateur teams sponsored by cities, towns and companies. Although these games are supposed to be purely for fun, foreigners may be surprised at how seriously they are taken. Americans care a great deal about winning.

ACTIVE SPORTS

Not every American man hunts and fishes, but many more do than in the world at large. We have some wild country and fairly clear streams left, and our frontier days, when hunting and eating were intimately entwined, were not so long ago. There are still rural families who count on bagging their annual deer to get through the winter. Most current hunting, however, is for the sport—the opportunity to be outdoors stalking living things through swamp, bush, stream, or woods.

Fishing is popular with a large cross-section of the population, and unlike in England, 'shooting' is not a

Going fishing with the fellows represents heaven to many American males.

particularly upper-class pursuit. The elite may ride to the hounds, but families with racks of rifles over the fireplace are not usually the heirs to old money.

The rich have often re-channelled their killing instincts and are satisfied to go out with their tennis rackets and golf clubs to expensive country clubs. Tennis and golf, however, are by no means restricted to the monied classes. Public golf courses can be inexpensive and public tennis courts are usually free.

Sailing, motor-boating, windsurfing, hang-gliding, skiing, kayaking, snowmobiling, mountain-climbing, water-skiing, and hiking are a few other avocations that allow Americans to exert themselves outdoors. Many people feel the need to have the best and newest equipment for each sport.

Formal Dancing

Just when it seemed that the only waltz any of us would ever see would be in reruns of *War and Peace*, old-fashioned dancing is back with a vengeance. Check listings in your local paper and you're apt to find classes and evenings of salsa, tango, rumba, swing, waltz, fox trot, folk dances of many kinds and more. All ages are enthusiasts and partners often aren't required.

GAMBLING

Not so very long ago, gambling was only legal in Nevada and Las Vegas, Nevada, became synonymous with gambling. Las Vegas remains the mecca—although it increasingly invests in other family entertainment—but some kind of gambling, if only a state lottery, is now widespread. Atlantic City, New Jersey, is a lesser, East Coast version of Las Vegas. Some states allow just certain card games or a state lottery or off-track betting.

Big casinos are still illegal in most states, with one exception. Because Indian tribes are considered sovereign nations and not subject to state laws, they may operate casinos on 'tribal lands'. This has enriched many tribes, while at the same time impoverishing a number of their patrons and sometimes causing great distress to the surrounding communities. It has certainly expanded the number of people whose hobby is 'gaming'.

And a Few Other Avocations

Whatever you might like to do, there are groups of people doing it all around the USA. Knitting is booming, and kindred souls gather at knitting shops. A remarkable number of weavers and quilters are at work. Book clubs of every kind are proliferating. Use a Mac computer? There are lots of clubs for you. Photography? Bird-watching? Hiking? Boat-building? Singing? Painting watercolors? Flower arranging? Writing? You name it. You'll find courses, stores and companions all ready to welcome you.

TRAVELING AROUND

If you want to actually see the USA once you're here, you've got a lot of traveling to do. In fact, unless you've got unlimited time and money, you might start by narrowing down your itinerary. Buy a guidebook to the USA and read it. Then decide what appeals the most to you.

To some people, the natural wonders are the top attractions. The great national parks—the Grand Canyon, Zion, Yellowstone, the Everglades, Acadia, Yosemite and many others—are each unique. Others would rather be in New York City than in the 'Wild West'. Many people love San Francisco, and even Los Angeles has its devotees. You will probably be happy with wherever you go, and I don't have space here to advise on the choices, other than to suggest that unless you truly love hot weather, that you stay out of the South in the summer.

In fact, in some ways summer isn't the best time to travel anywhere because lots of places are hot, families are on the go as the kids are out of school, and vacation spots are crowded. On the other hand, everything's open, you don't need to worry about winter clothes, the evenings are delightful, and swimming is great. But in summer, make reservations well in advance at popular places.

Camping

The USA is a great camping country. There are many campgrounds—private and in state and national forests and parks. In summer, you need reservations; for most of the national parks, you can call (800) 365-2267 or visit: http://www.recreation.gov. States each have their own services. If you don't have Internet access, go to a camping store, where you will be able to get information. You need to take precautions in campgrounds (lock valuables in your car), but they are reasonably safe.

How to Get Around America
Flying

The fastest way around the country is by plane, but flying can be very expensive. One-way flights are exorbitantly priced, except for a few airlines that don't penalise the one-way traveller—Southwest is excellent for short hops and hops around a large part of the country. Jet Blue, good for cross-country flights and from the Northeast to Florida, is well-liked as well for its low prices and wide seats.

Your overall best bet for booking is to search the online travel agencies—the best known are Eexpedia, Travelocity, and Oorbitz. For rock-bottom lowest prices, you could try Priceline. There you can make a bid on an undetermined flight to a determined destination. It's very cheap and very possibly, you'll get a real bargain, but you need to be flexible.

Trains

Amtrak is the name of our national long-distance railroad. Trains are clean and well-maintained, and many have dining cars worthy of grander days. Because Amtrak trains are often delayed by freight trains, which own the tracks, they frequently are behind schedule. But if you're not in a hurry, Amtrak is a glorious way to see the country. It's three days coast-to-coast; in 36 hours you can take the incomparable California Zephyr from San Francisco through the Sierra and Rocky Mountains to Denver, Colorado. Seat prices are modest, but if you want a bed, they skyrocket. Packages are available. Call 800-USA-RAIL or go to their website: http://www.amtrak.com.

Buses

Local train companies serve the suburban areas of some cities, but the majority of towns only have a bus going through them (and some don't even have that). Buses are cheap and some of them attempt luxury travel with snacks and movies. (*See the* Resource Guide *for specific information*.) Coach tours are a different category from scheduled buses, and you may

Americans like to roam. Some retired people spend many months of the year living in their recrreational vehicles, travelling from campground to campground, constantly socialising with different people.

find them ideal for both sight selection and economy. Many different companies organize them, and often advertize in Sunday newspaper travel sections. Green Tortoise is a unique one that delights mostly youthful travelers who don't mind sleeping all together on the ground.

Autos

Driving is the American way to go, and for convenience it's hard to beat. You can rent a car, lease one, or even buy a used car and sell it when and if you leave. One other bargain way to see the country is to sign up for a drive-away car, which means you deliver somebody else's car to a distant place. There are numerous companies making the arrangements (see the yellow pages or http://www.autodriveaway.com). You'll need to make a deposit, pay for gas and deliver the car within a stated amount of time; drive-aways are not for those who want to linger long or to deviate far from the beaten path, but if what you want is to drive from, say, NYC to LA in ten days, a drive-away can be perfect.

The highway system allows you to cover a lot of ground fast. Even-numbered highways are east-west, and the odd-numbered are north-south. Numbers increase as they go east and north—so I-5 is West Coast and I-95 East Coast. If you're going to be driving much, you'll find joining AAA a bargain at US$ 55 a year; they provide maps, guidebooks, travel advice, tow service, and more.

INTERNET ACCESS

Cyber cafes are proliferating. Many cafes offer free wireless. Starbucks isn't one of them; you have to sign up with one of their providers. If you can't access your e-mail on the web, you might want to open an account (free) with Yahoo or Hotmail. Most public libraries offer free internet access, as do some hotels. If you're traveling with a computer with Wi-Fi and have an account with T-Mobile hotspot, you can connect at any Starbucks.If you've got your own laptop and have to plug it in, you are likely to need an adapter for American current.

SPECIAL EVENTS

I can't begin to list the festivals across the USA. Everything from art, blues, folk music, crafts, Shakespeare, race cars and juggling to corn, potatoes and chilli has a festival. A web site, festivalusa.com helps you search them out wherever you are going to be. It can be even more fun going to an obscure, minor festival in a small town than to a giant, famous one.

County fairs are ubiquitous in the summers, and these will bring you up close to the real America. A fair worthy of the name should have ferris wheels and merry-go-rounds, an arcade of games, shows of livestock and culinary arts, tractor pulls, sheepdog trials, and constant entertainment in the grandstand. For many children, the fair is the high point of the year.

Athletic types can join marathons, bike tours, Ironman contests, or other such workouts. If you feel like doing Irish jigs or spending a week at Balkan Music and Dance camp, there's a place to do it. There are also any number of opportunities for spiritual uplift, from Catholic retreats to AA conferences to Zen meditations. You can find them all on the web.

HOLIDAYS

Each holiday has its own particular flavor, but most of them only arouse excitement insofar as they provide an excuse for a holiday from work or school. Only Christmas and Thanksgiving inspire great expectations. Whether you think the USA has a lot of holidays or very few depends on where you come from.

The Major Holidays
Christmas

'Tis the season to be jolly,' says the Christmas song. December 25, remembers the birth of Christ and is the biggest holiday of the year. Its celebration goes far beyond its religious origins, and most of the festivities have little to do with religion. In fact, the holiday may originally have been a pagan celebration of the winter solstice (December 21), when the days start to get longer again.

Christmas calls people home from far away to be with their families, and each family has its own Christmas rituals. Although Jews and members of some other religions may prefer not to, most houses have a decorated Christmas tree, and people cook (or buy) special foods for the season—Christmas cookies, plum puddings, fruitcakes. Everybody is expected to have a family or family substitute at Christmas time; it is the only time of year that some families see each other. It is also a particularly depressing time of year for those who are alone.

The central ritual of Christmas is the exchanging of gifts that are intended to represent the 'goodwill towards men' that Christ preached. Every year, voices rise to protest the insane commercialism of Christmas, but nothing has dimmed the enthusiasm for gift-giving. As a nation of shameless consumers a holiday centred round shopping suits us very well.

Charitable giving is at a peak at Christmas as well. 'Blessed are the poor,' said Christ, and so it's a time of year when many people feel inclined to brighten the lives of the less fortunate. An abundance of fine dinners are offered to the poor and homeless on Christmas; the charitable institutions try to emphasise that the need goes on all year.

Christmas Merrymaking

A fair proportion of the year's parties are thrown at Christmas time. As Christmas takes place the week before the new year begins, the holiday spirit does not diminish even after Christmas. Christmas parties can be given any time between December 6 and December 29. 'Open Houses' are popular, some given on Christmas Eve or Christmas Day.

Family traditions vary. Some people open their presents on Christmas Eve, and some wait until Christmas Day. There are many church services on Christmas Eve; Midnight Mass is popular (usually held at 11:00 pm). Throughout the Christmas season there is much singing of Christmas carols, lovely songs well known to most Americans. Special concerts play Christmas music and Handel's *Messiah* can be heard everywhere.

Christmas is a big event in the USA and department stores and hotels put up elaborate decorations in the weeks leading up to festival. Here, busy shoppers admire the lights while looking for gifts on 5th Avenue in New York.

Door-to-door Christmas carol singing is a lovely holiday tradition.

Usually a big dinner makes its way to the family table sometime between 1:00 pm and 7:00 pm on Christmas Day. You, as a foreigner, whom everyone will feel sorry for if you are far from family, may well be invited to one of these. You may wish to bring a bottle of wine or champagne or flowers or a potted plant—the poinsettia is the Christmas flower.

New Year's Eve
Our calendar elects January 1 as the first day of the new year. The big celebrations are held the evening of December 31. Parties should be gala, and you are supposed to drink champagne and kiss everybody at midnight. Some of us prefer to go to bed at 11:00 pm and start the new year well rested, but the young and romantic feel that on this night of nights they must have a date and preferably be in love. New Year's Day, January 1, is subject to a round of open houses but can properly be celebrated very quietly—nursing a hangover or in making grandiose New Year resolutions (such as giving up smoking or losing weight).

While most companies only give workers a day or two off at Christmas, it's a time when many people take personal vacation days. The week before Christmas and New Year's Day is not a time anyone should seriously expect to get much business done. Those of your business partners who haven't flown to the homes of distant relatives may be in the mountains skiing or in the tropics swimming. Not everything grinds to a halt, but you are unlikely to find a full quorum of decision makers on the scene.

Thanksgiving

On the fourth Thursday of November, Americans celebrate Thanksgiving and remember a supposed feast between the Indians and the Pilgrims in 1621. Had the Indians not befriended the Pilgrims during that winter, the Pilgrims would have starved. In recognition of this alliance (and ignoring all the bloodshed that followed) and of the success of the Mayflower settlement, Americans have a harvest feast.

A big turkey (wild turkey was an Indian delicacy) is central to Thanksgiving. Surrounding the turkey, one expects to see

The members of this family have flown in from all parts of the country to be together for Thanksgiving.

stuffing, cranberry sauce, potatoes, squash, pumpkin, and mincemeat pies. Whether or not the Pilgrims enjoyed the same foods, these dishes are all New England specialties that grace nearly every table at Thanksgiving.

It is as important to have somewhere to go on Thanksgiving as it is on Christmas. Some businesses are closed both on Thanksgiving, a Thursday, and the next day, a Friday, enabling people to travel great distances to join their families. However, other than wishing others a Happy Thanksgiving, Thanksgiving is not nearly as demanding as Christmas. No gifts or celebrating other than the dinner itself are required. It is a generous holiday, and many families welcome those who haven't a family of their own nearby.

Calendar of Holidays

The USA has ten federal holidays observed countrywide. Four are set by date:

- January 1   New Year's Day
- July 4   Independence Day
- November 11   Veterans Day
- December 25   Christmas Day

If any of the above fall on a Saturday, then Friday is usually observed as a holiday. Similarly, if one falls on a Sunday, then Monday is usually the holiday.

The other six holidays are set by a day of the week and the month:

- Third Monday in January   Martin Luther King's Birthday
- Third Monday in February   Washington's Birthday
- Last Monday in May   Memorial Day
- First Monday in September   Labor Day
- Second Monday in October   Columbus Day
- Fourth Thursday in November   Thanksgiving

The Minor Holidays

The significance of the minor holidays is mainly the long weekend they provide—many are observed not on their actual date but on a handy federally mandated Monday.

A few of them are marked with parades, but the only celebration for most people is in sleeping late. Not all of them provide even that. On many of these holidays the ordinary worker works, but banks, schools, and government offices are closed. Stores are usually open and often have big holiday sales.

- **New Year's Day**
  January 1. Businesses closed. A popular time to hold an Open House.

- **Martin Luther King Day**
  January 16, the birthday of the great civil rights' leader, celebrated on the closest Monday. The degree of observance varies from one city and state to the next. Often a school and government holiday, but most businesses are open.

- **Presidents' Day**
  The birthdays of Abraham Lincoln (February 12) and George Washington (February 20) are combined in one convenient mid-February Monday, awarding a welcome long weekend in the middle of winter. Theoretically, Franklin Roosevelt is included in the celebration, but few people realize it.

- **Valentine's Day**
  St. Valentine was the patron saint of lovers and on February 14, people give cards, candy, and flowers to loved ones. Children often give cards to everyone they know. Not an official holiday.

- **Easter**
  A Christian holiday celebrating the day that Jesus rose from the dead. Children color Easter eggs and have Easter egg hunts and often receive chocolate bunny rabbits or baskets of candy and toys. The date falls on a Sunday anywhere between late March and late April. Easter heralds the beginning of spring.

A Memorial Day parade in a small town brings out anyone who has served the country in the armed forces and still has a uniform to wear. Many flags are waved.

- **Mother's Day**
  The second Sunday of May. A day to pay tribute to Mother, with cards, flowers and restaurant dinners.

- **Memorial Day**
  A national holiday on the last Monday of May; commemorates the Americans who have died in war and kicks off summer. A good day for a barbecue/picnic.

- **Father's Day**
  The third Sunday of June. Not as important as Mother's Day, but still the fifth largest card-sending occasion.

- **Fourth of July**
  A national holiday. On July 4, 1776, the Declaration of Independence was signed. Also called Independence Day, it's another good barbecue day. Official celebrations consist of fireworks displays; most private fireworks are now illegal, but many people set them off anyhow.

- **Labour Day**
  The first Monday in September and the occasion for the last barbecue of summer; a day of honour (and rest) for the worker. The school year traditionally starts a day or two after Labour Day, although in fact it may start in late August.

- **Columbus Day**
  October 12, the day in 1492 when Christopher Columbus landed in the New World.

- **Halloween**
  October 31, the evening that children put on costumes and go out 'Trick or Treating,' which means that if you don't provide treats when they knock on your door, they will enact a dirty trick on you (such as writing on your windows with soap). It's a good idea to stock up on some Halloween candy (wrapped) to hand out, but you probably don't really need to worry about the tricks. It's the parents who do the worrying now—that some atrocious person will give their child poisoned food. For this reason, parents usually supervise their children's rounds very closely.

- **Veterans Day**
  November 11. Honours all those who have served their country in the armed services. Celebrated the same day as Armistice Day/Remembrance Day in other countries, commemorating the signing of the armistice that ended World War I.

Everyone loves to eat. Crowds throng 9th Avenue in New York City as the road is closed off to traffic for its annual food festival.

'Language exerts hidden power, like a moon on the tides.'
—Rita Mae Brown

HOWEVER DIVERSE THIS COUNTRY MAY BE, there is only one universal language in the United States: English. Some foreigners never learn it because they speak a language, such as Spanish, that is widely spoken in certain districts. But while 35 million people here speak Spanish, the rest do not, so once Spanish-only speakers leave the Spanish community, they're in trouble.

Writing English

In written communication, the formal style is always used in the work place or when you're writing to a stranger or an elder. However, the pervasiveness of email and cell phone text messaging has given rise to a new, abbreviated style of writing. This abbreviated vocabulary will substitute 'CU' for 'See you', 'How R U' for 'How are you', or 'AEAP' for 'As early as possible'. Learning this is a purely voluntary and possibly trivial exercise for anyone over age 40 but may be essential for the young.

You, presumably, speak English well or you wouldn't be reading this book. If you speak extremely well, you even recognise the accents of different regions. But you don't have to. None of our accents are so extreme that people can't understand each other, and a large number of the people in every region speak without a trace of the local accent. The American population has moved around so much that in cities nationwide most people speak Standard American English, otherwise known as 'broadcaster' English.

Many accents, though regional, are really more affected by social strata than by geographics. They mainly survive in rural areas and among the less educated, less cosmopolitan elements. You may be more likely to hear them in the movies than in your travels. But here's what to look for:

The South boasts a very notable accent—varying in different areas of the south—and one that still dominates even in sophisticated circles. The speech is slow, with vowels dragged out, consonants dropped and 'I' pronounced 'ah'. "How y'all? Ah'm fahn." Next to this, the fast, clipped speech of a Northerner sounds cold. The New York accent is famous. An r is often dropped, th becomes d and ir becomes oi: 'doity-doid street'. The classic Boston accent drops r's and pronounces an **a** as **ah**. So you get "Pahk the cah in Hahvahd yahd."

Hip-Hop Lingo

And for those who like to keep their finger on the pulse of pop culture, there is a certain type of slang that is prevalent today, derived from hip-hop and rap music. It is often punctuated with explicit language and derogatory terms, and as such, it is now common practice and legally responsible for record labels, advertising, music videos, and television programs featuring hip-hop or rap to provide warnings that the language may be too graphic for younger audiences.

The difficulty with learning this form of English is that as soon as a term gets too mainstream, it's immediately replaced by another word, which one can only assume is an ongoing effort by the very hippest to keep everyone else in the dark. "Ay yo trip" now means "check this out" and "Fo shizzle ma nizzle" is saying "For sure my friend," but these terms could be forgotten by the time this book is published. It's best for newcomers to stick with standard English, unless you're here to work for MTV.

A Western accent is an amalgam of many and not easily placed. Then there are numerous localized accents—Maine, Louisiana, Ozark, and Appalachian are all distinctive. An

African-American accent is not only distinctive, though similar to a Southern accent, but has its own syntax and some particular vocabulary.

ENGLISH FOR SUCCESS

Speaking correct English is important for progressing upward both professionally and socially, but correct English is not nearly as hard to learn as, for instance, correct Japanese. Unlike many other languages, forms of address don't vary according to addressee and the structure doesn't change for different settings.

However, we do adapt the tone and grammar according to the situation or the audience. Within standard English, one can use the formal style or the informal style of speaking, depending on whom you're addressing. It is considered polite to speak standard, formal English when addressing someone older than you are, someone you don't know very well, or someone in a position of authority (like your boss). 'How do you do?' 'How may I help you?' 'To whom would you like to speak?'

When you're speaking to a friend, you can instead say, 'Hey, how are ya? Whatcha need?' without fear of being inappropriate, provided your friend speaks to you in a similarly casual manner. That ubiquitous, youthful word 'whatever' is best reserved for the informal situations.

Etiquette demands that you use 'gender-neutral' terminology in all situations, rather than accepting the male as the standard. This means you say 'chairperson' instead of 'chairman', 'firefighter' instead of 'fireman', etc. Awkwardly, we also don't want the third person singular always to be a he. So we say, "If someone calls, tell them to call back"—it's grammatically incorrect but politically correct.

ESL

Foreigners who want to learn and improve their English have many different vehicles from which to choose. Most local community colleges will offer English as a Second Language (ESL) courses for relatively low cost and there are many for-profit companies that offer specialised language courses, with either in-class, multimedia, or online instruction that can be personalized depending on your needs. Conversational, business-oriented, intensive, total immersion, and accelerated learning are now convenient options. And, for the temporary visitor or tourist, the local bookstore will usually carry a large variety of books, audiotapes, and computer programs that provide basic English instruction.

Language Schools

- **Agape English Language Institute for Internationals, USA**
  Instruction in English for academic and professional needs in 12 locations. TOEFL preparation, communication skills, university and college preparation, and business English.
  Website: http://www.aeliusa.com

- **American Language Programs**
  Immersion programs in twelve cities including Honolulu and Vancouver. Offers homestays and business and special English courses.
  Website: http://www.alp-online.com

- **Berlitz**
  With more than 450 centres in more than 60 countries, Berlitz offers language instruction for business or personal enrichment through a variety of vehicles.
  Website: http://www.berlitz.com

- **Converse International School of Languages**
  Intensive ESL courses for international students and professionals in California cities, with separate programs for teens.
  Website: http://www.cisl.org

- **English Language Center**
  Courses in Boston and Los Angeles with varying levels of intensity and English-Plus programs such as "English + Surfing."
  Website: http://www.elcusa.com

- **Interlink Language Centres**
  ESL programs at four American universities. Offers information on homestays.
  Website: http://www.eslus.com

- **FLS International**
  Intensive English programs, homestays and study-tour programs on college and university campuses.
  Website: http://www.fls.net

- **Language Studies International**
  Locations in San Diego, New York, Boston, and Berkeley/San Francisco with weekly start times. Offers ESL programs, TOEFL and TOEIC test preparation, and business English courses.
  Website: http://www.lsi-america.com

Many foreigners speak excellent English but are still hard for Americans to understand. If you'd like people to forget you're not American, you may have to work on your accent. Listen to yourself on tape and ask a native speaker for honest feedback.

If you do want 'accent modification', there are schools and tutors to help you. A speech-language pathologist will analyze your speech and pinpoint where it varies from Standard American English. A popular and low-priced book is *American Accent Training* by Ann Cook, which comes with five CDs. She discusses such matters as 'staircase' phrasing, which defines the rise and fall of sentences. Much of sounding American (besides being able to pronounce the 41 basic sounds), she asserts, is in the sound units. Americans don't say 'Bob is on the phone'. They say 'Bäbizän the foun'. The right intonation, stress and rhythm are all part of building the all-American sound. And with it, you will get invited to a lot more of those all-American parties.

You can also subscribe to an online "American Accent Training" for US$ 199. Visit their website at http://www.americanaccent.com

AMERICAN CONVERSATIONAL STYLE

It is hard to generalize about conversation in America. We have the full range of talkers—chatty, taciturn, forthcoming, secretive. Conversation is generally less lively than in the Latin countries, where everyone talks at once. When someone talks here, everyone is expected to listen, no matter how dull the talker may be. But there are countries where the conversation is far more careful and deliberate than ours.

In the search for conversational material, work is a good bet. In many countries, it is not seemly to ask, 'What do you do?' Not so here. We are so often defined by our work that we are happy to talk about it. But if work proves unproductive, you might try, 'What do you do in your spare time?'

We are not on the whole a reticent people. Some observers have noted that we are freer than Asians in discussing emotions and feelings, but more secretive about factual matters. Still, you can safely inquire about wives or husbands, children, geographical background, hobbies, and habits. Ethnicity is a subject of some interest and Americans will inquire about the ancestry of others.

A highly personal conversation can take place on the basis of short acquaintance, but it will not indicate that a lasting friendship has been established. Americans can form relationships very quickly, but they don't often go deep. We constantly encounter new people we will never see again. Therefore we don't need to worry that our familiarity will entice them to become burdens to us. Airplanes are famous for inducing intimate conversations, doubtless because no follow-up is expected.

While few Americans will mind any questions you may ask—particularly if they are in the spirit of intercultural research—you may find they are delicate about asking you questions. One Chinese friend of mine says, "Americans aren't interested in other people. They don't ask questions."

My other Chinese friend says, "Ah, that's not true. They just find things out in a more roundabout manner."

We worry about invading people's privacy, and we also have the idea that foreigners aren't used to personal inquiries. So some Americans may chatter on about trivialities because they don't dare to plunge into deeper territory, but they will happily take your lead given an opening. Others will resolutely talk about safe and superficial subjects until the cows come home. And still others have much to say on important but impersonal subjects, which interest them more than personal ones. (This distribution is probably not unlike the differences anywhere.)

What we have very little of are pre-cut conversational rites. Even when engaging in small talk, you have to make up your own lines.

Bluntness and Tact

Americans can be very straightforward, which may be discomfiting to people from more circuitous cultures. Here, if your neighbor thinks your apple tree is encroaching on his garden, he will tell you, rather than hint at the subject. If you claim New York is the capital of the United States, you will quickly learn you're wrong (it's Washington, DC). A supervisor who thinks you're making too many mistakes will let you know.

"I love writing English," says a Brazilian. "It's so direct."

The bluntness is somewhat tempered by language. Besides a profusion of please's and thank you's, a well-spoken person will make his points politely. 'Would you mind if I borrowed your atlas' not 'Lend me your atlas'. "Perhaps you could be more careful," says the supervisor to the blunderer. "I think you're a bit off there," to the person who added two and two and got five. The meaning is still clear, but a little delicacy of language leaves some respect for the other person's feelings. 'I don't think you're quite right about that', goes down better than 'No, you're wrong'.

Criticism

Friends do not often directly criticise each other, and people who do not 'mind their own business' are disdained. Even parents aghast at their grown children's behavior may choose to say nothing rather than alienate their offspring. "They have to live their own lives and make their own mistakes," say the parents with a sigh. Popular psychology insists that people's behavior comes from deep, unconscious motivations and people can't change until they understand why they act the way they do. So, according to this theory, only a professional therapist can help them. You, their friend, would only make them angry and unhappy by offering unwanted advice.

Style of Talk

Americans admire someone who thinks fast and always has something to say. Among friends, there's apt to be a lot of cheerful banter going on. This volubility and enthusiasm makes some Chinese distrust Americans and consider them insincere. If someone has something to say about everything, how much could she really know?

Some French writers have noted that the conversational style of African-Americans, with its lively repartee, is closer to the French manner than what they consider the more plodding delivery of the white American. Ask an American a question, they say, and you'll get a long-winded answer.

It's true that most talk isn't lighthearted exchange for us; it's informational exchange, and we assume you want all the data you can get. In some cultures, people will take the opinion of a trusted friend. Not us. We want the facts so that we can make up our own minds. As nearly every cultural observer has noted, Americans love statistics.

What we do not like is silence. Should everyone in a group run out of things to say, an anxious pall descends until somebody saves the day by producing a subject. Almost any subject will do. By no means are all Americans slick talkers. There are those, often young males, who do not seem to have developed much verbal ability at all. Yet if you can find the right subject, they suddenly come to life. Other non-talkers may be depressed or lacking in confidence. These people often respond well to kindness and your interest in them.

Some foreigners think some American space-fillers very silly: 'Have a nice day,' 'Have a good workout,' and the phone message that ends with, 'Have a beautiful day.' Such directives are perhaps not very sincere, yet they are well-meant.

Talking About Me

Compared to some peoples, we can be very boastful, and we see nothing wrong with stating our credentials frankly. However, smart conversationalists keep an edge of self-deprecation in their comments: 'The company chose me to go to China so they'd have some peace in the office for a while.' Or: 'That was a lucky shot. I'm really a terrible golfer.' You are, incidentally, not supposed to agree.

SAFE AND UNSAFE SUBJECTS

You won't find Americans quick to take up the subject of religion, which is considered a personal matter. As a newcomer to the country, you could certainly ask about religious habits, but Americans who meet at parties do not inquire about each other's faiths.

Politics are discussed among people who are in relative agreement, but when a group is far apart, politics becomes a subject to be avoided. On the whole, we dislike argument. Unlike the French, who consider a verbal battle refreshing, we become personally insulted by disagreement. If an argument breaks out, we try to smooth it over or break it up.

A German who has many friends here says he is amazed how rarely the conversation turns to subjects of national or world interest. Part of the reason is that Americans are not on the whole well-informed on world matters. While it is not impolite to broach large subjects and hope for a response, you may find that conversation soon returns to harmless and painless topics. Many of these are questions of taste. Did you like such-and-such a movie? What do you think of the food at that new restaurant? Do you like Mexico? How do you like the weather? Through discussing mutual likes and dislikes, we find out whether this is our kind of person. American society is classed by tastes as much as by anything else.

Compliments are always in order. 'What a pretty dress... I love your earrings... Great tie!' (But not, 'How much did you pay?') We keep the compliments flowing even with close friends and family. The recipient should accept the compliment graciously by looking very pleased and saying,

'Oh, thank you'. The tale of the item in question often provides further talk.

Most of the people you meet will be glad to hear about your country and about your impressions of America. You can be frank. We've become accustomed to criticism in recent years, although of course it's always tactful to mix a few positive comments in with the negative. ('The bus stations are awful, and I hate the food, but the people are friendly.')

Gestures

Many Americans, eager to be understood, will use all possible means of communication, including lively gesturing with the hands and arms. The hands are intended to add emphasis and conviction, but only rarely are they lifted higher than the shoulders. Other Americans, often of Anglo-Saxon origin, do not consider gesticulation dignified and can be even somewhat wooden in their movements. Gestures are anything but universal, sometimes bearing opposite meanings in different cultures, so the language of gestures is an important one to learn. Several of our most well-meaning signals are obscene in other countries.

- Headshaking—Up and down is yes and from left to right is no.
- Waving—The arm is held upward, palm outward, fingers stretched out. The hand moves from side to side in a V pattern. Can mean hello or goodbye.
- Snapping fingers—An attention-getting motion, not gracious, but not vulgar. May also mean, 'I just remembered something.' Don't snap fingers to call a waiter.
- Arms folded across chest—Not rude or arrogant but could mean, 'I'm waiting.'
- Striking forehead—Somebody who strikes his or her own forehead with an open palm is saying, 'How stupid I am.'

There are two subjects that may rapidly bring conversation to a halt: age and money. Only as a newcomer might you plead innocent of these sanctions. If you insist on asking someone's age, it's best to lower your voice, inquire 'Do you mind if I ask your age,' then immediately respond with 'Heavens! You look much younger!' All adult Americans are mad to look young. Actually, many of them do.

- Bowing—We don't do it.
- Pointing to own chest—'Do you mean me?'
- Hitchhiking—Hold arm away from body, make a fist, then extend thumb. Not a vulgar gesture, as in some parts of the world.
- Come here—Hold arm forward, make a fist, palm up. Extend thumb and forefinger and wiggle forefinger.
- Hand wag—Fingers out and palm down. 'It was so-so.' Indicates lukewarm response to something.

Finger Signs
- Thumb to nose—Very rude. Shows defiance.
- Crossed fingers—'Good luck' or 'Hope for the best'. Among children, there is a code that a lie is not a lie if the fingers are crossed.
- Pointing with forefinger—'Look that way.'
- V-sign—Either 'We have won,' or 'We will win.' Also, 'Peace'. Palm can face forwards or backwards.
- Thumb pointed up—Success.
- Thumb pointed down—Failure.
- One or both index fingers pointed upwards from fist—'We're number one.' Used mainly at sporting events.
- Middle finger stuck up from fist—An obscene gesture of contempt.
- Circle made with thumb and forefinger, other fingers sticking up—'Okay.' 'It's a go.'

Income is a very hush-hush subject, and while we may spend a great deal of time wondering how much other people make, we don't say so. This may be because, all evidence to the contrary, we hold to the idea that people are actually paid according to their worth, and we don't care to have that figure as public knowledge.

We do not inquire about how much people paid for things either, unless we have a good reason to do so. ('I'm shopping for a new car myself. Could you tell me what that one cost you?') People who have got a great bargain are glad to volunteer the cost, but they hate to be caught overpaying.

You also should not poke too obviously into someone's class background. You do not ask, 'What did your father do for a living?' To ask where someone went to college, you need a cue. ('Ah, you rowed on the Charles River; did you go to Harvard')

Sex is, as in many cultures, best approached with discretion. Most direct questions are taboo, and probably people will grow uncomfortable if you are overly frank in presenting your own history. All appearances to the contrary, we don't take sexual matters for granted, and men who talk of their conquests are not thought very honourable. Women usually discuss methods of birth control only with close friends.

You do not inquire into someone's sexual orientation. 'Are you gay?' is a forbidden question.

When all other conversation fails, there are always sports and the children to fall back on. If you are male, an interest in the fortunes of the local football and baseball teams may serve you well at parties.

DOING BUSINESS IN AMERICA

CHAPTER 9

'I'm a great believer in luck, and I find that
the harder I work the more I have of it.'
—Thomas Jefferson

'THE BUSINESS OF AMERICA IS BUSINESS,' said President Calvin Coolidge in 1927. That statement is even more valid today. Of all the ways to occupy one's time, work is the most important. Elsewhere, the sickness of a grandmother or the problems of a cousin would be reasonable excuses for taking a day off. Not so here. Nearly every other element of life is sacrificed before the work part.

Foreigners generally surmise that it's because 'the dollar is king' that Americans are so work-crazy and that the unabashed fever for moneymaking overrides the finer feelings. There's some truth to this, but there's more than money driving the worker.

THE VALUE OF WORK

A belief in progress, a sense of infinite resources and an emphasis on tangible results contribute to unbounded enthusiasm for undertaking new projects. As an American's self-image is dependent on action, even personal wealth does not inhibit the work ethic.

To work well and hard is a high value. Although there are many who do neither, they are not the people who win the admiration of their peers, nor the ones who rise to the top. Those who want to command respect apply themselves diligently. No matter how splendid someone might be on other fronts, she does not wish to be thought remiss as a worker. Better to be labelled a bad daughter or a thoughtless friend. Self-esteem is bound up in achievement, and when people lose their jobs or retire they often become depressed, even when money is not a problem. The more successful the person, the more likely it is that his life revolves around his or her career rather than around home and family.

A degree of unfettered ambition, one that might even be found unattractive in other countries, is admired here. An Englishman would not care to be known as 'all business'. An American would. At the bottom of the career ladder, where people serve fast food for minimum wage, people work hard, but the job does not overlap into leisure hours. The higher one rises, the more all-consuming the job becomes.

Company Operations: The Bottom Line

The company is in business for one reason: to make a profit for the owners—individuals or stockholders—and to make more profit than could be made if the capital were invested otherwise. This is not simple as many businesses are up against cutthroat and global competition and must keep prices low or lose market share.

This single-minded dedication to profits leads to ruthless operations. American companies are quick to throw out the old and bring in the new. Typically, they make only short-range plans and want fast profits. Since the eighties, when the USA became the world's biggest debtor nation, more and more companies have felt under attack. Publicly held companies are subject to unfriendly takeovers. Most companies do not feel stable enough to make their workers too comfortable, and job security is not a feature of American worklife.

While some companies engage in shady practices, most stay within the law. There are famous examples of those that did not (the former CEOs of WorldCom, HealthSouth, and Enron are currently in prison), but these companies went way beyond usual procedures and were not typical of US business. You are unlikely to be asked to engage in illegal operations in U.S. companies. But you may find your company's policies rather heartless.

In countries such as Japan, social benefits are part of national and corporate philosophy; companies factor in the higher costs of keeping everyone employed and using goods made at home, etc. The extra costs are paid for through higher consumer prices. The American viewpoint is that the citizen/consumer, who is also the worker, is best served by the lowest prices. In the process, workers may lose their jobs but the deserving will find other ones. Thus by an 'invisible hand', the economy is directed to function in the most efficient manner—at a cost of much upheaval and dislocation.

It has taken a long time to convince the public that free enterprise does not mean a company should be free to pollute the air, foul the rivers and destroy the forests. Such problems, of course, are not unique to this society.

EXECUTIVES

Life at the top is very different from life at the bottom, except in one regard—it can be just as insecure. Mistakes are not easily forgiven, and even a long-time employee in the highest ranks can be summarily dismissed. (Those at the top, however, will probably leave with a very handsome severance package, whereas lower down, a few weeks' pay may be the most the worker can hope for.) Those closely associated with the ousted executive may be out the door as well, leading to Byzantine politics in which underlings try to keep lines of communication open to several factions within the company.

Democracy has little place in the American corporation. Important decisions are made at the top, usually in secrecy, and based on a heavy weight of facts and figures. The chief executive officer may take complete responsibility for a key decision after thrashing it out in executive meetings.

As few people are involved, a decision in the USA can be made quickly. However, it may take longer to implement than in a system in which everyone was involved beforehand in making the decision. If a venture goes bad, the person who championed it can be fired, which would not occur where there is consensus management. The person fired could be the chief executive officer.

Business life is tense. Few American companies can stand still and reap the rewards of America's one-time advantages. The playing field has levelled, and foreign companies are successfully competing. It's a rare executive who is in a position to relax.

Executive Life

For his trouble, the fellow (it almost certainly is a man) at the top is extremely well-compensated. The differential between top and bottom salaries in the USA is extraordinary and even in companies doing badly, chief executives collect millions of dollars a year in pay, stock options, and bonuses. Despite the downturn in the U.S. economy, executive pay continues to rise, and those at the very top now take home 500 times as much as the average worker. Furthermore, taxes in the highest income bracket have been reduced. Millionaires are now commonplace.

Amiability is not a prerequisite for rising to the top, and there are a number of chief executive officers with legendary bad tempers. It is not the boss's job to worry about the well-being of his subordinates (although the man with many enemies will be swept out more quickly in hard times); it's the company he worries about. His business savvy is supposed to be based on intimate knowledge of his company and the industry so he goes home nightly with a full briefcase. At the very top—and on the way up—executives are exceedingly dedicated.

The American executive must be capable of enough small talk to get him through the social part of his schedule, but he is probably not a highly-cultured individual or an intellectual. Although his wife may be on the board of the symphony or opera, he himself has little time for such pursuits. His reading may largely concern business and management (American companies are often trendy in their attempts to keep up with the latest innovations in business methods), despite interests in other fields. Golf provides him with a sportive outlet that combines with some useful business socializing.

These days, he probably attempts some form of aerobic exercise to 'keep the old heart in shape' and for the same reason goes easy on butter and alcohol, substances thought to contribute to taking highly stressed executives out of the running. (These health endeavors may be favorite conversational subjects.) But his doctor's admonition to 'take it easy' falls on deaf ears. He likes to work. He knows there are younger men nipping at his heels. Despite the occasional newspaper article about the executive who gives up the rat race, few actually are eager to be put out to pasture.

They may, however, be quite willing to move on to greener pastures. Corporate head-hunting, carried on by 'executive search firms', is a growth industry. America has great faith in individual talent and dynamic, aggressive executives are so in demand that companies regularly raid each other's managerial ranks.

EMPLOYEE LIFE

"In Argentina I worked just as hard," an Argentinian architect complained, "but work wasn't as stressful or competitive as it is in the USA. There you feel part of a group that helps each other, but here you feel disposable."

Foreign employees of American companies sometimes feel the lack of spoken praise, which is often felt to be superfluous here. Good work is noted and rewarded with salary increases and promotions or in these days of stagnant salaries, it simply may not be noted at all. Bad work is usually quickly brought to the employee's attention.

Competitive tension here goads the workers on, but it also causes a high level of anxiety. Individual effort prevails over teamwork. When results are quantifiable, many companies give awards to the most productive workers, thus pitting one worker against another. If a decision is made because one person's point of view prevailed, that person is held responsible for the outcome and will get the credit if the idea succeeds—no matter how many people helped implement it. If the idea fails, the person will also shoulder the blame. While there's always some give and take among people who work together, the level of trust in an office may be low.

Company loyalty is also rather slight, and people identify themselves by their job ('I am a bank manager') rather than by company name. Co-workers may speak very derisively of the company among themselves ('Thank God it's Friday and I'm outa here'), although it's understood that this doesn't affect the quality of their efforts. Within the company, while one might have some loyalty to one's manager, one would not be expected to put one's own job on the line for him or her. It is to yourself that you are expected to be true.

Despite the stress level, many foreigners find the American work climate very satisfying, particularly ambitious people who felt stymied in their own cultures. "America is the best place for work," says a British woman, now rising in corporate ranks. "Working so hard is very stimulating, and I find my job exciting and rewarding." Even many of those who complain about the relentlessness of the pace admit they would be bored in a more restful atmosphere.

CORPORATE CULTURES

In stereotype at least, office atmosphere varies from coast to coast. New York is frenetic, pressured and more formal than elsewhere; the Midwest is conventional and methodical; the West Coast allows a degree of nonconformity. But you can also expect to find laid-back offices in New York and formal ones in Los Angeles. Even in Midwestern Chicago, you'll come across eccentricity.

Beyond locale, particular companies are known for distinctive 'corporate cultures'. There are those that pride themselves on creating a family atmosphere and provide employees with unusual security. Many companies run bowling leagues and baseball teams, and on weekends the employees' children paddle in the company pool. (But even some of these old-style companies, such as IBM, have been laying off large numbers of workers.)

Some companies make a point of giving employees an enormous amount of autonomy ('We don't care what you do or how you do it, just get results.') There are companies that emphasise creativity and others that are very disciplined; some have rigid chains of command and others almost imperceptible chains. Many, goaded on by those books and courses on management, are constantly dreaming up new ways of organizing and issuing new work flow charts.

The human factor may anywhere override a particular company's stance. The manager of one department in a company may develop strong team spirit, whereas another whips up a deadly competition. In the end, however, both managers must produce results.

Hiring

The process of interviewing and hiring for job vacancies usually is an even-handed one. If no one is on the spot for an opening, the company announces a job opening on its own website and usually on others as well—or other websites pick up the announcement. Generally, only low-level jobs are still found in newspaper classifieds, though their online classifieds may prove to be some help.

Some of the most popular websites are monster.com, hotjobs.com, and craigslist.org. Often you can post your resume on the website but don't expect a lot of response from that. Dice.com is the leading site for tech jobs; other industries have specialty web sites as well. If you think you can command a salary of more than US$ 100,000, try http://TheLadders.com.

You must have a resume that states your qualifications and experience. For a small price, you can get help in creating one at pongoresume.com. Be sure to have someone with good editorial skills proofread it for you; to get an interview you need an impressive resume and usually it is sent with a cover letter. Be formal, polite, and enthusiastic in any correspondence or telephone conversation you have with a company. Do not use text-message slang

Applicants with the most promising records are invited in for interviews and get a chance to demonstrate ease of manner, enthusiasm, experience, and ideas. This is not the time for undue modesty (although one should not sound like an unbearable braggart). There are many books of advice for the job seeker, and the newcomer to America would be wise to consult the literature. By law, women and minority applicants must be given equal consideration.

Although connections are not necessary even for the best jobs, the person who comes recommended has an edge. However, in the end, nobody will hire you just because you are so-and-so's niece or nephew. Even if you are, your qualifications will have to be at least as good as the competition's. In some cases, a relationship could be a drawback as nepotism is looked on unfavorably. The main thing a company is usually looking for is somebody who has done exactly the same sort of work before.

Despite the opinion of many business journalists that the MBA's (persons holding degrees in business administration) are wrecking American business with their narrow, methodical, cold-blooded methods and although they are disdained by many old-line entrepreneurs, these MBA's are much in demand and those from the elite schools start with very high salaries.

Personnel Policies

Company employment policies are nearly all neatly codified and presented to the new employee at the time of hiring. Although a company has the fundamental right to dismiss an employee at any time, recent lawsuits have caused most companies to carefully document the procedure the procedure leading to firings. Minorities, the disabled, and older people can sue for wrongful termination.

Work hours, vacation time, breaks, pension plans, sick leave, and rights are itemized and administered with impartiality—no matter if one person has a dying mother, and another develops disabilities. Mitigating factors may be tolerated for a time, but the employee who can't meet the standards can expect eventually to be dismissed.

There are, of course, exceptions to the impersonal approach and many cases of companies that have stuck by their workers through thick and thin. But even then, the bosses will probably excuse themselves by saying, 'She was too good a worker to lose. We knew she'd be back some day'. Whether true or not, nobody would want to admit that a business decision had been tilted by purely human considerations.

Office Relationships

Most offices are informal, with lots of joking around, back-slapping and breeziness. Office doors are usually left open, unless a meeting is in progress. Although everybody knows perfectly well who the boss is—and subtly jockey for attention—the deference paid is less obvious than in more hierarchical societies.

For many people, the workplace becomes a substitute for the community that is fast disappearing from urban life. It's in the office that gossip, recipes, and names of barbers are exchanged and where someone will listen to how your date went last night. The department will take you out to lunch on your birthday and send you flowers when you're bereaved. The young and single may drink together, rent ski cabins in the winter, and set up blind dates for each other.

Nonetheless, it's a transitory community. Few groups stay intact for long. The members bond together for a while, but the ties are fragile and often don't outlast a regrouping. Americans are good at the quick relationship—thick today, gone tomorrow. After all, in the course of a career, a vast number of paths cross and it would be impossible to keep up with all of them.

Managers do not routinely involve themselves in their subordinates' personal lives. They may indulge in some friendly chat on personal subjects, but they do not consider themselves responsible for anyone's emotional well-being. This is not pure hardboiled indifference but reflects also the respect for privacy, which so often in American life takes primacy over other needs. The American viewpoint is that the worker has a right to conduct his personal life however he sees fit as long as it does not affect his job performance. Despite the separation of job and life, many workers keep pictures of wives, husbands, children, and dogs on their desks, a practice some foreigners find very odd.

Initiative Before Deference

The hierarchy is not rigid in most offices. Managers encourage ideas from subordinates and subordinates may contradict their superiors. Promotion is by no means orderly, and tomorrow you may be reporting to someone who reported to you yesterday.

It doesn't hurt to be pushy and aggressive (within reason). The theory is that if you're aggressive in your own cause, you'll exert yourself for the company too. You can get away with stepping on a few toes on the way up, although it's wise to cultivate supporters as well.

One large California computer company runs a special course for its Asian-born employees, a course popularly known as 'rudeness training'. The intent is to teach those from non-confrontational cultures how to be direct and assertive towards clients, co-workers, and to their own bosses.

The Job Hop

As companies are constantly reorganizing, retrenching, and being bought and sold, they have many occasions to lay off workers. They may do so regretfully, but they feel no compulsion to go on supporting the unprofitable employee. Companies have been so ruthlessly 'downsizing' for the last couple of decades that it seems that every remaining employee is doing the work of two or three people. Those who do have jobs live in fear of losing them, and when the axe does fall, people are usually asked to clear out their desks quickly.

The workers on their side are always free to improve their situations by looking out for new jobs. In fact, this is about the only right an individual (unless a member of a union, as are only 13 per cent of American workers) has in a corporation. So workers are quick to move if a better opportunity presents itself. Were company fidelity alone to cause someone to reject brighter prospects, her colleagues would probably think him or her stupid. After all, someone who doesn't move voluntarily may end up moving involuntarily.

However, options are limited for job seekers. Many manufacturing jobs have been lost in the past decades, so blue-collar (manual) workers especially have limited choices. Many of the newly created jobs in our economy are in the service sector and poorly paid. The federally mandated minimum wage at this writing is US$ 6.55 and will rise to US$ 7.25 in

July 2009. The highest state minimum wage is presently US$ 8.00 an hour. A minimum-wage worker is worse off now than he was thirty years ago. White-collar workers may make decent salaries and even receive benefits, but downsizing, mergers, and market fluctuations keep everyone hopping. Furthermore, white-collar jobs have been following blue-collar jobs overseas recently, a shock to the middle-class.

DOING BUSINESS WITH AMERICANS
Get to the Point

By all reports, the single greatest difference between business dealings in the USA and the rest of the world is the American eagerness to get to the point. Most peoples of the world don't negotiate with strangers. Therefore the first order of business is to get to know their callers, no matter how long it takes. Then they can decide if these are people they want to work with.

All this is a mystery to an American. Why sit around jawing and drinking cup after cup of coffee when you could be making deals? Certainly we want to know if you can deliver, the strength of your company, your resources. Why don't you tell us that instead of about the beauty of Tang dynasty vases? Then we can get down to how much, when, and who pays for what. At the end of several days when the American realizes that he and his new friends haven't yet lighted on one significant aspect of the business he came to talk about, he's ready to exit by the nearest window.

It's not that we're automatons. We're friendly, and we want to be liked. We're glad to have a little let's-all-relax chitchat at the beginning of a meeting. We'll even occasionally offer you coffee, if the company coffeepot isn't too far away. We'll take you out to lunch, but by the main course we expect to have the pleasantries out of the way and get down to brass tacks. We just don't think it's necessary to know someone very well to do business with them. After all, if we find we don't like you after we've done a little business, we can dump your company and try a different one.

Another reason that we want to get on with the business at hand is that it's what interests us. Whereas business people from other countries may be frankly bored with business and prefer to talk about other things, Americans are not. It's abstract conversations that bore us; the pragmatic American likes a conversation that is going somewhere. Stuck making small talk for hours, we're like racehorses shut up in the paddock. We long for a chance to show our stuff.

Tick Tock

In the mind of the American businessperson the clock is always ticking, and there are further worlds to conquer. Why spend any more time than necessary on this deal? We feel no need to be soul mates. We are not going to base this relationship on trust anyhow. We are going to base it on an elaborate, detailed contract which our lawyers will draw up.

During the workday, Americans are very precise about time. If you're ten minutes late for an appointment, you should apologize. If you're half an hour late, you should have a good reason. When you see your American host drumming his fingers and looking at his watch, wrap up the meeting quickly. And don't be insulted if he announces he has another meeting and unceremoniously turns you out of his office. Very likely he does have another meeting, and even if you're in the middle of a critical conversation, he has to be there on time. It doesn't mean that he's any less interested in your business.

Making Contact

As anywhere, when you're trying to get in the door it helps to have mutual acquaintances. But if you don't, the direct approach is perfectly acceptable. Find out who is in charge of the area of your interest and write, phone, or e-mail, stating your credentials and intentions. You may want to open negotiations at the top, by having your president contact the American company's president.

If you don't get a reply, follow up. It's helpful to have an exchange of correspondence before you arrive for a meeting so the Americans can consider your proposal and involve the right people.

Meetings are informal, and participants make their points forcefully.

If you're flying in for a meeting, be sure you have an appointment before you arrive. Americans keep tightly packed schedules, and should you arrive without appointments, you could discover that your important contacts have absolutely no time to see you—no matter how important you are.

Meetings

A lot of business decisions are made in meetings, which can be stormy. Those in attendance are expected to bring up objections, thrash out problems, and defend their positions. Those in a losing position are not supposed to brood about loss of face.

To many foreigners, the American approach is cold and rational; we like a proposal that is based on facts and figures. Of course, we want to know that you're reliable, but our main interest is price and we are incredulous to hear that in some cultures the business relationship is more important than the price.

Americans will appreciate it if you show up at a meeting armed with all the pertinent statistics and deliver a well-rounded pitch, including the data that proves what a great company you represent. It's a good idea to work in how great you are too, although you must be a little more offhand in forwarding yourself. Americans accept arrogance, but too much boasting can arouse doubts. "Doing business is completely different here," says a Japanese businessman. "I make my presentation, they ask questions and I'm done."

We favor fast-talking, smooth operators, which is why some of our most sparkling representatives fail in countries where fast talkers are distrusted. Humility goes a lot further outside the United States. The important thing here is to make it clear that you are a 'can-do' kind of person and that you understand what the Americans want.

Straightforwardness

Americans do not appreciate being 'strung along'. If, as is done in some countries, you offer pleasant reassurances that turn out not to be true, American business people will be highly annoyed—'Why the devil didn't someone tell us?' We want the straight scoop, the real story. If you can't deliver when you said you would (and June 1, means June 1, not sometime in June) tell us now so we can plan for it. We'll still like you better than the bunch that couldn't deliver and didn't tell us about it.

Those from the Far East may be shocked by the bluntness with which an American reports negative news. 'Sorry, but we got a better price from someone else,' or 'Those blouses were badly made.' In another culture your feelings would be considered more important than the truth, whereas we consider that we're doing you a favor by our straightforwardness. Now you know why you're not getting our business and can do something about it. And we've saved you from wasting your time in anticipation. But this can seem rude in some cultures.

Accountability

You may find the decision-making process fairly streamlined in an American company, compared to that in other countries. Certain key decisions will probably require an executive board's approval, but very often there are somebodies along the line with the authority to make lesser decisions. Who these people are is generally not a secret.

Business Entertaining

Americans can be lavish entertainers. We see the value in breaking bread with our counterparts from other countries and most executives have quite decent expense accounts. But few would care to be out every night. If you find yourself less royally entertained than in some other countries, it could be because most Americans prefer a steak and salad themselves to what they regard as the tedium of a five-course meal in a French restaurant.

As conversation isn't our favorite indulgence either, we assume that you too would be as glad to lie down and take off your shoes as to be dragged all over town. So a night out with American hosts will probably not be excessively long. Americans do not consider that they need to show their dedication to the company by sacrificing sleep.

If you are traveling with your spouse, be sure that your host knows it so that he or she won't be left out of evening plans. If the American wives (or husbands) don't appear, it is probably because they have business of their own, live in a distant suburb to which your host will be returning on the late night train, can't find a babysitter, or are bored stiff by business dinners.

Breakfast and Lunch

You may find yourself facing the business breakfast, favored by Americans who don't want to break up the business day, or who don't have enough lunches on their calendars to go around. If the thought of bacon and eggs at eight in the morning makes you sick, just have a roll and coffee. The point of the business breakfast is not to eat breakfast.

Lunches don't often last for much over an hour. Americans have never had the tradition of the long midday repast, and the practice of having a few drinks with lunch is long gone. At breakfast and lunch, the Americans will expect to talk business for at least part of the time; dinner can turn out to be purely social, particularly if couples are involved.

The person who did the inviting does the paying. If your hosts took you out the first time, you may wish to reciprocate and invite them the next. The Zagat restaurant guides are fairly reliable and have editions for many major cities.

Names, Rank, and Titles

Nearly everybody these days is on a first-name basis. If you prefer some other form of address, say so. One Japanese man, who after twelve years here still can't get used to strangers calling him by his first name, gives out his last name by itself, which Americans think is his first name.

Titles don't matter much in the business world. It's important to know who the company president is, but you wouldn't call him 'President Watson'. If you're not using a first name, say Mr, Mrs, Miss, or Ms (*See 'What Do I Call You' in* Chapter 4: Socializing With Locals)

You do need to know who the important people are at the meeting or else you may find yourself addressing your remarks to the distinguished looking older man who turns out to be the company bookkeeper rather than to the awkward-looking kid who happens to be the CEO. Try to listen carefully when the introductions go by. Of course, even in America, there's enough homage paid to the boss so that observers don't have to be too brilliant to figure out who counts.

Business Cards

Cards play a minor role in American business and may not come out until the end of a meeting. They are used mainly to pass on an e-mail address and phone number, not as credentials. Most people have them, however, and you should too, printed in English.

Dress

If you belong to one of the more conservative industries, such as banking, you will probably do best to wear the kind of conservative suits that Brooks Brothers and Paul Stuart are known for: grey or dark blue, understated and well made.

Nothing should be polyester or shiny, and the cut should be classic and conservative. Subtle tweeds are fine; pinstripes must be very narrow, barely perceptible as stripes. In the summer, a cotton khaki suit will do, although if you have a little panache you might get away with wearing seersucker.

You're safest in a white or light blue shirt. Drip-dry is acceptable as long as the naked eye can't tell the difference. Colored shirts with white collars are still a bit trendy. A tie cannot be flamboyant, and any bright colors should be discreet. The pattern should be small, as in little dots or vague stripes. Never wear jewelry.

Black wing-tip shoes are usually favored among conservative dressers, although loafers will probably not shock anyone. Belts should be black.

These guidelines are merely starting points, as business dress becomes more and more casual by the day. A few years ago, it was the prerogative of IT workers to shun ties, but now, according to a recent Gallup poll, only six percent of American men ever wear ties to work. When you know with whom you're dealing, you can adapt

Women are allowed more color and variations. Some executive women disdain suits in favor of colorful skirts or dresses (often worn with a jacket), but if you want to be entirely safe, a suit with a skirt, worn with a simple shell or a neck scarf and minimal jewelry, will take you anywhere. A good pantsuit is also fine for almost anything, except perhaps a fancy evening when most women want to look a little feminine. In the winter, boots are ideal footwear, and in summer, shoes with thick heels, rather than spikes, are preferable for anyone with much walking to do.

Gifts

Forget about graft. No respectable business greases palms. (Yes, there are occasional scandals involving the government, but they're far outside the norm.) An American who found that someone had left him a briefcase full of money would be struck dumb. Even gifts are unusual, except at Christmas.

Business Hours

The standard working day is 9:00 am to 5:00 pm, although for executives those are minimal work hours. On the West Coast, working hours are often 8:00 am to 5:00 pm, and anyone in the West doing much business with the East has to get an early start. West Coast stockbrokers are at work by 6:00 am (when it's 9:00 am on the New York Stock Exchange). Some cities with major traffic problems encourage flexible work hours ('flex-time') so that within one company some people might work from 7:00 am to 3:00 pm and others 10:00 am to 6:00 pm.

Many workers get only a half hour for lunch. It is very common to bring a sandwich and eat at one's desk or in a staff room. Hourly workers usually get 15-minute breaks morning and afternoon.

Americans try to keep their weekends for home and family. You might, however, be invited to someone's home on the weekend for a dinner, barbecue, or brunch.

Some urban dwellers have weekend homes in the country and leave early on Fridays to get to them. It is a very favored guest who is invited to the country home. If you are so honored, write a thank-you note to your hostess afterwards.

Vacations

American vacation time is extremely short compared to European and even many Asian allotments. It increases with length of employment; most people qualify for only a couple of weeks a year. Eventually, some may receive a month's vacation, but usually take a week here and a week there, being loathe to leave their offices for a month at a time. Because of the children's school holidays, summer is the commonest time for a break.

Frequently (life speeds up in more and more ways), people make the most of long weekends rather than take substantial vacations. Supposedly, fear of what will happen in their absences causes many people to settle for four-day holidays—just long enough for the New Yorker to fly down to the Caribbean.

Communicating

Americans are expected to answer their mail (postal and e-mail), and they'll expect you to answer yours. If you don't, you'll be thought unreliable. So even if you don't have an immediate answer, it's best to write and say so. Messages can be very brief.

The telephone is heavily used. Many, many questions that would call for a personal meeting in another country are resolved over the phone here. We can happily do business with people we have never met at all.

Assistants

Persons of importance have an assistant (sometimes still called a secretary) who takes care of their appointments and correspondence and who is a buffer between the person and those demanding to see him or her. It's helpful if the assistant likes you and you should learn his or her name. Although the assistant probably doesn't influence major decisions, he or she can forward your cause in various ways, not the least of which is in putting your phone calls through.

WOMEN IN BUSINESS

Although women are still rare in executive boardrooms, they are fast on their way up the ladder. Half the managerial positions in corporate America are held by women, and chances are good that your visiting foreign team will be meeting women who are doing the same job they are.

Some foreigners are not used to negotiating with women, but they should try to acclimatize very quickly or risk badly antagonizing a prospective business partner. Be sure that you are not in the habit of assuming that all women are underlings.

The correct procedure is simple: treat a woman as you would a man. This does not mean that you can't discreetly help her on with her coat after a business lunch, but you should ask her the same questions you would a man and give the same regard to the answers.

Allow a woman to pick up the check under any circumstances when a man in her position would pay. Don't

Women executives in the USA dress well and are confident of themselves. Many of them hold high positions and are even CEOs of companies. Treat all women as equals in a business meeting and never assume that the only female in the group is the secretary who is there to take notes.

take over in restaurants if she invited you; she understands a wine list. Do not be overly solicitous of her safety—she's used to going home alone in a cab. And do not, under any circumstances, make a pass at her unless you want to see your whole deal go up in a puff of smoke.

The truth is that it is tough for a woman in a man's world. One reason is that the one endeavor that society takes as seriously as 'worker' is 'mother', and the working mother constantly feels she is cheating either her job or her children. (The working father can be regretful he sees his children so little, but he isn't considered a bad father.) She will appreciate it if you don't make her job any harder for her. If working with women is a new experience for you, you may be pleased to discover what a pleasure it can be. Even in America, many women insist, to get ahead they must be twice as good as a man.

USA AT A GLANCE

CHAPTER 10

'Figures won't lie, but liars will figure.'
—Charles H Grosvenor

Official Name
United States of America

Capital
Washington, DC (District of Columbia)

Flag
Sometimes called 'Old Glory'. Thirteen horizontal red and whites stripes with a blue rectangle, containing 50 white stars, in the upper left-hand corner. The 13 stripes stand for the 13 original colonies, while the 50 stars represent the current 50 states.

National Anthem
The Star Spangled Banner

Time
The time difference from Greenwich Mean Time ranges from -5 hours on the East Coast to -8 hours on the West Coast. (This is decreased by an hour during Daylight Savings from April to October, when clocks are set back an hour.) Alaska is -9 hours from GMT, while Hawaii is -10 hours.

Telephone Country Code
1

Land
In size, North America is the world's third largest country. The North Atlantic Ocean borders its East Coast and the North Pacific Ocean is off its West Coast. To its north is Canada and to its south is Mexico.

Area
9,631,418 sq km (3,718,711 sq miles)

Highest Point
Mount McKinley (6,194 m/20,321 ft)

Major Rivers
The Mississippi-Missouri river system (6,260 km/3,890 miles long), is the longest in the US and the second longest in the world. From this river flow hundreds of tributaries, including the Red River, the Ohio, and the Arkansas. The Colorado River, Columbia River, Rio Grande, and the Hudson River are also notable.

Climate
Predominantly temperate climate in most parts of the country. The climate is arctic in Alaska and tropical in Florida and Hawaii. The Great Basin of the Southwest is arid and the great plains west of the Mississippi semi-arid.

Natural Resources
Bauxite, coal, copper, gold, iron, lead, mercury, natural gas, nickel, petroleum, phosphates, silver, timber, tungsten, uranium, and zinc.

Population
297,000,000

Ethnic Groups
In 2000, whites made up 75.1 percent, blacks 12.3 percent, Asian 3.6 percent, Amerindian and Alaska Natives 0.9 percent and native Hawaiian and other Pacific islanders

0.1 percent. 'Others' were 5.5 percent and 2.4 percent were of mixed origins.

Religion
Christian Protestantism, Roman Catholicism, Mormonism, Judaism, and Islam are the leading religions.

Languages
English is the official language while Spanish is spoken by 8 percent. Nearly 18 percent of the population speaks a language other than English at home.

Government
A federal republic with a constitution and a strong democratic tradition. There is a division of powers between the federal government and the state governments. The federal government consists of three branches: the executive, the legislative, and the judicial.

Administrative Divisions
Fifty states: Alabama, Alaska, Arizona, Arkansas, California, Colorado, Connecticut, Delaware, Florida, Georgia, Hawaii, Idaho, Illinois, Indiana, Iowa, Kansas, Kentucky, Louisiana, Maine, Maryland, Massachusetts, Michigan, Minnesota, Mississippi, Missouri, Montana, Nebraska, Nevada, New Hampshire, New Jersey, New Mexico, New York, North Carolina, North Dakota, Ohio, Oklahoma, Oregon, Pennsylvania, Rhode Island, South Carolina, South Dakota, Tennessee, Texas, Utah, Vermont, Virginia, Washington, West Virginia, Wisconsin, and Wyoming.

One district: District of Columbia

Outlying territories: Puerto Rico, the Virgin Islands, Guam, the Northern Mariana Islands, American Samoa, Wake Island, and several other islands. The United States also has compacts of free association with the Republic of the Marshall Islands, the Republic of Palau, and the Federated States of Micronesia.

Currency
US Dollar (US$ or USD)

Weights and Measures
Despite attempts, the USA still hasn't made the switch to the metric system. The following are rough equivalencies.

- Americans measure weights in ounces and pounds. There are 16 ounces in a pound. 1 oz = 28 g. 1 lb is about 1/2 a kg or 500 g 1 kg = 2.2 lbs.
- Lengths are in inches, feet, and yards. There are 12 inches in a ft and 3 ft in a yard. An inch = 2.5 cm. One m = 3.2 ft. One m = 1.09 of a yard.
- Distances are measured in miles. 1 mile = 1.6 km
- In cooking, Americans measure rather than weigh. Both liquids and dry foods are measured in teaspoons, tablespoons, cups, pints, quarts, and gallons. 3 teaspoons = 1 tablespoon. 16 tablespoons = 1 cup. There are 2 cups in a pint, 2 pints in a quart, and 4 quarts in a gallon. A litre is slightly more than a quart. 1 gallon = 3.8 litres.
- Temperatures are measured in Fahrenheit rather than Celsius. To change Fahrenheit into Centigrade subtract 32 and divide by 1.8. Freezing point is 32°F and boiling point is 212°F.

Gross Domestic Product (GDP)
US$ 10.99 trillion

Agricultural Products
Corn, cotton, fruits, grains, vegetables, and wheat.

Other Products
Beef, dairy products, fish, forest products, pork, and poultry.

Industries
Aerospace, chemicals, consumer goods, electronics, food processing, motor vehicles, mining, petroleum production and refining, steel, telecommunications.

Exports
Agricultural products, automobiles, capital goods, consumer goods, industrial supplies, and raw materials.

Imports
Automobiles, crude oil, consumer goods, food and beverages, industrial raw materials, machinery, refined petroleum products.

Ports and Harbours
Anchorage (Alaska), Baltimore (Maryland), Boston (Massachusetts), Charleston (South Carolina), Chicago (Illinois), Duluth (Minnesota), Hampton Roads (Virginia), Honolulu (Hawaii), Houston (Texas), Jacksonville (Florida), Los Angeles (California), New Orleans (Louisiana), New York (New York), Philadelphia (Pennsylvania), Port Canaveral (Florida), Portland (Oregon), Prudhoe Bay (Alaska), San Francisco (California), Savannah (Georgia), Seattle (Washington), Tampa (Florida), Toledo (Ohio).

ACRONYMS

AA	Alcoholics Anonymous. A self-help program for alcoholics.
AAA	American Automobile Association. Provides many services for travellers and drivers, including towing. Well worth joining.
ABC	American Broadcasting Corporation (one of the big three TV networks) / American-Born Chinese.
ACLU	American Civil Liberties Union. A membership organization that defends civil rights.
A/C	Air conditioning.
aka	As known as. For instance, Sean Combs, aka Puff Daddy and P. Diddy.
am & pm	The 'am' hours are from midnight to noon; 'pm' hours from noon to midnight. So, 3:00 pm is the middle of the afternoon, not the middle of the night. Americans rarely use the 24-hour clock.

ASAP	As soon as possible. Meaning, do it right away.
ATM	Automated Teller Machine, where you can make deposits and get cash. An ATM card is one that lets you access your bank account.
CBS	Central Broadcasting Service—one of the big three TV networks.
CIA	Central Intelligence Agency—does the international information gathering.
CNN	Central News Network—a cable news network.
CPS	Child Protective Services—the agency that will be called if someone suspects you're mistreating your children.
c/o	Care of; used when forwarding mail. Joe Smith c/o Jim Dandy.
DDT	A pesticide that had deadly effects on the environment. It's now illegal, but the residues remain.
DUI	Driving Under the Influence (of alcohol or drugs). This could get you to jail.
ER	Emergency Room—in a hospital.
FEMA	Federal Emergency Management Agency —takes charge in disasters.
FBI	Federal Bureau of Investigation— the national domestic spy agency.
FDA	Food and Drug Administration. A federal government agency that sets standards.
HMO	Health Maintenance Organization
ICU	Intensive Care Unit—where the most critically ill people in a hospital are cared for.
ID	Identification, such as a driver's licence or passport.
ICE	U.S. Immigration and Customs Enforcement
IED	Improvised Explosive Device
IRS	Internal Revenue Service, the agency that collects federal taxes.
K-12	Kindergarten through 12th grade.
MIA	Missing in action.
MTV	Music Television—the place to see hip music in action.

NASA	National Aeronautics and Space Agency—runs the space flights.
NBC	National Broadcasting Corporation—one of the big three network TV channels.
NIMBY	Not in My Back Yard. Describes fighting against projects that might otherwise be favored—such as homeless shelters—except that they are in one's own neighborhood.
PBS	Public Broadcasting Station—less advertising, more quality television fare.
R & D	Research and Development—a department in some companies, usually where new products are developed.
R & R	Rest and relaxation. As in 'I'm planning some R & R this weekend'.
SSN	Social Security Number. All working citizens and residents have one. If you're not eligible for a SSN, you can get a Tax Payer ID, which enables you to open a bank account.
VIP	Very Important person.
WMD	Weapons of Mass Destruction.

FAMOUS PEOPLE

Susan B. Anthony (1820–1906)
Renowned women's rights leader, abolitionist, and co-founder with Elizabeth Cady Stanton of the National Woman Suffrage Association, formed in 1869 to agitate for an amendment to the US Constitution to guarantee women the right to vote. The Nineteenth Amendment was finally passed by the Supreme Court in 1920.

Kobe Bryant (1978–)
Renowned basketball player, of the Los Angeles Lakers.

Warren Buffett (1930–)
Legendary stock market investor, CEO of Berkshire Hathaway, and philanthropist. His theory of value investing is summed up in his book, *The Warren Buffett Way*.

Johnny Carson (1925–2005)

Television entertainer who hosted the popular late night program *The Tonight Show* from 1962 to 1992.

Tom Clancy (1947–)

Best-selling novelist known for his spy and political thrillers with intricate, detailed plots. Nearly fifty million copies of his books—including *Hunt for Red October*, *Patriot Games*, *Clear and Present Danger* and *The Sum of All Fears*—have been printed and three have been made into movies. He is currently developing multimedia computer games based on his stories.

Bill and Hillary Clinton (1946– and 1947–)

Bill Clinton was the 43rd president of the USA and remains extremely popular. He is a magnetic speaker and a powerful force in Democratic politics. His wife, Hillary Rodham Clinton, went in 2001 from being First Lady to U.S. senator from New York State. She ran for president in 2007–2008 and came very close to winning the Democratic nomination, but was finally defeated by Barack Obama. Her candidacy broke new ground for U.S. women.

Walt Disney (1901–66)

Movie producer and pioneer in animated cartoons, who also developed theme parks in California, Florida, France, and Tokyo.

Dwight David Eisenhower (1890–1969)

Supreme Commander of the Allied Troops in Europe in World War II and 34th president of the U.S. Ike presided over the peaceful fifties and though a Republican warned against undue influence of the 'military-industrial complex'.

Benjamin Franklin (1706–90)

American statesman, printer, scientist. and writer. Franklin's role as key participant in the Federal Constitutional Convention of 1787 brought the Constitution of the United States into being. In addition, he was a renowned and inexhaustible scientist—inventing, among other things, bifocal glasses, the Franklin stove, and the harmonica—before conducting his most famous experiment: flying a kite in a thunderstorm. Franklin's invention of the lightning rod won him respect and recognition, as did his service as Ambassador to France. His autobiography is one of the most translated works ever written.

Bill (William Henry) Gates (1955–)

Chairman and co-founder of Microsoft, a top computer software firm. Gates co-founded (with Paul Allen) the company at age 19 and is now the richest man in the world.

Tony Hawk (1968–)

Champion skateboarder and developer of wildly popular electronic video games for Sony Play Station.

Thomas Jefferson (1743–1826)

Third President of the United States (1801–9), scientist, inventor, author of the Declaration of Independence, and founder of the prestigious University of Virginia.

Steve Jobs (1955–)

An icon in the personal-computer industry, Jobs (with Stephen Wozniak) developed the first Apple computer in 1976, the main competitor to Microsoft. After resigning in 1985, Jobs founded the NeXT Computer Company and in 1986 bought Pixar Animation Studios, a computer animation firm founded by George Lucas, becoming a multi-billionaire when Pixar went public in 1995. Jobs returned to Apple as interim chief executive in 1997.

Michael Jordan (1963–)

Generally considered the best basketball player in US history, Jordan led the Chicago Bulls to six NBA championships. He briefly interrupted his superstar basketball career for a stint as a baseball player with the Chicago White Sox.

Stephen King (1947–)

Bestselling and prolific writer internationally known for his horror stories and screenplays, such as *The Shining*, *Carrie*, *Misery*, and *Delores Claiborne*.

Abraham Lincoln (1809–1865)

The 16th US President, who preserved the union following the secession of the Southern states by leading the country through the long, bloody Civil War. In the course of it he issued The Emancipation Proclamation, freed the slaves and delivered the Gettysburg Address, one of the most famous and oft-quoted speeches in our history, detailing the hardships of war ('Four score and seven years ago our fathers brought forth on this continent, a new nation, conceived in Liberty and dedicated to the proposition that all men are created equal'). He was assassinated by John Wilkes Booth on April 14, 1865.

Vince Lombardi (1913–1970)

Legendary football coach, who led the Green Bay Packers to repeated success and after whom the Superbowl Trophy is named. Among his many colorful sayings were, 'Winning isn't everything; it's the only thing' and 'Show me a good loser, and I'll show you a loser'.

George Lucas (1944–)

Hollywood director, producer, and writer, best known for the films *American Graffiti* and *Star Wars*, which set a standard for the use of special effects in film-making.

Martin Luther King, Jr. (1929–68)

African-American clergyman, civil-rights leader, and winner of the Nobel Peace Prize. The Reverend King led many civil-rights marches in the South, while espousing non-violent resistance. In 1963, King headed the March on Washington, where he gave the famous 'I Have a Dream' speech. King was assassinated on April 4, 1968, by James Earl Ray. His birthday is celebrated as a national holiday.

Charles Manson (1934–)

A vicious cult leader of the sixties, Manson instigated hideous killings, including that of pregnant Hollywood actress Sharon Tate, that shocked the country. He remains in prison, his name synonymous with evil.

Joseph McCarthy (1909–1957)

A U.S. senator whose 1950s investigations of supposed communists smeared countless people and ruined many careers. McCarthy was finally exposed and condemned. The term 'McCarthyism' now refers to illegitimate accusations.

Franklin Delano Roosevelt (1882–1945)

Statesman, 32nd president (1933–45), and polio survivor, aka 'FDR'. Roosevelt's legacy was marked by his social and economic plan to rebuild the country after the Great Depression. This plan, known as the New Deal, set the tone for today's liberal Democratic party. After the attack on Pearl Harbor, Roosevelt led the country through World War II, dying just four weeks before the German surrender. His wife Eleanor Roosevelt, a strong voice for the poor and powerless, was widely-loved as well as controversial.

Jackie Robinson (1919–1972)

No African-American had ever been allowed to play major-league baseball before Robinson was chosen in 1947 to play for the Brooklyn Dodgers, thus integrating the sport. He became the target of venomous racial hatred, which he bore with grace while helping the Dodgers win six pennants.

A-Rod (Alex Rodriguez)

Great third baseman and home-run king, playing for the New York Yankees on a US$ 275 million contract.

Babe Ruth (1895–1948)

One of the greatest baseball sluggers of all time; 'The Babe' played for both the Red Sox and the Yankees.

Jonas Salk (1914–1995)

The discoverer of the vaccine against polio, which has virtually eradicated the disease in countries where used.

Arnold Schwarzenegger (1947–)

Born in Thal, Austria, Schwarzenegger as bodybuilder won five Mr. Universe titles, then became a star of Hollywood action movies, such as *Conan the Barbarian* and *The Terminator*. He burst onto the political scene when in 2003 he won election as California governor following the recall of sitting governor, Gray Davis.

Steven Spielberg (1947–)

Influential director of such blockbusters films as *Jaws, E.T., Jurassic Park, The Color Purple, Schindler's List* and *Saving Private Ryan*.

Martha Stewart (1941–)

Businesswoman and lifestyle entrepreneur, Stewart heads Martha Stewart Living Omnimedia, Inc., a multi-billion dollar company known for its magazines, television shows, cookbooks and housewares. In 2004, Stewart spent five months in jail after being found guilty of insider trading.

Ted Turner (1938–)

A communications and media mogul, Turner is best known for developing the first 24-hour Cable News Network (CNN), which changed the direction for news reporting forever. Active in philanthropic and environmental causes; divorced from actress Jane Fonda.

Mark Twain (pseudonym of Samuel Langhorne Clemens) (1835–1910)

Quintessential American author, humourist, narrator and social observer. His novel, *The Adventures of Huckleberry Finn*, is a classic in American literature.

George Washington (1732–99)

Known as the 'Father of His Country', Washington was the first President of the United States (1789–97) and Commander-in-Chief during the American Revolution.

Oprah Winfrey (1954–)

Television talk-show host, actress, producer, and head of Harpo Productions and Oxygen Media. Known for her honest accounts of her struggles with weight loss and a childhood marred by sexual abuse. Today, Winfrey is one of the most influential and wealthiest people alive.

Tiger (Eldrick) Woods (1975–)

One of history's top professional golfers, Woods has won fourteen major golf tournaments and was the highest-paid athlete of 2007. Of multi-racial heritage, he is one-quarter Chinese, one-quarter Thai, one-quarter African American, one-eighth Native American and one-eighth Dutch. He calls himself a "Cablinasian"—Caucasian, Black, Indian, and Asian. Woods has greatly increased the attention paid to golf.

Frank Lloyd Wright (1867–1959)

America's most famous architect, whose work defined 'modern' architecture.

PLACES OF INTEREST

Florida Everglades

A marshy, low-lying subtropical savanna area in Southern Florida spanning 4,000 sq miles (10,000 sq km), the Everglades is home to massive mangrove forests and a large alligator population. The Everglades receive an annual average rainfall of more than 60 inches (152 cm), mainly in the summer.

Golden Gate Bridge

One of the world's most beautiful bridges, the Golden Gate spans the sea between San Francisco and Marin County in California. Built in 1933–37, the bridge is 9,266 ft long (2,824 m) and 4,200 ft high (1,280 m) at its tallest point. Walkers and drivers both enjoy spectacular vistas.

The Golden Gate Bridge in San Francisco.

Grand Canyon National Park

One of the seven natural wonders of the world, the canyon was carved by the Colorado River and shows the region's geological evolution through erosion patterns, rock formations, and mineral deposits. At 1.6 km (1 mile) deep, from 6.4–29 km (4–18 miles) wide, and 349 km (217 miles) long, the Grand Canyon has been and continues to be home to a variety of native American peoples and a place of unrivalled beauty.

Mount Rushmore National Memorial

Spanning 1,278 acres (518 hectares) in the Black Hills of Southwestern South Dakota, sculptor Gutzon Borglum carved on the face of a mountain the likenesses of four US presidents: George Washington, Abraham Lincoln, Thomas Jefferson, and Theodore Roosevelt, each about 60 ft high (18.3 m) and visible for 60 miles (97 km). Borglum died in 1941 and his work was finished later that year by his son Lincoln. In all, it took 14 years to complete.

Statue of Liberty

Marking the entrance to New York City, the 305-ft-high (93 m) statue was designed by the French sculptor FA Bartholdi and inscribed with a famous sonnet by Emma Lazarus welcoming immigrants to the United States. Originally commemorating the alliance of France with the American colonies during the American Revolution, now it is known as the beacon of liberty.

The Alamo

Former mission in San Antonio, Texas, the Alamo was the site of a famous siege in 1836 during the Mexican-American War. The 187 defenders of the Alamo held off a much larger force for ten days but were finally overcome and all were killed. The cry 'Remember the Alamo!' drove Texans on to an ultimate victory.

Yosemite National Park

A national park in East Central California spanning 61,266 acres (308,205 hectares). Located in the Sierra Mountains, the park was founded in 1890 on the behest of John Muir, a naturalist who was awed by the beauty of the glacier-formed region. Among the notable mountain peaks, such as El Capitan, there are also many lakes, rivers, streams, and waterfalls, including Yosemite Falls, the highest in North America, with a drop of 2,425 ft (739 m).

Yellowstone National Park

The first national park, established in 1872 and spanning 2,219,791 acres (899,015 hectares) through Montana, Wyoming, and Idaho. Located on the Continental Divide in the Rocky Mountains, Yellowstone National Park is characterized by its mountain pools, rugged topography, and volcanic activity—Old Faithful, Yellowstone's famous geyser, erupts every 40 to 70 minutes.

CULTURE QUIZ

Here follows a few situations over which some foreign visitors have been known to stumble. What would you do?

SITUATION 1

You are a man employed by a large company, and many of your co-workers are women. Where you come from, strong barriers separated men and women and you find you really like the looseness between the sexes here. To show how much you like working with women, you:

Ⓐ Touch them often, draping an arm around the ladies' shoulders, or taking hold of a hand or arm.

Ⓑ Compliment the women constantly on their hair, clothes, and pretty smiles.

Ⓒ Compliment your female colleagues on their good work.

Comments

Although a lot of contact is permissible between men and women in this society, the office is not a dating situation, and women should be treated professionally. Too much of **Ⓐ** could get you in hot water; you could even face charges of sexual harassment. **Ⓑ** will simply be found annoying. **Ⓒ** will be pleasing to one and all.

SITUATION 2

You want to have a telephone installed quickly at your new apartment. You should:

Ⓐ Call the telephone company and accept the first appointment for installation that you're offered.

Ⓑ Appear in person at the telephone company's offices and explain how important it is that you get a phone promptly.

Ⓒ Find someone with connections to the phone company who can see that you go to the top of the list.

Comments

Ⓐ is all you need to do. Most businesses serve their customers impartially on the basis of first-come, first-served. Your phone is likely to be installed within a week.

SITUATION 3

A friend has invited you to dinner at a nice restaurant. You dine well, and at the end the waiter brings the check and puts it in the middle of the table. You expect your friend to pick up the check, but he (or she) doesn't. You wait, and the conversation grows slow, and still he (she) doesn't. You are getting very tired and are beginning to think that you're expected to pick up the check. What do you do?

Ⓐ Grit your teeth and wait some more.
Ⓑ Pick up the check and pay it.
Ⓒ Pick up the check and say, "Shall we split it?"

Comments

Ⓒ is the most reasonable course of action. You could also just produce your share of the check, based on what you ate and drank.

You may have been justified in expecting him to pay, particularly if he selected the restaurant. But people often propose meals together without intending to pay for the other person. If your friend happens to be a client of yours, he might be hoping you'll pay, but if the dinner was his idea he should not expect you to. Unless you're very sure someone is paying for you, take enough money to cover dinner when you go out.

SITUATION 4

In the college cafeteria, you meet an American and fall into a long and revealing conversation. You are new in the USA and lonely. Here, you think, is a real friend. You exchange phone numbers, but your new friend doesn't call. The following week, you see her again in the cafeteria, but although she smiles and says 'hi' in a friendly way, she passes by your table to sit with other people. You feel very hurt. What has happened?

Ⓐ She found out more about you and decided not to pursue the friendship.

Ⓑ Much as she enjoyed the conversation, it wasn't necessarily meaningful to her. The rapport the two of you quickly achieved does not make her think of you as a special friend, and having an intimate conversation does not commit her to future closeness.

Ⓒ She has so many intimate conversations that she has forgotten all about this one.

Comments

Ⓑ is the most probable answer. You'll have to build up more of a shared history before you become anybody special to her. Why don't you call her? This may prove to be a real friendship some day; it just isn't one yet. **Ⓒ** is a possibility as well.

SITUATION 5

A friend is visiting your house when the phone rings. It is someone you don't hear from often and you are anxious to catch up on their news. What should you do?

Ⓐ Ignore the visiting friend in favor of the telephoning one and have a nice, long chat. Apologize when you hang up.

Ⓑ Express your happiness at hearing from the caller, then explain that you have company and ask when you can return the call.

Ⓒ You shouldn't have answered the phone at all.

Comments

Either **Ⓑ** or **Ⓒ**. Not answering the phone is easier if you have an answering machine. A live visitor should always take precedence over the one who dropped in by phone. As Americans allocate their time carefully, they will resent their visiting time with you being idled away while you talk to someone else. Even if there are other people around to entertain, guests will not like being treated as second fiddles.

SITUATION 6

While visiting the USA on business you would like to make contact with Company X. How do you go about it?

Ⓐ Find out who is in charge of your area of interest and write to him or her well in advance of your visit. Suggest what you might do for Company X. If the response is positive, set up a precise appointment before leaving home.

Ⓑ Step in at Company X's office during the course of your visit and ask to see the president.

Ⓒ Call a day or two in advance and make a date to visit with anyone who's around.

Comments

Ⓐ is best. As Americans hate to waste time, they're not apt to see you unless they have good reason to believe it's worthwhile. You can chance **Ⓒ** sometimes, but your odds are poor of seeing anyone consequential. **Ⓑ** is fairly hopeless, although out of politeness some minor functionary may see you. As a person with demonstrated time to spend in waiting, you will be assumed to be of little importance.

SITUATION 7

You hire a nanny. Although you consider her wages very high, you are glad to have her as she is sensible and reliable. However, it distresses you that she calls you by your first name. You don't want to hurt her feelings, but you wish she would call you Mrs. Ayashi. Can you ask her to?

A No. She would be too insulted at the suggestion. She hasn't called anyone by their title since her schooldays.

B Yes, but you must ask tactfully.

C Yes, just tell her you think it is very rude of her to call you by first name.

Comments

B Tact should spare hurt feelings. You might bring up the subject at a happy moment when you are offering some kind of treat so that she will realize that you bear her no ill will personally.

If she is a mature woman, we assume that you have taken care to call her Mrs. XX, rather than by her first name. You should explain to her that in your country only people who have known each other for a very long time are on first name terms and while you hold her in high regard, you cannot get used to the sound of your given name coming from someone you met so recently. You might add that you know this is not the custom in the USA and you understand that she does not mean to be rude. If she is a great deal younger than you, you may call her by her first name while explaining that where you come from younger people always address older ones by their title.

DO'S AND DON'TS

DO'S

- Wear dress-up clothes to a funeral.
- Keep track of your place in line at the cash register when shopping. Even if the line is invisible, everyone will know who is first, next, and so on.
- Help with the housework, even if you're a man. Americans think men who don't are being unfair. Your wife will come to believe this too.
- Thank your hosts who have entertained you by calling, emailing, or sending a note.
- Send or bring a present if good friends have a new baby. The present might be a meal for the family.
- Encourage your children to go to college even if they aren't academically inclined. College is very important in the USA.
- Have a shower or bath every day.
- Ask if it's all right to smoke before you light up, wherever you are.
- Shave your underarms and legs below the knees (for women), if you want to Americanize.
- Say "God bless you" or "gesundheit" when someone sneezes. It's an old custom that is supposed to keep vital forces from escaping.
- Go see a therapist if you feel very depressed, anxious, or distraught. It doesn't mean you're crazy, and therapists have techniques that are very helpful.
- Ask questions if you're unsure or confused about anything. People will be happy to help you.
- Arrive 10–15 minutes late to a dinner party.
- Make reservations at busy restaurants by calling first.
- Say 'no ice' if you don't want it; otherwise your drinks will come with it.
- Try to learn something about the rules of football and the name of the local team. Whether they win or lose is a great source of conversation.
- Pay your traffic and parking tickets.

- Take time to rest when you can. Just being in a foreign culture and remembering all the different ways of doing things is tiring.

DON'TS

- Try to bribe police or other officials.
- Arrive late for a wedding.
- Yawn, if you can help it, as yawning indicates boredom. If you must yawn, cover your mouth.
- Stick out your tongue at anyone.
- Expect your children to support you in your old age.
- Be hurt if your children want to leave home when they're 18. For American children, it's natural.
- Spend too much time watching television, playing video games, or cruising the Internet. These are addictions.
- Buy illegal drugs from people on the street. That drug seller could be an undercover cop, and you could go to prison.
- Hitchhike. It's not safe. And don't pick up hitchhikers either.
- Change into your bathing suit on the beach.
- Take your shoes off when you go in someone's house. And don't put your feet on the furniture either.
- Make derogatory comments about ethnic or racial groups.
- Ask people how much money they make or have or how much their new car or house cost.
- Feel obligated to check your coat in restaurants or museums.
- Start eating at a meal until everyone has been served.
- Drop in to see people at their homes without calling first.
- Tip customs officials, police, airline personnel, store clerks, room clerks, receptionists, or elevator operators. (*See 'Tipping' in the* Resource Guide)
- Be rude. Americans are straightforward but polite.

GLOSSARY

ace	Do really well. 'I aced that exam.'
African-American	The preferred term for American blacks.
awesome	Much over-used term by youths, meaning 'very good'.
baby boomer	The large generation of people born between the end of World War I and 1965. This was a period of high birth rate, which will soon produce a very large senior group.
black	The color of mourning; often worn at funerals.
carpool	Go together in a car. 'Three of us carpooled to the meeting.'
catch-22	Term that titled a popular novel, describing a paradox in which the solution to a problem causes an equally serious problem.
classifieds	Paid listings for jobs, etc., in newspapers or on the Internet.
clean	No drugs or evidence of crime. 'The police frisked him, and he's clean.'
college	An institution of higher learning that students attend after high school. A four-year course may earn a student a B.A. (Bachelor of Arts) or a B.S. (Bachelor of Science).
cop	Policeman or policewoman.
cruelty-free	Products that do not use animal products and are produced without being tested on animals.

class of 2007	In college, people are divided up according to the year they graduate (or are supposed to graduate). As college is supposed to take four years—although it often takes more these days—someone who starts college in September of 2003 would be referred to as 'in the class of 2007'. If he drops back a year, he would then become 'the class of 2008'.
first floor	In the USA, the first floor is the ground or street-level floor. The second floor is one flight up.
86	Throw out, get rid of. As in, 'He was so drunk, the bar '86ed him.'
generation X, gen X	The post-baby boomer generation, i.e. born after 1965.
green card	The document allowing a foreigner to live and work in the USA.
hasta la vista	Spanish for 'see you later'.
like	Teen language, meaning 'say' or 'said'. As in 'I was like 'let's go to the mall,' but Mom's like 'not before you clean your room.''
9/11	September 11, 2001, the day when terrorists attacked the World Trade Center and the Pentagon (Defence Dept. headquarters). It is often referred to now without explanation, as in 'Since 9/11, people have been more insecure'.
mañana	Spanish for 'tomorrow'.
medicare	Government-paid health care for people 65 and over.

pharmacy	Place to buy prescription drugs, as well as toiletries and sometimes nearly everything you might want. Also called 'drug stores' but not 'chemists'.
rehab	Rehabilitation; used to described a place that treats drug and alcohol problems. 'The Betty Ford Center is a famous rehab.'
'right to bear arms'	The phrase from the US constitution that gun supporters think justifies them in insisting that guns should be legal.
sappnin?	Teen version of 'What's happening?'
shrink	Psychiatrist or other kind of psychotherapist. From 'head shrinker.'
social security	The pension that most workers get from the government, currently at age 65.
strike out	A baseball term meaning to fail.
toll-free numbers	If instead of an area code, a phone number has the prefix 800, 888, 877, or 866, the call won't cost you anything. The most common toll-free number is 800; the other numbers were added recently because the 800 numbers were all taken. A 900 number, on the other hand, indicates a very high-priced call.
24/7	Twenty-four hours a day, seven days a week, i.e. all the time. As in, 'I've been working 24/7'.
Uncle Sam	The US government. For example, 'Uncle Sam takes a lot of my money'.

university	An institution of higher learning that includes a four-year college, as well as advanced schools of study (graduate schools).
vegan	A vegetarian does not eat meat; a vegan does not eat meat, fish, or dairy products.
wassup?	'What's up?' in teen talk. Sometimes pronounced 'Zup'.
whatever	'Who cares?' in teen talk.
X	The symbol of a kiss, which you might use in signing a letter. Also used by teachers to indicate an answer is wrong. Used with an O, the O signifies a hug.
x-rated	Pornographic.
zip code	The five-number suffix used in all US addresses. Properly, a four-number code follows the zip code, narrowing down the location still further.

RESOURCE GUIDE

EMERGENCIES
911 is the emergency number nearly everywhere in the USA. This will bring you police, the fire department, or an ambulance.

ENTRY REQUIREMENTS
Customs: When entering the USA, you may bring in 1 litre of alcohol, 100 cigars (not Cuban), and 200 cigarettes without paying duties. You may bring in bakery items and certain cheeses but not meat or meat products, fruit, or vegetables.

Pet dogs and cats may be brought into the USA, subject to health inspection; dogs coming from a country not free of rabies must have a rabies vaccination certificate issued at least 30 days before departure. Individual airlines may require health certificates.

You may bring in a generous number of household items for your own use and gifts of up to US$ 100 in value. Do not bring in firearms unless they're for hunting; these you must take with you when you leave. All drugs must be clearly labelled, in reasonable quantity and accompanied by a prescription or doctor's statement that you require them. If you bring in more than US$ 10,000 in cash, money orders, or traveler's checks, you must file a report with customs.

Immigration
The website of the US Customs and Immigration Service (http://uscis.gov) will lead you to the source for application forms and answers to many questions. The American Immigration Center at http://www.us-immigration.com (800-814-1555 or from outside the country call 505-891-1555) provides information and sells do-it-yourself kits for processing your own applications.

Passports

All nationalities need passports to enter the USA. If you lose yours, notify both the police and your home embassy.

Visas

Under the recent Visa Waiver Program, people from certain countries can enter the USA for business or pleasure for up to 90 days without a visa. You must come on an airline that belongs to the program. Visas are generally available for people who want to stay for up to six months as tourists or visitors; it is a great deal harder to get a visa that will allow you to work here. Students must be accepted by an American school before applying for a student visa. In all, there are some 40 different kinds of visas; you should apply in the U.S. consulate of your home country before you depart. It is possible to change your visa status after you arrive by applying to the INS. New strictures have been added since 9/11, particularly for people from countries that 'harbor terrorists'. It is now extra-important to be sure that all your papers are exactly in order.

For information: http://travel.state.gov.

TRANSPORTATION
Buses

Usually the cheapest way to get around. Greyhound (800)229-9424, http://www.greyhound.com, crisscrosses the country. Trailways is an association of regional bus lines with separate phone numbers, which you can find at http://www.trailways.com.

Driving
Auto Insurance

Most states require it in order to register a car, which you must do at the state Department of Motor Vehicles (DMV). You'll want to shop around for a policy and decide how much insurance you want. It is also useful to join AAA, which provides road service when you break down, as well as maps, guidebooks, and trip-planning advice. AAA also sells automobile insurance, as do many other companies.

Drivers' Licences

Drivers from most countries can use their home driver's licences in the USA for up to a year. An International Driving Permit is useful for drivers whose licenses don't have a photo on them, particularly young-looking people needing to prove they are old enough to buy alcohol and go to nightclubs.

Gas

Most gas stations are self-serve. You will have to get out of the car, pay at the pump with a credit card or inside the station with cash or credit, and then follow directions to fill the gas tank yourself. You will also have to wash your own car windows and add oil, air, and water yourself. A few gas stations still have islands labelled 'Full Serve'; gas prices are higher at these.

Parking

When you're parking on a street, look around for signs announcing parking hours. Curb color has meaning: Red—no parking; Blue—handicapped only; White—unloading only; Green—very short-term parking. Your car can be towed away if you park illegally and you will find getting it back most inconvenient. Parking meters usually don't need coins after 6:00 pm and on Sundays; read the fine print on the meter for the hours.

Rental Cars

Drivers are usually required to be 25 years of age, though some companies will allow 21–25-year-olds to rent with an additional charge. You also need a valid driver's licence and a credit card. The rental company will try and sell you accident insurance; you may be covered through home insurance or even a credit card, but unless you are sure of this, buy the additional insurance.

TRAVEL
Budget Accommodations
In major cities, you can usually find reasonably priced lodgings in a YMCA or YWCA. There are also many hostels sponsored by Hostelling International–American Youth Hostels (http://www.hiayh.org) across the United States. These can be pleasant and sociable, but you won't get much more than a bunk. For budget hotels, there are numerous guidebooks, such as *Let's Go USA*. There are also hotel brokers that discount empty rooms at very large savings if business is slow. 800-USA-HOTEL [(1-800) 872-4683; http://www.1800usahotels.com] has nationwide service, as does Quikbook [(1-8000 789-9887; http://www.quikbook.com]. Central Reservation Service specialises in Boston, Orlando and San Francisco: (1-407) 740-6442 from within the United States and (1-800) 894-0680 from overseas; website: http://www.roomconnection.com.

Camping
At http://www.recreation.gov, you can book reservations for campgrounds all over the country and of every type. Want a campground near Kansas City on a lake with a water hookup for your 60-foot RV? Or to pitch your tent in Yosemite? In a few seconds you'll have pictures, descriptions, directions, and available dates. Most spots are about US$ 20 a night. By phone, you can make reservations for state parks at 800-444-PARK and for national parks at 800-365-2267.

Directions
Mapquest (http://www.mapquest.com) is a remarkable website that delivers precise directions to almost anywhere.

Flying
Since March 2007, new restrictions apply to liquids, aerosols, and gels—even lipsticks and mascaras. These must be taken through security in individual containers of 100 ml (3 oz) or less. They should be collected together in a quart-size plastic bag (about 20 cm x 20cm or 8" x 8") and carried separately from other luggage. However, there are exceptions

for reasonable amounts of baby products and medicines. If you want to bring a drink on the plane, you have to buy it after passing through security. Also, do not try to take on board knives, long scissors with pointed tips, box cutters, or anything else that could conceivably be used as a weapon. For more specifics, see http://tsa.gov.

Pets

Most airlines will allow you to bring a dog or cat along at a cost of US$ 80 and up, but rules vary according to the weather (too hot and they can't come) and the airline. Most bus lines don't allow pets at all and neither does Amtrak.

Trains

Amtrak is the national railroad company, and you can travel from the Atlantic to the Pacific on it in comfort, or speed up and down either coast on Amtrak trains. Amtrak offers 15- and 30-day passes with unlimited stopovers for foreigners at attractive prices. Call 800-USA-RAIL or see: http://www.amtrak.com.

HEALTH
Dental clinics

Private dentists do almost all dentistry. The larger cities have dentistry schools that run low-cost clinics, but the process of being treated by them is lengthy.

Dental Insurance

Much less common than medical insurance, which 17 percent of Americans lack.

Fluoride

Most of the tap water has added fluoride, which has greatly reduced cavities among children.

Health insurance

For stays under six months in the USA, buy travel insurance from a company in your home country (a travel agent can help you). If you're getting a job in the USA, be sure your employer will provide health insurance. If you do not have insurance through an employer, school or other family member, you will have to purchase it. There are numerous companies. The largest is Blue Cross/Blue Shield at http://www.bluecares.com; (800) 333-0912.

Health insurance is very expensive but the price of getting sick and paying the bills yourself is astronomical. You can buy medications online (usually from Canada or Mexico) at reduced prices.

Health threats

The threat of disease in the USA is no greater than in any other developed nation, despite increasing tuberculosis, seasonal outbreaks of flu, and an upsurge in cases of measles. Food-borne diseases originating in meat, such as E Coli 057 and salmonellosis have also increased.

Nature presents some threats. Mosquitoes, which are worst at dawn and dusk, are bothersome but rarely dangerous. Ticks, unfortunately, can carry Lyme disease—a chronic debilitating condition. Lyme Disease is endemic in the Northeast and upper Midwest; lolling in the grass on a summer's day in those areas is not as carefree as it once was. You now want to wear shoes and socks and inspect your body for ticks daily—ticks bite you and hang on. If you remove them within 24 hours you should be okay. If you're going into the woods, get somebody to identify poison ivy and poison oak for you. Both can cause horrible, itchy rashes. Learn about rattlesnakes before you go hiking in the West. More information available at:

http://www.cdc.gov/travel.

Take the proper precautions regarding sexually transmitted diseases here as everywhere in the world. Not only must you beware of HIV but Hepatitis C is rampant as well, as are various infections.

HMO & PPO

An HMO (Health Maintenance Organisation) is a company that provides complete health care to its members. People who belong to an HMO are discouraged from using doctors outside the HMO's own providers. The advantage is that HMOs are cheaper than plans that allow you free choice of doctors.

A PPO (Preferred Provider Organisation) provides a method of insurance that limits members to seeing only the doctors that are enrolled in its plan.

Vaccinations

No vaccines are specifically required to enter the USA, but if you're planning to stay, you ought to see a physician and discuss vaccines you might need. It helps if you have brought your medical records from home.

Before starting school, children must have proof of immunisation against diphtheria, measles, polio, rubella, tetanus, pertussis, mumps, and Hepatitis B (in some states).

Disabilities

Thanks to the American Disabilities Act, facilities for the handicapped are good. Public places are supposed to provide access and rest room facilities for people in wheelchairs. However, older systems of public transportation (like the New York subway system) predate modern construction standards. City streets usually have ramps at curbs. You must not leave your car in such a way as to impede wheelchair crossings.

If you're traveling in a wheelchair, you will find a lot of help from *The Traveler's Guide To Wheelchairs*. A useful website for travelers with disabilities is http://www.sath.org (the Society for Accessible Travel & Hospitality).

HOUSE & HOME
Buying a home

You'll find useful information on the website of the US Department of Housing and Urban Development at:
                         http://www.hud.gov.

- Electricity
  110–120 volts AC, so European appliances generally need an adapter and a dual-voltage switch. European TVs, VCRs, and DVD players will not work here.

- Garbage Collection
  Nearly every community has some regular collection; sometimes the city pays, sometimes you do.
- Moving
  There are numerous companies that come to your house, pick up your things and take them to your new house—or to storage. If you are making a major move, you might want to get several price quotes before choosing a company. Be wary of unknown companies quoting ultra-low bids. They have been known to hold people's goods hostage for additional payments.
- Telephone
  To have one installed, call your local phone company and make arrangements. Because long-distance companies have been deregulated in recent years, you will have to select the carrier you want. It probably won't make much difference which one you choose, but you may want to consider one that gives you low rates for international calls. A cheap alternative for international calls is to dial 1016868-011, followed by country code and number.
- Television
  Before cable television, all TV stations were broadcast over the airwaves. Some still are, and these are the giants on your TV dial: ABC, CBS, NBC, and PBS. You may be able to receive these with just an antenna. But these days, there's a lot of competition from cable stations, which require you to pay monthly charges for a cable hookup or to get a satellite dish. There are two primary satellite providers: Dish Network and DirecTV. You get what you pay for, with substantial additional charges for stations like HBO.

  As of early 2009, all broadcast stations will have switched to digital broadcasting, and old (analog) TVs will need a converter box.

- Water
  The tap water everywhere is considered quite safe to drink, although many people buy water, which they consider purer and better tasting. In fact, testing generally shows that the tap water is superior.

Services
- Childcare

  Agencies are listed under 'child care' or 'babysitting' in the *Yellow Pages*. On the Internet, Craig's list is a good source. Always ask for personal references and check them.
- Housecleaners

  Most people get their house cleaners from personal references, but you'll find a great variety of cleaning services in the *Yellow Pages*. Craigs list, again, is a good source. You don't need a licence to open a cleaning service, so you should try and get a recommendation.

MONEY
Currency
American bills come all in the same size and color, so look carefully before you part with them. You will see US$ 1s, US$ 2s (extremely rare), US$ 5s, US$ 10s, US$ 20s, US$ 50s and US$ 100s. Coins come in a 1 (penny), 5 (nickel), 10 (dime), 25 (quarter) and, rarely, 1 dollar. There is little relationship between the coin's size and its value, so watch carefully here too.

Exchanging money
Credit cards provide a good and up-to-date exchange rate. Most ATM machines take the Star and the Cirrius networks. If you plan to withdraw money from a credit card account, be sure you have your four-digit PIN with you.

Income Taxes
The federal tax is the largest. It is a sliding scale according to income; the highest rate (income of above US$ 357,700) currently is 35 percent. Some states also have income taxes, but they are much lower than the federal tax. There is also a Social Security/Medicare tax that takes 15.3 percent of up to US$ 102,000 from a paycheck and pays for retirement and health care of those aged 65 and over. Americans generally hate taxes even more than people in other countries. President George W. Bush ran for president promising to 'give your money back to you'.

Sales tax

A tax added on to every purchase is a primary way that states and localities collect revenue. This amount is not included in the stated price of the item. The amount, from 4–8 percent, varies from place to place and a few states have none. If you are having something mailed to a location outside of the sales tax region of the store where you bought it, you needn't pay the sales tax. Groceries are rarely taxed.

SHOPPING

Except in very rare circumstances, you don't bargain but pay the sticker price. For most goods, you will pay more than the stated price because of added sales taxes. You can return most goods within a reasonable amount of time, if you keep your sales receipt. Supermarkets are astonishingly large and carry nearly everything you might want. There are few specialty shops, so even when you just want a bottle of milk, you may still have to go to the supermarket. Store hours vary; many foreigners are surprised at how early stores close. You will doubtless find a mall very early in your stay. Malls are the result of cars—built for parking and outside of city centers. Going to them provides the prime recreation for many people.

Store Hours

They vary widely. Some department stores are open 10:00 am to 9:00 pm every weekday, closing at 6:00 pm on weekends. Others normally close at 6:30 pm, except on Thursdays, when they stay open until 9:00 pm. Some supermarkets are open 24-hours a day. Many drugstores close at 9:00 pm, others at midnight.

In some communities, everything closes early. Smaller speciality stores may be closed on Sundays, especially if they are located in business districts.

TELEPHONE
Numbers

All numbers have first a three-number area code, followed by seven numbers. Usually, you dial '1' before the area code.

Generally, you do not have to dial the area code if you are calling someone within the same area code, although in NYC, you do.

Calling

Pay phones cost 35¢ to 50¢ a minute for local calls; long-distance calls are much higher. You can save money by buying phone cards instead. Or you may want to get a cell phone for your stay. If you do not want to sign a year's contract, you can buy a new or refurbished cell phone from a wireless phone company (AT&T does this) and rather than signing a contract, you can buy prepaid phone cards for your calls. Prices vary from about 12¢ to 35¢ a minute. You can also rent cell phones from cellular/satellite phone rental companies, but the rates are exorbitant. Sprint will rent you a phone on a monthly basis. It costs US$ 10 more a month than with a yearly contract. Plans start at around US$ 40 a month.

Hotel calls

Charges for calls from a hotel room phone can be very high. Inquire before you make any.

Information

To get a local phone number, call 411. For another area code, dial the code and 555-1212. The charge for information is usually US$ 1.50. You can get free information from 1-800-FREE411, but you'll have to listen to a couple of ads. Telephone directories are often divided into residential and personal sections; there is then another section (or in large cities, another book) called the *Yellow Pages*, which lists services and vendors alphabetically. A local phone book is always excellent reading, full of useful information.

TIPPING

- Airport
  Electric cart transport: US$ 1–2
  Skycap: US$ 1 per bag (transport or curbside check-in)
  Wheelchair assistance: US$ 3–5

- Barber or beautician: 10–15 percent
- Casino Dealer: US$ 5–100 when you leave. If you win a jackpot, tip everyone in sight lavishly, including the security guard.
- Coat check: US$ 1
- Emergency Roadside Assistance: US$ 5–20, depending on the service.
- Hotel
  Bellhop: US$ 5 for taking you to your room
  Chambermaid: US$ 1–2 per night
  Doorman: US$ 1 for hailing a cab
  Flower delivery: US$2–5
  Hotel room service: 10–15 percent of bill
- Manicurist: US$ 2–5
- Massage therapist: 10 percent
- Movers: US$20–50; For a big move, give 10 percent of total cost to team leader to divide
- Pizza Delivery: US$ 2–5 depending on distance
- Restaurant counter server: 10 percent
- Waiter: 15–20 percent
- Rest room attendant: 50¢–US$ 1
- Shampoo person: US$ 2-5
- Taxi drivers: 10 percent of bill
- Tour bus driver: US$ 1–2
- Tour guide: 10–15 percent of tour cost
- Ushers: Do not tip
- Valet parking: US$ 2–5

MISCELLANEOUS
Weather
- http:// www.worldclimate.com gives you average temperatures and rainfall
- http://www.nws.noaa.gov gives you current conditions and forecasts in the USA.

- **http://www.anything.com** is a website that has references to excellent sites for everything from airlines, credit cards, and travel to medicine, cooking, and maps.

Drinking

Rules for sale of alcohol vary from state to state and county to county. Some places are altogether 'dry', i.e. no alcohol is sold. Generally, you can buy wine and beer more freely than stronger liquor, but you must be 21 years old to buy it.

You can get in a lot of trouble if you are picked up driving with a high blood alcohol level, which roughly speaking means more than a couple of small drinks in a couple of hours. You are also not to have an open bottle or can of alcohol in your car.

Gambling

Gambling is only allowed in select places, such as Atlantic City and Nevada, which includes Las Vegas, and on Indian reservations, which escape state laws. State lotteries are further exceptions to laws against gambling, as is racetrack betting.

Legal Matters

http://www.nolo.com is a great fount of legal information, on everything from probate to divorce to Internet law to small claims court.

Lost & Found

Each company, whether bus, train, taxi company, airline, hotel, theatre, restaurant, or other public place, has its own system for holding lost property. Contact them if you lose something. Your chances of getting it back are quite good. You can also try the police.

Mail

Post offices are usually open from 9:00 am–5:00 pm, though large ones may have self-service sections that are open for longer hours. You can have mail sent to you c/o General Delivery at the main post office of whatever city or town you are in; you will need to pick it up personally. Letters should all include the five-figure zip code. Delivery takes one to three days within the continental USA. As of this writing, the domestic rate for a one-ounce letter is 42¢.

Each additional ounce is 17¢. Postcards are 27¢ (large ones 42¢). Package rate varies according to distance. Domestic (books and tapes) media mail is a great bargain at $1.33 per pound and 45¢ for each additional pound. Express mail is expensive but promises overnight delivery. Most international letters (up to 1 ounce) are 80¢. For precise details see: http://www.usps.com.

A number of private mail handlers have sprung up, with names such as Mail Boxes Etc. and Postal Plus. These charge extra for their services but are fast. They will wrap your packages as well as ship them; they generally also have copiers available, provide fax services and provide FedEx shipment.

Envelopes: How to address

```
Your Name
Your Street Address                    Stamp
Your City, State, Zip Code
            Recipient' s Name
            Company's Name
            Street Address
            City, State, Zip Code
            Country (if outside the USA)
```

Newspapers

There are three newspapers of importance in the USA: *The New York Times, The Washington Post* and the *Los Angeles Times. The Wall Street Journal* is widely read in business circles. Most cities have their own newspapers.

Police

Policing responsibilities are divided among state, county, and city forces. There is no national police force other than the FBI (Federal Bureau of Investigation), which concentrates on major interstate crimes. You are only likely to meet the state police if you speed on a state highway. County governments have sheriffs' departments, and if you are robbed you will deal with them or the local city police force.

Radio

Radio frequencies are divided into AM and FM. The classier stations—National Public Radio, classical music—are nearly all on FM.

Smoking

Foreigners are frequently put out by the hostile attitude toward smoking in the USA. We simply consider other countries backward to allow smokers to freely pollute the air.

The laws vary greatly both by state and by town. California, Connecticut, Delaware, Massachusetts, New York, and Rhode Island have laws barring smoking in all workplaces and public places, including restaurants and bars. Other states have few laws against smoking, but local ordinances may prohibit smoking in public places or require non-smoking sections. You must be at least 18 to buy cigarettes, and even older in a few states. (*For the etiquette of smoking in private homes, see 'Smoking' in Chapter 5: Settling In*)

FURTHER READING

The following recommendations include only those books that I feel would be most helpful to foreigners trying to understand Americans and their way of life. It is, of course, far from a complete reading list.

American Cultural Patterns. Edward C Stewart and Milton Bennett. Intercultural Press. 1972. Revised 1991.
- A classic study of American beliefs and behavior. Thorough and academic.

American Mania: When More Is Not Enough. Peter C Whybrow. Norton, 2005.
- How materialism and neuropsychiatry combine to produce overwork and overconsumption—and what can be done about it.

American Ways. Gary Althen. Intercultural Press, 2003.
- An easy-to-read and thorough review of American attitudes and customs by a foreign student advisor. A new, updated edition.

American Born Chinese. Gene Luen Yang. First Second Books, 2006.
- A graphic novel (comic book) that became a surprise hit and the first such ever nominated for the National Book Award. Interwoven tales, focusing on a boy who is the only Chinese in his class.

Bowling Alone: The Collapse and Revival of American Community. Robert D Putnam. Simon & Schuster, 2000.
- A wealth of active civic organizations were a strong force in America's success. Putnam, a Harvard sociologist, demonstrates the decline of 'social capital' in the last 30 years and pleads for a revival, saying that social connectedness is better than Prozac for what ails us.

Catfish and Mandala. Andrew X Pham. Farrar, Straus, and Giroux, 1999.
- While bicycling through the land of his birth, Vietnam, Pham reflects on his adopted country: 'But now, I miss the white, the black, the red, the brown faces of America... their idealistic search for racial equality, their bumbling but wonderful pioneering spirit'.

Class. Paul Fussell. Touchstone, 1983.
- Not only does Fussell insist that America has a class system, he describes in minute detail the elements that separate the strata. A most amusing book and thoroughly practical for anyone who seriously wishes to rise socially.

Cultural Misunderstandings. Raymonde Carroll. The University Chicago Press, 1988.
- If you're just going to read one book on cultural differences, this is the one. Compares French and Americans, but the points are universal.

Dance of Life. Edward T Hall. Anchor Books/Doubleday, 1983.
- An anthropologist explains why time is perceived so differently in various cultures and why Americans go by the clock.

Democracy in America. Alexis de Tocqueville. NAL, 1991 (first published in 1835).
- De Tocqueville wrote about the uniqueness of America, and many of his observations remain apt today.

Do You Speak American? Robert MacNeil and William Cran. Doubleday, 2005.
- A companion volume to the PBS television series of the same name, demonstrating that regional accents in the U.S. are thriving.

Domestic Manners of the Americans. Fanny Trollope. Oxford University Press, 1984 (first published in 1832).
- Mrs Trollope, a lively writer, found Americans ignorant and parties dull, but she grants that the USA was a fine country to get ahead in.

Gig: Americans Talk About Their Jobs. Bowe, Bowe and Streeter, eds. Three Rivers Press, 2000.
- In their own voices, 127 Americans talk about their work—drivers, fast-food workers, salespeople, teachers, artists, and more—with great forthrightness and humor. A fascinating book for anyone contemplating a career in America.

Host Family Survival Kit. Nancy King and Ken Huff. Intercultural Press, 1997.
- A guide for Americans who are sheltering exchange students, but equally useful in helping the students understand the hosts. Includes a good description of the culture shock process.

In Search of Self in India and Japan: Toward a Cross-Cultural Psychology. Alan Roland. Princeton University Press, 1988.
- A psychoanalyst who worked with American, Japanese and Indian patients discovers very basic differences in family attachments.

Laughing Without an Accent. Firoozeh Dumas. Randon House, 2008.
- To the delight of all who loved *Funny in Farsi*, Dumas (who moved to the U.S. from Iran at age seven) is back with an equally funny, follow-up saga.

Living and Working in America: A Survival Handbook. David Hampshire. Survival Books, 1998.
- A thick, detailed book full of specifics on everything from highway driving to shoe sizes. The breezy, frank style makes it as interesting as it is useful.

Lost in Translation. Eva Hoffman, E. P. Dutton, 1989.
- A beautifully written account of life in America by a Polish-born refugee.

People's History of the United States. Howard Zinn. Perennial, 2001.
- History from the point of view of the poor and powerless.

The Big Squeeze: Tough Times for the American Worker. Steven Greenhouse. Knopf, 2008.
- Focuses on American workers, concentrating on the stresses under corporate America. Very readable, by a *New York Times* correspondent.

The New First Dictionary of Cultural Literacy: What Your Child Needs to Know. E.D. Hirsch, 2004.
- From the Bible to Harry Potter. As handy for adults as for children, this book, with almost 3,000 definitions, is intended to make a well-educated sixth grader out of anyone.

Understanding America: The Anatomy of an Exceptional Nation. Peter H. Shuck and James Q. Wilson, eds. Public Affairs, 2008.
- Ten distinguished scholars contributed chapters to this excellent volume, which examines the USA in ten different areas and describes the forces that make it so different from other nations.

'What We Think of America': Granta 77, April 2002 issue, London. Ed. by Ian Jack.
- Perspectives on America in the post 9/11 era by distinguished writers from Lebanon, India, Serbia, the Middle East, Europe, Chile, China, Canada, Australia, Turkey, and Malaysia.

ABOUT THE AUTHOR

Esther Wanning was born in Boston, Massachusetts, and is descended from New England Yankees on both sides of her family. She grew up in a rural setting but spent her young adulthood in New York City, where she worked as a magazine and travel book editor. After a short stint as a teacher, she moved to San Francisco, where she continued editing and writing. She now lives in Marin County, California.

She has written for numerous publications and, in addition to *CultureShock! USA*, is the author of *Surviving Without Cigarettes* and *The Art of Maryland*. In true American fashion, she returned to school in mid-life and earned a master's degree in counselling psychology. While continuing to write, she now also works as a psychotherapist.

INDEX

Titles in the CultureShock! series:

Argentina	France	Russia
Australia	Germany	San Francisco
Austria	Hawaii	Saudi Arabia
Bahrain	Hong Kong	Scotland
Beijing	Hungary	Shanghai
Belgium	India	Singapore
Bolivia	Ireland	South Africa
Borneo	Italy	Spain
Brazil	Jakarta	Sri Lanka
Britain	Japan	Sweden
Bulgaria	Korea	Switzerland
Cambodia	Laos	Syria
Canada	London	Taiwan
Chicago	Malaysia	Thailand
Chile	Mauritius	Tokyo
China	Morocco	Turkey
Costa Rica	Munich	United Arab
Cuba	Myanmar	Emirates
Czech Republic	Netherlands	USA
Denmark	New Zealand	Vancouver
Ecuador	Paris	Venezuela
Egypt	Philippines	
Finland	Portugal	

For more information about any of these titles, please contact any of our Marshall Cavendish offices around the world (listed on page ii) or visit our website at:

www.marshallcavendish.com/genref